X k4

OVERTURE
TO
OVERLORD

OVERTURE
TO
OVERLORD

by

Francis Mackay

Pen & Sword
MILITARY

First published in Great Britain in 2005 by
Pen & Sword Military
an imprint of
Pen & Sword Books Ltd
47 Church Street
Barnsley
South Yorkshire
S70 2AS

ISBN 085 052 8925

A CIP catalogue record for this book is
available from the British Library

Typeset in Sabon by
Phoenix Typesetting, Auldgirth, Dumfriesshire

Printed and bound in England by
CPI UK.

Pen & Sword Books Ltd incorporates the imprints of Pen & Sword
Aviation, Pen & Sword Maritime, Pen & Sword Military, Wharncliffe
Local History, Pen & Sword Select, Pen & Sword Military Classics and
Leo Cooper.

For a complete list of Pen & Sword titles please contact
PEN & SWORD BOOKS LIMITED
47 Church Street, Barnsley, South Yorkshire, S70 2AS, England
E-mail: enquiries@pen-and-sword.co.uk
Website: www.pen-and-sword.co.uk

This book would not have come about if, in days long gone, Major John Farrell TD had not talked about the Hopkinson Mission, and the late Squadron Sergeant Major Bob Bennett MM, BEM, one of David Stirling's originals, had not mentioned 6 SAS. Nor would it have come about if I hadn't read an old notebook found in my ancient bergen. I was lucky to have known some of the originals, so this book is really theirs.

Contents

Acknowledgements

This book is based on notes and jottings collected over more than fifty years, almost from the start of my involvement with HM Forces. Over the years many people provided information about many aspects of Special Operations and Special Forces, a small amount of which appears here. Some of these people have passed on, others are alive and well, most preferred to live anonymously and I see no need to change that now.

My particular thanks go to the following: Robert Bickers, Senior Lecturer, Department of History, Bristol University, an acknowledged expert on old Shanghai, for information about Messrs. Fairbairn and Sykes, and the Shanghai Municipal Police; Major Bob Bragg, formerly of 12/13th Battalion Parachute Regiment (TA), for enthusiastic cooperation from the earliest stages of this project, and for allowing open access to his unique collection of material about worldwide airborne, amphibious, Commando and Special Forces operations and training; Harry McClure, Curator, Army Physical Training Corps Museum and Association for information about bayonet fighting; David Buxton for delving in the National Archives and contributing much information from his archive on SOE and SD missions; Ron Clarke, Chairman of the Harrington Aviation Museum Society, Kettering, Northamptonshire; John Farrell, ex lance corporal, Phantom, and later major, 23 SAS Regiment TA, for information on the early days of Phantom; Luigi Cortelleti, Arsiero, Italy, for information about the Tandura Mission, and Dale Hjort, an authority on British military operations in Italy during the Great War, for introducing me to the role Captain William Wedgwood Benn played in that feat; Major Michael Jodeluk for information gleaned from his father about the Polish Resistance movements in Northern France, and the training of the Bardsea teams; Louis Meulstee, Holland, an international authority on Second World War British, Commonwealth and Allied Army wireless equipment and author of the *Wireless for the Warrior* series of books; Doreen Smith for information on the wartime National Pigeon Service, and the photograph of the 'flying agent' insertion system; Harry Pugh, Arlington, Virginia, former member of the 82nd Airborne Division and US Special Forces, and Don Strobaugh, Mesa, Arizona, for copious information on parachute, glider and special operations forces, including detailed studies of the awards of wartime Polish parachute badges and combat wreaths; Tom Ensminger, author of the detailed accounts of the USAAF Carpetbagger Bomb Group and its operations, *Spies, Supplies and Moonlit Skies, Volumes I and II*; John M. Smith of the Flore Heritage Society for information about the NORSOG at Brockhall and Fawsley Park, and to his brother, Captain P.B. Smith, for permission to use the photograph of the building; Adrian Mettem, of Stuart Turner Pumps Ltd., for information about, and a photograph of, the Portable Steam Generator; Mrs Diana Matthews, JP OBE, Chairman, Windermere Nautical Trust, for information about the only SOE Seaplane Glider ever constructed, carefully preserved in the Windermere Steamboat Museum, Bowness-on-Windermere, Cumbria; Susan Smith, Secretary, Friends of Loudoun Kirk, for information about the travels and travails of the Belgian SAS men; Martin Sugarman, Assistant Archivist, Association of Jewish Ex-Servicemen and Women, for information about the Special Interrogation Group.

In the distant days of my youth my father and an uncle, marine engineers to trade, spoke of Shanghai in the roaring days, including the briefings given by the Municipal Police to merchant marine personnel. In later years two venerable officers of the Argyll and Sutherland Highlanders, Major General Sir Freddy Graham and Captain (ex-Corporal) Jimmy Robertson, spoke of similar briefs, and self-defence training, used to fortify soldiers against the rigours of Saturday nights in the stews behind the Bund. Another uncle had survived three years as a subaltern on the Western Front and the Irish War of Independence, and later served in the Fort William Battalion of the Home Guard. He helped scour the wet hills of Lochaber for 'enemy paratroops', men (and some women) from a variety of nations and organizations training at the Commando Basic Training Centre, Achnacarry, and other places, and guarded the tunnels and bridges of the West Highland Railway Line against 'saboteurs'. His family were Ayrshire miners, a canny breed, and when visiting thereabouts I learned much about the doings of the French SAS Regiments in the months before D-Day. The men said 'Humph, aye', and changed the subject, the ladies said much more, later, when the men were out of the way. Squadron Leader Bruce Blanche provided the Tempsford photographs and much useful information about SD squadrons and air operations, and Flight Lieutenant John Campbell did the same for navigation, Eureka, Rebecca and Gee. More recently Klemen Luzar, of Mrna Pec, Slovenia, provided much information about Austro-Hungarian special troops and guerrilla forces, not all of which could be included here. A number of NATO colleagues helped scour their national archives, and provided other information.

I have tried at all times to be as accurate as time and access to records allows, hence my occasional caveats of *possibly*, and *probably*. If anyone knows better I will be happy to hear from them via the publisher. My considerable thanks to Charles Hewitt and Henry Wilson of Pen & Sword Books Ltd., for their ready agreement to this book, and for their patience during difficult times.

I have tried to make this book not only informative but readable and hope to have succeeded in both aims.

Francis Mackay,
Scotland,
April 2004

Glossary

I have used well known place spellings e.g. Kabrit, not Al Kibrit. Ranks are those held at the time mentioned in the text and decorations have not been listed for the sake of brevity.

1CIA	*1e Compagnie d'Infanterie de l'Air*
ACAS	Assistant Chief of the Air Staff
ACIU	Allied Central Interpretation Unit
A/DP	Director, Intelligence, Security & Propaganda Section, SOE
AFHQ	Allied Forces Headquarters
AFV	Armoured Fighting Vehicles
AILS	Air Intelligence Liaison Sections
ALM	Air Liaison Mission
AMGOT	Allied Military Government of Occupied Territories
APJI	Assistant Parachute Jump Instructors
APTC	Army Physical Training Corps
ASD	Air Staff Director
AST	Assault Ships, Transport
ASW	Anti-Submarine Warfare
BAFF	British Air Forces in France
BCRA	*Bureau Central de Renseignements et d'Action*
BEF	British Expeditionary Force
BIA	*Bataillons d'Infanterie de l'Air*

CCC	Congressional Country Club
CEFN	*Corps Expéditionnaire Français en Scandinavie* (The French part of the Allied force sent to Norway in 1940)
CI	Counter Intelligence
CIGS	Chief of the Imperial General Staff, head of the British Army, up to 1949
CLET	Clandestine Laboratory Entry Teams
CLS	Central Landing School
COI	Coordinator of Information
COMINT	Communications Intelligence
COS	Chief of Staff
COSSAC	Chief of Staff to the Supreme Allied Commander
CQMS	Company Quartermaster Sergeant Major
CTC	Combined Training Centre
CTR	Close Target Reconnaissance
D Section	Short-lived (1939) covert operations branch of MI6
D/M Section	1939 covert operations section of (technically) Directorate of Military Intelligence; forerunner to SOE
DCIGS	Deputy Chief of the Imperial General Staff
DCO	Directorate of Combined Operations
DDMI	Deputy Director of Military Intelligence
DF	Direction Finding
DMI	Director of Military Intelligence
DMO	Director of Military Operations
DQMG	Deputy Quartermaster General
DS	Directing Staff (of a UK/Commonwealth military exercise)
DSD	Director of Staff Duties
DSO	Distinguished Service Order
DZ	Dropping Zone
EMIA	*Etats Major d'Infanterie de l'Air*
FBGB	*Force Belgique en Grande Bretagne*
FSHQ	Field Service Headquarters
FUSAG	First US Army Group

G(R)	Cover designation for the Directorate of Special Operations of the Middle East branch of SOE
G(RF)	General Staff Section (Raiding Forces)
GCCS	Government Code and Cipher School, later GCHQ
GOC	General Officer Commanding
GPR	Glider Pilot Regiment
GS (R)	General Staff Research Section
GSO1	General Staff Officer Grade One
HRT	Hostage Rescue Teams
ISIC	Inter Service Intelligence Committee
ISLD	Inter-Services Liaison Department; cover name for MI6
ISSB	Inter Service Security Board
ISTDC	Inter-Services Training and Development Centre
JCS	Joint Chiefs of Staff
JIC	Joint Intelligence Committee
Joe	Short for 'Joe Soap'. RAF and SOE slang for agent to be delivered into hostile territory
JPS	Joint Planning Staff
KOSB	King's Own Scottish Borderers
LAD	Light Aid Detachment
LG	Landing Ground
LMG	Light machine gun
LRDG	Long Range Demolition Group
LZ	Landing Zone
Maquis	The French resistance
MCR-1	A small radio receiver developed for clandestine operations
MI (R)	Military Intelligence, Research
MI10	Wartime secret deception service, the designation later applied to the department dealing with enemy weapons
MI19	Wartime secret interrogation service
MI8	Wartime secret radio security service
MI9	Wartime secret Escape and Evasion service
MNBDO	Mobile Naval Base Development Organization

MT	Motor Transport
MTB	Motor Torpedo Boat
MU	Maritime Unit
NATO	North African Theatre of Operations
NNMC	National Naval Medical Center
NORSOG	Norwegian Special Operations Group
NREF	North Russia Expeditionary Force
NWEF	North-West Expeditionary Force
OG	Operations Groups
OKH	*Oberkommando des Heeres* (German Army High Command)
OKW	*Oberkommando der Wehrmacht* (German Armed Forces High Command)
OPs	Observation Posts
ORBAT	Order of Battle
ORs	Other Ranks
OSS	Office of Strategic Services
OVRA	*(Organizzazione di Vigilanza e Repressione Antifascista)* Italian Secret Police
PIAT	Projector Infantry Anti-Tank
PJI	Parachute Jump Instructors
POL	Petrol, oil and lubricants
PPA	Popski's Private Army, otherwise No. 1 Long Range Demolition Unit
PTC	Parachute Training Centre
PTI	Physical Training Instructor
PTS	Parachute Training Squadron
PWE	Psychological Warfare Executive which carried out clandestine propaganda operations around the world
PzKw	*(Panzerkampfwagen)* German tank
QVR	Queen Victoria's Rifles
R & D	Research & Development
RASC	Royal Army Service Corps
Ratline	Escape routes/underground railways organized by agents
RHQ	Regimental Headquarters

Ringing the Bell	In the early days of British military parachuting if, when using a floor exit, the parachutist pushed off too vigorously and hit face or helmet on the opposite side of the hatchway he (or she) had 'Rung the bell'
RMR	Royal Marines Reserve
RNVR	Royal Naval Volunteer Reserve
RSM	Regimental Sergeant Major
RSR	Raiding Support Regiment
RTU	Returned to Unit – administrative action applied to a volunteer for special duties found to be superfluous to requirements or unsuitable
RV	Rendezvous
SACEUR	Supreme Allied Commander Europe
SAS	Special Air Service
SASC	Small Arms School Corps
SBS	Special Boat Service
SD	Special Duties
SF	Special Forces
SHAEF	Supreme Headquarters Allied Expeditionary Force
SIG	Special Interrogation Group
SIGINT	Signals Intelligence
SIS	Secret Intelligence Service
SLOC	Seaborne Lines of Communication
SMP	Shanghai Municipal Police
SOE	Special Operations Executive
SRS	Special Raiding Squadron
SSRF	Small Scale Raiding Force
STC	Special Training Centre
STS	Special Training Schools
SWAT	Special Weapons and Tactics teams
USCG	United States Coast Guard
USMC	United States Marine Corps
WE	War Establishment
WPA	Works Progress Administration, part of Roosevelt's New Deal programme

Introduction

Opening Movements

By dusk on 4 June 1940 Operation Dynamo was over. A motley flotilla had removed some 300,000 Allied personnel from France and Belgium, and a few days later Operations Cycle and Aerial collected the remainder from Bordeaux and Brittany. On 17 June the French government settled in Vichy, a small spa previously famous only for mineral water and an associated method of cooking carrots. Premier Reynaud resigned, and the new administration sought an armistice. Germany had injured France almost to the point of death, and proceeded to rub salt into the wound; the Articles of Armistice Agreement was signed in the same railway carriage, parked on the spot as in 1918, in the Forest of Compiègne. Insult was heaped on injury when the coach was displayed to crowing Germans and pensive neutrals in Berlin.

The Armistice saw one moment of farce. The Italian Army attacked the Maginot Sud but stalled before the ceasefire sounded. Mussolini hurried forward to join his Fascist legions but when descending the Mont Cenis Pass saw a tricolour still flying over a mountain fortress. Fort la Turra, garrisoned by two subalterns and fifty conscripts and reservists, was undefeated. Mussolini, a former conscript wounded on the horrific Isonzo Front, recognized courage when he saw it, and the little garrison marched out with the full honours of war. Italian spin-doctors unwisely broadcast this chivalrous gesture to a sniggering world; an Army Corps stopped up by some old men and boys.

*   *   *

The French had little to celebrate for years, the *quatre années noires*. Their attenuated country was run by a cabal which exchanged *Legalité, Egalité, Fraternité* for *Famille, Travaille, Patrie*; but whose *Patrie* was questionable. The Armistice terms required retention of the million plus French prisoners of war in Germany and Italy for an unspecified period, massive reductions in the armed forces, and dismemberment of the secret service and its wireless monitoring system. French people of all classes and political persuasions faced a growing horror – that the occupation was permanent.

But in Britain some senior figures realized that one day an Allied army would have to cross the Channel and defeat the Germans on the field of battle. Adolf Hitler also seemed to know there would be a day of reckoning in France:

> *Führer Headquarters*
> *23 March 1942 1616*
> *OKW/WFSt/Op.Nr.: 001042 g.Kdos.*
> *Directive No. 40*
> *Subj: Command Organization of the Coasts*
> *General Tactical Instructions for Coastal Defence:*
>   *Coastal defence is a task for the Armed Forces, and requires particularly close and complete cooperation of all the services.*
>   *Timely recognition of the preparations, assembly, and approach of the enemy for a landing operation must be the goal of the intelligence service as well as that of continual reconnaissance by Navy and Luftwaffe.*
>   *Embarkation operations or transport fleets at sea must subsequently be the target for the concentration of all suitable air and naval forces, with the object of destroying the enemy as far off our coast as possible. However, because the enemy may employ skilful deception and take advantage of poor visibility, thereby catching us completely by surprise, all troops that might be exposed to such surprise operations must always be fully prepared for defensive action. Counteracting the well-known tendency of the troops to relax their alertness as time goes on will be one of the most important command functions. Recent battle experiences have taught us that in fighting for the beaches—which include coastal waters within*

*the range of medium coastal artillery—<u>responsibility for the</u>
<u>preparation and execution of defensive operations</u> must
unequivocally and unreservedly be concentrated in the hands
of <u>one man.</u>*
   signed: Adolf Hitler

That is exactly what happened, but before then the Axis had been
defeated in North Africa, due in part to various Allied Special
Forces. Further east Russians, Poles and Czechs, also helped by
secret warriors, tore the heart out of several Axis army groups and
pushed them relentlessly westwards. But for the Western Allies the
outcome of the war, and the future political shape and stability of
Europe, would be decided on the coast of Normandy.

The aim of Operation Overlord was to secure a lodgement on
the Continent from which further offensive operations could be
developed, and was one part of a strategic plan for concerted
assaults from Britain, North Africa, Italy and Russia leading to the
defeat of Germany. The lodgement was to include the Cotentin
peninsula and the port of Cherbourg, essential for supplying the
beach-head and subsequent operations. In March 1944 Hitler, with
one of his uncanny flashes of insight, decided the Allies would land
on the Cotentin and Brittany peninsulas. Accordingly, the defences
of the central area, the Cotentin, were strengthened in May 1944,
days before the landings took place.

Overlord, the greatest military operation in human history,
started almost four years to the day after the Allied evacuation from
Dunkirk, and ended on 19 August 1944 when General Eisenhower
took command for the final assault on Germany.

If Overlord failed it might never be attempted again. Everything
hinged on the first few hours of the invasion, and anything that
could be done to prepare the way was important. That included
raising secret armies and forces for one thing – to help defeat of the
German Army in the west.

This book describes some lesser-known aspects of these secret
formations prior to the Overlord landings, and starts, surprisingly
perhaps, before the Great War.

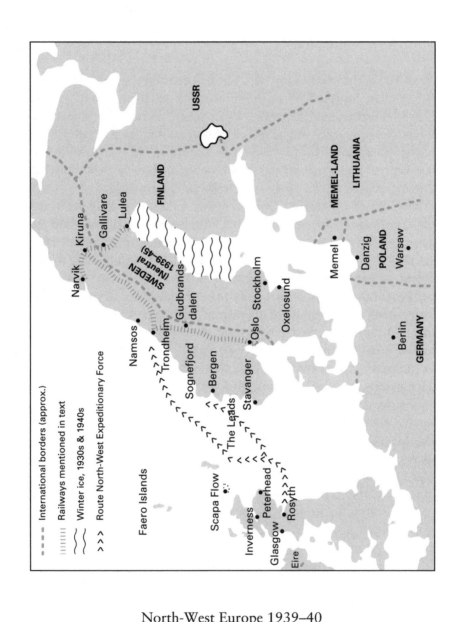

North-West Europe 1939–40

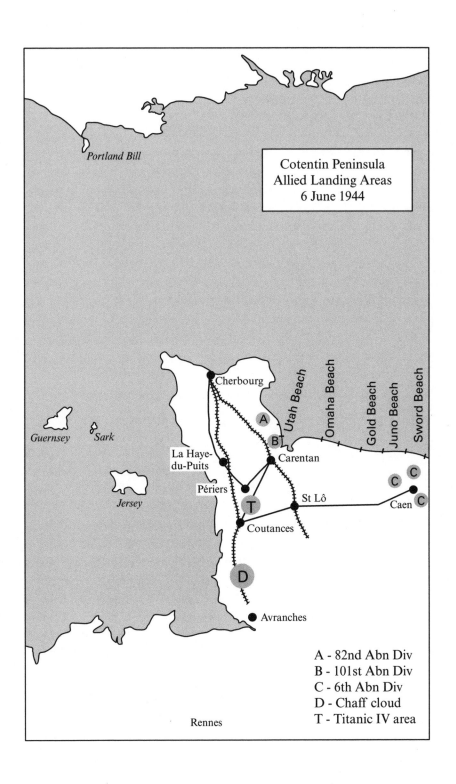

Portland Bill

Cotentin Peninsula
Allied Landing Areas
6 June 1944

Cherbourg

Utah Beach

Omaha Beach

Gold Beach

Juno Beach

Sword Beach

A

B

Guernsey

Sark

La Haye-
du-Puits

Carentan

Périers

C

C

Jersey

T

St Lô

Caen

C

Coutances

D

Avranches

A - 82nd Abn Div
B - 101st Abn Div
C - 6th Abn Div
D - Chaff cloud
T - Titanic IV area

Rennes

Chapter One

Preparations for War

Between 1899 and 1919 the British Army changed from a small, professional force usually employed as colonial constabulary, into a massive all-arms fighting force, manned mainly by hostilities-only personnel. It started to change in South Africa where important lessons were learned at the hands of Boer Commando leaders such as Christian and Piet De Wit, Koos De La Rey and Denys Reitz. The British copied their enemy's deep-penetration raids and raised small units for specific tasks, reconnaissance (Rimington's Tigers), observation (Lovat's Scouts) and raiding (Steinaecker's Horse). Heavy losses from enemy action and disease made the Army turn to the scorned Volunteers, and found they made good, if critical, soldiers. Women also appeared in the field and criticized the supply and medical arrangements, a heresy compounded when they were proved right.

Lessons Learned

Between the end of the Boer War and 1914 the British Army also changed weapons, tactical doctrine, structures and uniforms to prepare for a major European war. The government modernized other aspects of defence. In 1903 the Royal Naval Volunteer Reserve, Royal Naval Reserve (fishing and merchant service personnel) and Royal Marines Reserve were formed. In 1904 the Committee of Imperial Defence appeared, in 1907 the Territorial Army, then the Junior (public schools) and Senior (universities)

1

Officers Training Corps in 1908. The ladies were not forgotten, or to be precise, did not let themselves be forgotten and, in 1907, formed the FANY, First Aid Nursing Yeomanry, still in existence at the time of writing, still confident of their opinions – and usually right. The Secret Service Bureau was formed in 1909 as part of the War Office, and later spawned the Secret Intelligence Service. From 1908 the Army and Navy were encouraged to involve the reserves in home defence plans and tactics, including staff rides, coastal cruises, war games and exercises. Many regular officers found reservists, Home, Dominion and Empire, were capable of expressing constructive ideas on tactics, equipment and mobilization plans, again to everyone's benefit. However few part-timers understood or appreciated the need for good administration, and recognized that if mobilized it would take months of training and practice to bring them anywhere near to the regular forces standards of fitness, endurance, weapon handling, musketry and minor tactics, not to mention discipline. Many of the South African lessons were assimilated into Army tactical doctrine, training manuals and courses of practical instruction. One example was the use of infantrymen for reconnaissance in country where cavalry could not operate, such as the North-East and North-West Frontier Provinces of India. The Indian Army used native levies to scout ahead of columns operating in the Himalayan foothills, units such as the Assam Rifles, Zhob Militia and the South Waziristan Scouts. They were technically a sort of tribal gendarmerie, rarely moving outside their recruitment and patrol areas, but manned by hill men who were superb scouts, observers and trackers, and their reconnaissance was vital to the safety of British or Indian battalions operating in mountainous terrain.

Prior to 1914 British battalions in frontier areas trained platoon-sized forces of scouts to act in hostile territory. 'Infantry Scouts' were trained intensively in scouting, observing, assessing tactical situations, and signalling, by British and Indian military and civilian instructors. The syllabuses covered military, or topographical, sketching, map-reading and map-making, with practical sessions in unfamiliar terrain. These included plotting routes across unmapped territory, and noting wells, springs and seepages, with sketches and notes on access for man and beast, and estimates of the volume of water produced in twelve hours. Also practised was measurement and recording of gradients and the type of surface and its possible resistance to large numbers of metal-shod animals and men. One vital subject was assessing the conditions for forage-laden camels and mules; animals cannot judge the width of their load, only of their own width through a defile, or on a path along the face of a cliff. This material was used to compile 'march books', showing routes, gradients, defiles, water points, villages, watch towers, tribal boundaries, and as much other information as possible to help military forces operate in the wild borderlands, and indeed anywhere.

The Infantry Scouts also spent a considerable amount of time in the field and around the cantonments practising signalling, using semaphore with hand-held flags, and Morse code using heliographs by day and signal lamps at night. A photograph taken in the Himalayan foothills during 1909 shows a very young but self-possessed Second Lieutenant Bernard Law Montgomery sitting among men of 1st Battalion Royal Warwickshire Regiment. The group is described as 'fifty hand-picked men, training as reconnaissance Scouts', and look remarkably fit and confident. During his time in India, Montgomery developed a deep interest in reconnaissance and communications. Much later, in southern England after Dunkirk, then in North Africa and North-West Europe, his interest became almost an obsession, leading to his espousal of units that could help him know what was happening on the 'other side of the hill'. At one time or another these included the Long Range Desert Group for observation and information on the conditions for armoured vehicles, the Special Air Service Regiment for strategic raiding, and Phantom (No. 1 General Headquarters Liaison Regiment) for fast accurate information from the front. (The Russians had developed scouts in 1886. These were *Okhotnichaya Komanda*, literally a 'hunting group'; small teams to be available in times of tension, transition to war and for 'special duties' such as forward reconnaissance, static observation, and path-finding. The Germans and the ever-innovative Austro-Hungarians had followed suit by 1914.)

Across the Atlantic, between the Confederate surrender at Appomattox in April 1865 and entry into the Great War in April

1917, American forces were also only involved in limited warfare. That included the Indian wars, the Battle of the Little Bighorn, neo-colonial incursions into the Philippines, Cuba and other Caribbean islands, and the pursuit of Pancho Villa after the raid on Columbus, Texas, (March 1916). That long chase saw the first US Army operational use of motors and aircraft and was in many ways good preparation for the Great War. Once in Europe the Army and Marine Corps quickly adapted to the demands of modern warfare, and did well against German and Austro-Hungarian forces in France and Italy.

Mobilization

By 1914 most European governments recognized that a major war was inevitable. Many had introduced conscription to maintain large standing armies and larger reserve ones, and laid plans for rapid mobilization to win the first round, which sometimes meant a pre-emptive attack. That required what that unlettered but tactically astute Confederate cavalryman Nathan Bedford Forrest described as 'Git'n thar fustest with th'mostest', which in turn meant swift, efficient mobilization. That was in itself an (almost) irrevocable act of war, and therefore a legitimate excuse for potential enemies to mobilize in turn, perhaps even more quickly than the first party. The main requirement was awareness of enemy intentions, such as pre-mobilization activity including discreet bustle around headquarters, supply centres and printing works (Russian mobilization notices were printed on sullen red paper; even illiterates knew what they meant), while Army remount staff would be meeting with horse dealers and forage merchants. To detect such signs in potentially hostile territory meant spying, the second oldest profession and widely practised throughout Europe before1914.

In 1906 Germany completed the famous Schlieffen Plan, a complex strategy for defeating first France, then Russia, in one short, violent war fought in two stages and on two fronts. It assumed both nations would mobilize slowly and at different rates, allowing a pre-emptive German thrust through Holland, Belgium and the

French Channel ports to forestall British intervention. To quote Field Marshal Schlieffen, 'When you march into France, let the last man on the right brush the Channel with his sleeve'. After defeating the French near Paris the German forces would move east by train to defeat the Russians, hopefully along the banks of the River Niemen, well away from the granaries and horse farms of East Prussia. To be successful the plan required rapid, flawless mobilization encompassing three million troops, 600,000 horses and 11,000 train journeys, and a complex, rigid timetable. (The plan was later modified and weakened; the Russians cheated and mobilized quickly and the rest is history.)

To find out if their enemies were mobilizing the Germans organized an espionage system for the frontier zones of France and Russia; 'Tension Travellers'. These *Spannungs Reisende* were apparently innocent businessmen, many with dual nationality and foreign passports. All were carefully selected, trained in observation and information gathering, and briefed on signs of pre-mobilization activity. A simple communications system was created, based on the international telegraph system. Messages were passed to business houses in neutral countries; information was embedded in innocent business traffic, usually enciphered with commercial codes. The *Spannungs Reisende* were to operate to a tight timetable which required them to return to base, or to a safe house in neutral or potentially hostile territory, for debriefing within a specific period. They were predecessors of Allied surveillance organizations of the Second World War; the Norwegian, New Guinea and Pacific island coast-watchers, and the Sussex and PROUST road watching teams, described later.

Sabotage

The Germans also developed sabotage teams to interfere with what the Italians call the *Primo Balzo*, 'the first rock', as in mountaineering; the first movement of troops in a military campaign. Teams of disguised pioneers (assault engineers) would operate inside foreign territory to delay or disrupt enemy timetables, operating from safe houses established with help from disaffected citizens in

5

Belgium (Walloons were supposedly pro-German), eastern France and Russian Poland. The teams were to sabotage railway tracks and structures such as bridges, water standpipes, sand-drying furnaces, coaling stations, and points; anything required to move troops forward into blocking positions. The sabotage teams apparently also had training in 'counter-scorch' techniques; stopping or hindering enemy demolition of facilities vital to a swift and orderly advance by the German Army. The Germans had planned defensive sabotage and scorched earth operations in frontier areas should an enemy offensive 'git thar fust'.

Guerrilla Warfare

During the Great War there were numerous cases of clandestine warfare, including guerrilla groups and not just Lawrence's Arabs. In northern Albania a certain Austro-Hungarian officer, *Oberst* Nopsca, organized guerrilla forces to harry the Allies. (Special Forces personnel are sometimes a little larger than life. Franz, Baron Nopsca von Felso-Szilvas was a self-taught palaeontologist, geologist, biologist, highly respected scholar of Albanian culture and clan law and a talented linguist. He was also a spy, motorbike enthusiast, homosexual, would-be King of Albania, a murderer – and a suicide.) Austro-Hungary had extra-territorial rights in northern Albania, the *Kultursprotektorat*, guardianship of the minority Catholic Mirdite clans in the otherwise Muslim Gheg tribal confederacy. The Austro-Hungarian *Evidenzbüro*, the security and intelligence service, exploited this to establish an espionage, propaganda and guerrilla network throughout Albania, controlled through couriers and supplied by naval Motor Torpedo Boats. The guerrillas acted as an outer defence screen for the U-boat base at Kotor, one of the finest natural anchorages in the world. (The worst-ever month for U-boat sinkings in both world wars was May 1917; 860,000 tons, one third in the Mediterranean, mainly by Austro-Hungarian and German U-boats operating from Kotor.) The RAF bombed Kotor from airfields near Otranto; in August 1918 aircrew of 226 Squadron were warned about the hazards of falling into the hands of the guerrillas, not knowing the Austro-Hungarian authorities offered a bounty for live pilots and observers, and death for any murdered ones. The guerrillas also harassed Italian Army engineers building a supply road from the Adriatic coast to the Salonika front, which was used nearly ninety years later by NATO forces in Kosovo and Macedonia.

The First Military Parachute Descent?

During the summer of 1918 the Italian, British, French and American forces in Italy were planning a final offensive against Austro-Hungarian defences along the River Piave. The RAF helped the Italians make what they claimed was the first military parachute descent, spies in civilian clothing having been dropped in France since 1915. British assistance included an MP turned observer, later pilot, Captain William Wedgwood Benn and a Canadian fighter ace, Major Billy Barker. They helped solve the problem of dropping agents in the right place at the right time; in France some missions were aborted when the agent declined to leave the aircraft without 'encouragement'. With an Italian engineer, they devised a 'downward ejection seat' for a Savoie-Pomilio twin-engined bomber, usually flown with an observer/gunner in the nose, pilot amidships and another gunner aft. (Savoie-Pomilio aircraft were unreliable; Italian pilots claimed SP3 meant *Sepolcro Per Tre* – tomb for three.) The parachute was packed inside an inverted saucer-like container slung under the aircraft; when 'ejected' the agent's weight extracted the canopy.

The system was tested with dummies and found to work satisfactorily but there was no trial ejection, nor any landing practice, for the agent, Lieutenant Alessandro Tandura. He was to be dropped (in uniform) onto a mountain pasture near the Austro-Hungarian GHQ outside Vittorio, a small town in a very deep valley north of Venice. The aircraft was to depart from the RAF airfield at Villaverla, near Vicenza, about fifty miles from Vittorio. The route roughly followed a well-used railway line leading to a ruined railway bridge over the River Piave near Nervesa, then picked up an enemy operated section of the line to a junction, then along a branch line to Vittorio. William Benn and his Italian colleagues sited searchlights and wireless trucks at six waypoints along the route. When the searchlight crews received a wireless signal from William Benn flying in the bomber, the searchlights were tilted to point straight up, and illuminated in turn. The operation was to coincide with British, French and Italian activity in the mountains a few miles north of the flight path, and the artillery barrages and counter-barrages would, it was hoped, divert the Austro-Hungarians' attention. In addition the aircraft was armed with some bombs to be dropped around Vittorio.

The flight went without a hitch; the searchlights were illuminated in accordance with the plan, the ejection seat worked, and Alessandro Tandura arrived safely near Vittorio. He made contact with his family, built up a network of informers, agitators and saboteurs. Information was passed back by homing pigeon, and Allied aircraft made at least one re-supply drop of money, material and pigeons to the original drop zone. It was a bold attempt, unknown outside Italy.

William Benn returned to the colours in 1939, and flew on some missions before being grounded as overage for active service; he was sixty-three. His two sons also became pilots, and for a brief spell there were three Wedgwood Benn pilots in the Royal Air Force. Sadly the eldest son was killed in a flying accident caused by faulty instruments; but the other, Anthony, survived. William Benn ended the war in the Allied Military Government of Occupied Territories, AMGOT, in Italy.

Chapter Two

The Unquiet Peace

After 1918 the British Army was rapidly run down, yet still required to garrison much of the Empire, conduct battlefield clearance in Europe, and contribute troops to multi-national plebiscite monitoring forces in such diverse places as Silesia, new Baltic nations and Syria. All provided peacekeeping experience. It was also engaged in the Irish War of Independence, then as an onlooker of the Irish Civil War; both provided lessons used later to help agents operate in occupied Europe.

As a precaution in case of another major war, in 1924 the Army organized the Army Officers Supplementary Reserve, an inexpensive system for creating a pool of junior officers, based on the (re-named) Universities Officers Training Corps. Undergraduates joining the OTC could be granted a Supplementary Reserve commission, six weeks training each summer with their sponsor regiment or corps and then train annually thereafter as circumstances allowed. In 1937 a young Scottish SR officer, Archibald David Stirling, joined the Scots Guards after going down from Cambridge. He was following a family tradition; his eldest brother, William, was with the First Battalion, and another brother, Hugh, was about to join the Second Battalion. David Stirling did not take to life at the Guards Depot so took himself off to do some exploring. Later he and Bill, in different ways, contributed significantly to the development of special operations forces around the world.

At the opposite end of the command spectrum from the SR scheme, but also in 1924, the Chiefs of Staff Committee was established to advise the Cabinet on defence policy and to co-ordinate military planning and operations. The Committee was initially preoccupied maintaining a credible defence system in times of financial stringency, and preparing to defend the Empire, and also some fragments of China. These were British trading concessions, including Shanghai, where the British presence influenced some aspects of Allied special operations, and many people around the world have felt the effects – in more ways than one. Between the world wars Shanghai was one of the most degenerate and violent places on earth; one British officer called it a 'preview of the Damnation'. It was said of Shanghai that you could hire any kind of villain, from nailers-up-of-notices to nailers-up-of-Christs, and you could buy anything, from a used handkerchief to the robes of an archbishop – with the archbishop and his conscience inside them. Much evil was done with subtlety, thus the assassination of a corrupt French official, famously duplicitous, poisoned at his retire-ment banquet. Shanghai was no place for the fainthearted and policing it was far from easy. It was patrolled by the Shanghai Municipal Police, operating under the long-established principle of extraterritoriality, whereby citizens of nations with trading treaties were subject to the laws of their home countries rather than the laws of the host state. The Shanghai Municipal Police was therefore a cosmopolitan force, with Americans, Britons, Canadians, Chinese, Germans, Indians, Irishmen and Russians in its ranks, and recruited many ex-servicemen as it provided a better life and retirement than could be found at home. Leading from the front was the order of the day, but policing Shanghai was dangerous and many young officers and NCOs were crippled or killed before they had learned how to survive in the squalid streets and lanes of the settlements. The Shanghai police faced not just ordinary criminals but also Triads, Communist, Japanese and Chinese Nationalist activists, and gangs of disaffected youths bent on social disruption, while the Chinese population in general did not want foreigners present and were rarely inclined to be helpful. All reacted violently to police interference, but some erred seriously by severely injuring a young constable called William Ewart Fairbairn.

Bill Fairbairn was born in Rickmansworth, Hertfordshire, in 1885, and in 1902 enlisted in the Royal Marine Light Infantry where he developed an interest in physical fitness, and the once popular sport of bayonet-fighting; fencing with dummy rifles fitted with spring-loaded, button-tipped 'bayonets'. The British and Japanese Armies were the main proponents of this demanding sport; the former initially trained by an Italian fencing master who demanded absolute silence except in the final lunge. The Japanese sought success over style; in the 1904 Shanghai Garrison Skill-at-Arms Competition their team shrieked, yelled and gyrated its way to victory. Fairbairn, serving on the China Station, was impressed, and also being more interested in winning than style developed a life-long interest in Japanese martial arts.

In 1907 Fairbairn reached the end of his enlistment and joined the Shanghai police, flourishing until injured. He resolved to beat the gangs at their own game and, while still recovering, started to study under several masters, including a Professor Okada, once Judo tutor to the Emperor of Japan and advertising himself as 'Shinnoshindo-Ryu – Jujitsu Instructor and Bone Setter'. Fairbairn was taught street defence by Inspector Ogushi, head of the SMP Japanese section, and also earned a Third Degree Brown, and Second and First Degree Black Belts, at Tokyo's Kodokan Judo University. He learned wrestling, western, Siamese and Chinese boxing, Savate, dockside and bar-brawling techniques from soldiers, marines and seamen. Fairbairn was very professional in his approach to his work and, in 1920, spent four weeks (of his home leave) with the New York Police Department. He walked the beat, raided gambling dens, patrolled Central Park, and helped question suspects in the notorious Tombs; the Manhattan Criminal Courts Central Booking Office. He made many friends in the NYPD, some of whom he met later in life – and in very different circumstances.

In 1923 Fairbairn was posted to the SMP Training Section to teach shooting and unarmed combat. To learn fully what trainee policemen needed to know to survive on the streets he carried out some careful operational research, reviewing police incident reports and hospital records, and interviewing street-fighters and anyone who could help policemen survive and impose respect. The SMP was in the reality business, not practising martial arts, and Fairbairn was following what was to be an article of faith among

Special Forces (and any really professional group); 'you'd go out of your way to pick the brains of a one-armed char-wallah if it helps you do the job better . . .'. He was later assisted in his research by several volunteer SMP officers, including a British businessman called Eric Sykes. There is something slightly mysterious about Eric Sykes. He served in the British Army during the Great War, including training at the Second Army School of Sniping, near Ypres, and was an Infantry Scout and sniper on the Western Front, and later a big game hunter in India. In Shanghai he ostensibly worked for a firm of estate agents, but also represented the Remington and Colt arms companies in Eastern China, and is thought to have worked for Harry Steptoe, SIS Head of Station in Shanghai. Photographs show a distinct likeness to the fictional secret agent George Smiley; pleasant-looking, round-faced, and innocently bespectacled but, like the equally unprepossessing Fairbairn, Sykes was lethal. He joined the SMP in 1926 as a volunteer constable but was soon promoted sergeant in charge of the Sniper Section. He improved sniping methods and tactics for the SMP and developed its close quarter pistol shooting methods, using principles developed by American gunfighters such as Cullen Baker, Wild Bill Hickock and Wyatt Earp – look, tilt, shoot from the hip for really close shooting (up to ten feet), or look, tilt, point, shoot for anything up to thirty feet. As with Fairbairn and unarmed combat, Sykes adopted what worked, not what was orthodox, and encouraged policemen to find their way of hitting the target, in time, every time.

The SMP established a special training facility, the Mystery House, to train policemen in house-clearing and close quarter shooting and weapon skills. It featured moving targets, booby-trapped doors and steps, steep and twisting stairways, a cellar reached by a tunnel of decreasing width and height. It also featured moving targets and dummies to help develop snap-shooting and snap-responses. Although it could be hair-raising, its systems were changed frequently but randomly making it popular, and an efficient training 'theatre'. A sniping range was also built along somewhat similar lines; both were copied by Allied forces in Europe and elsewhere. Finally, Fairbairn and Sykes could do what they taught better than anyone else on the streets as well as in the gymnasium or shooting range, and they were inspired and confident trainers of trainers.

Special Forces

The SMP was an elite force, but within its ranks it had two special units, the Reserve Unit, and the Sniper Section. They dated from February 1925 when Chinese strikers attacked a police station, and harried officers shot several demonstrators, provoking extensive and prolonged riots. Afterwards the SMP appointed Fairbairn to organize a mobile force to contain and control civil commotion peacefully. He formed and trained the Reserve Unit, or 'RU', mobilized as required from specially trained volunteers, full or part-time, from across the force. The Sniper Section worked closely with the Reserve Unit, providing very visible marksmen and counter-sniping protection, which helped defuse many tense situations. There were more riots, and dead rioters, but none shot by the police. The role of the RU was extended to cover the movement of high-value goods, close protection for VIPs, guarding courts during major trials, handling abduction and ransom cases, and closing (trashing) illicit stills and chemical laboratories. The SMP Reserve Unit encompassed elements of many of today's protective services (and in some countries, military or para-military), special operations units, such as SWAT (Special Weapons and Tactics) teams, HRT (Hostage Rescue Teams), and CLETs (Clandestine Laboratory Entry Teams). The result of that sound, innovative training was a better disciplined and more confident police force, capable of holding its own on the streets of Shanghai.

In order to ensure that police weapons and ammunition were properly maintained and secured Fairbairn established the SMP Central Armoury, managed by a former lieutenant colonel in the Imperial Russian Army, Nikolai Pavlovich Solntseff. Civilian shooting clubs, and military and naval units deployed to Shanghai or patrolling the Yellow Sea also used the Armoury. There were two military formations in the Settlements, the Shanghai Volunteer Corps and the Shanghai Defence Force. The part-time SVC was a multi-national force which one time or another featured an

13

American cavalry squadron, British-Eurasian, Chinese, English, Filipino, Italian, Jewish, Portuguese and Russian sub-units. There was also a Scottish infantry company, dressed on occasion in full Highland dress and marching to the sound of bagpipes, which greatly impressed the Chinese. During times of tension, treaty nations with warships on the China Station supplemented the SVC and the SMP with marines, and infantry units from nearby colonies or concessions, from 1927 loosely grouped into the Shanghai Defence Force. Incoming troops, and the crews of naval and merchant ships, were briefed by SMP officers on the dangers of Shanghai. One US officer serving with the 15th Infantry at the 'unofficial' but busy US Concession at Tientsin, was a certain Major George Catlett Marshall, who saw something of Shanghai in his travels, and would have been briefed by the SMP. As General George Marshall, confidant of Roosevelt, he recalled and encouraged the use of Fairbairn as an instructor of the OSS.

Troops from every unit in Shanghai, and crews from naval and merchant vessels – in the pirate-infested Far East all merchant ships carried small arms – frequented the SMP training unit, ranges and armoury; few armies had anything like them at that time. The visitors were not only armourers seeking workshop facilities and gunsmiths' gossip, but servicemen interested in weapons, close quarter shooting, and unarmed combat. Solntseff's workshop converted bayonets and hunting knives into close defence weapons for anyone; in the 1960s veterans of the Shanghai and Wei-Hai-Wei garrisons referred casually to carrying shortened, sharpened but sheathed bayonets when 'walking out'. Fairbairn designed a dagger for self-defence. Solntseff made four examples, one of which was presented to Fairbairn by two US Marine Corps lieutenants, Samuel Yeaton and George Moore. It formed the basis of the famous Fairbairn Sykes No. 2 Fighting Knife, which features on Special Forces and Commando badges and arm patches around the world, and appears on the NATO conventional symbol for Special Forces units.

Fairbairn and Sykes were not the only members of the SMP to develop close quarter combat skills. One of their protégés was an Irishman, Sergeant Dermot Michael O'Neill, and a top Judoka,

14

ranking 5th Dan with the Kodokan. He joined the SMP in 1925, and at the end of his engagement in 1938 went to Japan as head of security at the British Embassy in Tokyo, where he continued to study the martial arts. He later unexpectedly served again with Bill Fairbairn, far from Shanghai.

During the Second World War Bill Fairbairn, Eric Sykes, Pat O'Neil, or instructors they had trained, taught thousands of servicemen and agents of both sexes how to defend themselves and attack an opponent. It will never be known how many enemy personnel were killed with knife, fist or foot, but the main benefit was the self-confidence inspired by possession of these skills.

Fairbairn and Sykes retired from the SMP and from China in 1939. The SMP continued to police the city until the Imperial Japanese Army invaded it in 1941. The Japanese introduced their own vigorous ways of policing but could not cope. They allowed the SMP to carry on until 1943, a situation bizarre even by the elastic standards of Shanghai.

Apart from forming a base for a gladiatorial school and being a fabulously rich trading centre, Shanghai had other uses. It was the hub of the north-west Pacific rim that was, in part, why various nations thought it worth stationing so many troops there. It was also, for the same reason, awash with spies, commercial, political and military, including those of the two superpowers, Britain and America.

Spying

After the Great War all forms of Communications Intelligence, COMINT, continued to be used and developed. The British Government Code and Cipher School, GCCS, was formed in 1922 from the remnants of the wartime Admiralty and War Office organizations and, with the SIS, was placed under control of the Foreign Office. Sections of the school were provided for the three armed services, and in 1925 a wireless interception and decryption facility was based on a warship stationed in Shanghai.

During the 1920s the US Navy also based a similar listening-post in Shanghai, operating as an outstation of the main base in Peking;

all that despite the assertion by the then US Secretary of State, Henry Stimson, that 'gentlemen do not read each other's mail'.

The Japanese were also hard at work in the same area, and were the main target for electronic warfare operations. The British (with considerable help from the Royal Australian Navy), the Americans and, it is thought, the Italians and French, broke the main Imperial Japanese Navy code, JN-25. That was a real feat as wireless traffic was in Morse code, and the Japanese version included twenty-five additional combinations of dots and dashes to transmit Anglicized versions of Japanese ideograms. The Japanese also stepped up their HUMINT (human intelligence) collection across Asia, paying particular attention to ports, anchorages and beaches. Groups of 'businessmen' and 'authors of guide books' toured the coasts of the Pacific and Indian Oceans, busy with cameras, notebooks and measuring tapes, and buying maps and topographical surveys. The Japanese, with a growing population but limited resources of land, food and raw materials had ambitions about many places, especially China, where they made their first major move.

In 1937 a young officer in the Royal Engineers, Lieutenant Michael Calvert, was posted to the British Army training staff of the Shanghai Volunteer Corps. He spoke Cantonese, having learnt it in less than two years while attached to the Hong Kong Royal Engineers. Shortly after arriving in Shanghai he witnessed the Japanese amphibious assault on Chinese defences at Hangchow Bay, near the International Settlement. The assault involved troop-carrying landing craft which were launched in pairs from a stern dock in a large ship, which was also equipped with side doors and ramps for offloading vehicles, including light tanks, onto quays. This was the purpose-built assault ship, the *Shinsu Maru*, launched in 1933 and the forerunner of present day Landing Ships, Dock (LSD). It was ordered and paid for by the Japanese Army, not the Imperial Japanese Navy. The Japanese armed forces fought what, at times, seemed like separate wars from 1930 until 1945. The IJN had used 'civilian fishing parties' to reconnoitre and plot the approaches to the levees and beaches where the Hangchow landings took place. Calvert submitted a report on the assault to the War Office but never heard whether or not it had been received.

16

Eight years later Brigadier Michael Calvert DSO commanded the SAS Brigade in northern Europe.

Military developments were not confined to the Far East. A series of interesting developments took place in the UK, initiated by the growing realization that another world war was inevitable.

Modernization

The Chiefs of Staff Committee had moved on from preoccupation with financial stringency to coping with new threats to peace, especially Nazi Germany and Fascist Italy, the hubs of an 'Axis of Steel, linking Berlin and Rome, around which all else will revolve' (Mussolini, 1936). One British response was the Inter-Service Intelligence Committee (ISIC), formed in January 1936 as a sub-committee of the Chiefs of Staff Committee. In July it became the Joint Intelligence Committee (JIC), and two years later, in July 1939 when war was imminent, passed to Foreign Office control. Another War Office response, not unrelated to the birth of the JIC, was the General Staff Research Section, or GS (R). It initially consisted of one officer, directly responsible to the Deputy Chief of the Imperial General Staff, and authorized to 'research into tactics and problems of organization, with a mandate to go where he liked, talk to anyone and not to be bothered with files, memos and telephone calls'. In other words, free from departmental or regimental responsibilities, the dreaded 'secondary duties' of HM Forces, so able to devote all his energies to research. The topics to be studied were selected by the DCIGS, the Director of Military Operations and Director of Military Intelligence, and confirmed by the CIGS on behalf of the Army Council. The topics were considered by the top echelon of the British Army to be of high importance; they were not, as has been suggested elsewhere, left to the discretion of the researcher nor was research on each topic confined to one year. By spring 1938, GS (R) had produced five reports, including *Reorganization of the War Office, Organization of Armoured and Mobile Units and Formations* to *Training of the Army*, and was completing a sixth. The DCIGS was considering the next subject when matters elsewhere dictated the decision.

That same spring the SIS extended its passive role of intelligence collection into active interference in the affairs of other nations. The Head of the SIS, Admiral Sir Hugh Sinclair, obviously with the knowledge and approval of his masters in the Foreign Office, asked the War Office for the loan of an officer to report on ways of disrupting Axis military and economic systems in times of tension, transition to war, and war. In April 1938 Major Lawrence Grand, Royal Engineers, was seconded to SIS, a few days after the Austro-German *Anschluss* ('connection'). He submitted his first report in May, outlining possible targets and methods of attack, both physical and psychological. He stressed these were wartime missions, but that agents would have to be positioned in or near the target areas prior to hostilities. The report also identified such preparatory moves as developing and stockpiling sabotage material, selection and reconnaissance of targets, training agents and creating an infrastructure of bases abroad. The concept was accepted, with one major proviso – that initial targeting should be limited to certain strategic materials essential to Axis war-making capability, namely Swedish iron ore and Romanian oil, and that operations should be confined to sabotage of shipping and handling equipment.

The ore was critical to Axis arms production; eight million tons were imported annually by Germany in 1937, a figure likely to be dwarfed in wartime. It was mined at three sites, Kiruna and Gallivare in the far north, and Nykopping, near Stockholm. The northern ore was exported through the ports of Lulea in summer and Narvik, in Norway, during winter; the southern ore went out via the ice-free port of Oxelosund. The ore-carriers offloaded at German Baltic ports such as Rostock, Lübeck and Kiel, or as close to the Ruhr as they could reach by sailing up the Rhine. Romanian oil went by river to Austria, Czechoslovakia and southern Germany, or by sea to northern Germany, Italy and Spain, considered likely to join the Axis. Grand's secondment was extended to enable him to form a new branch of SIS, Section IX, for offensive operations.

The same topic was being discussed in the War Office. The DCIGS, the DMO, and the DMI and, as it was so momentous, it must have also been in consultation with the CIGS, General Lord Gort, were deciding how the Army could match the work of Section IX. It is unlikely the issue was raised formally with the Secretary of State; the Cabinet had ordered the armed forces to refrain from studying anything like expeditionary forces or warlike operations in relation to Europe. Therefore GS (R) was tasked with studying an apparently innocuous topic, *Considerations from the recent wars in Spain and China with regard to certain aspects of Army Policy*; a reasonable subject for general research, but concealing an unwritten addendum, something like, 'Report on the methods, resources and outcomes of recent guerrilla wars'. The topic demonstrates that senior officers of that era were aware of the changing nature of war, and sought alternatives to 'conventional', i.e. Western Front, warfare.

The reading list devised for Study No. 7 included several books about the Boer War, including a best seller, *Kommando,* by Denys Reitz, published in Britain during 1932. Throughout the 1930s it exerted considerable influence in British military circles including the TA; in some units it was required reading for officers, and in one or two London ones recommended to all ranks.

While the British were taking these first steps towards developing special operations capabilities, the Germans were already active and successful. In 1920 they raised a Special Forces unit in Silesia to influence the plebiscite under the innocent name of *Industrieschutz Oberschlesien* (Upper Silesian Industrial Protection Service). It was later re-named *Deutsche Kompanie*, and produced a subsidiary offshoot, the *Sudetendeutsche Freikorps*, for work in the Czech lands of Bohemia and Moravia. Throughout the spring and summer of 1938 these organizations conducted operations in the Sudetenland, agitating for self-determination for the German minority.

GS (R) Report No. 7 appeared in late summer 1938 and was studied by several senior officers, including the CIGS-designate, General Sir Edmund Ironside. He spoke seven languages and during the Boer War, among other missions, made a covert reconnaissance into German South-West Africa masquerading as a Boer carter, complete with Cape cart and a span of oxen, to accompany a German military expedition suspected of aiding the Boer forces from a safe base, field hospital and rest area. He later experienced irregular warfare and political agitation in North Russia (1919), Ruthenia (1920, with the British Military Mission to Eastern Hungary), Iraq (1920), Persia (1921) and India, (1930), when Gandhi started the 'Quit India' civil disobedience campaign. In late summer 1938 Ironside was about to take post as Governor of Gibraltar when he was suddenly summoned to the War Office and offered a very special, short term task in Germany.

Munich

On 15 September the British Prime Minister, Neville Chamberlain, met Hitler at Berchtesgaden for talks about the alleged Czech suppression of the German minority in the Sudetenland. One by-product of the Berchtesgaden meeting was a lengthy minute from General Hastings Ismay, Secretary of the Committee of Imperial Defence, for the British Cabinet, dated 20 September and concluding that '. . . from the military point of view, time is in our favour, and that, if war with Germany has to come, it would be better to fight her in say 6–12 months' time, rather than to accept the present challenge'. That meant Chamberlain playing for time and also added urgency to Grand's work.

On 22 September Chamberlain and Hitler met again and agreed to hold a four-power conference at Munich on 29 September to resolve the Sudetenland issue; the Czechs would be present, but not allowed to sit at the top table. Mussolini and Edouard Daladier, Prime Minister of France, joined Hitler and Chamberlain in Munich, where between 27 September and 14 October General Ironside was 'specially employed', accompanying Neville Chamberlain; anyone speaking seven languages would have been very useful at Munich. The meeting produced not only Chamberlain's declaration of 'Peace for our time', but agreement to allow the Germans to occupy the Sudetenland a few days later, in early October. It also gave Hitler and Stalin apparent confirmation of the French view 'Mieux vaut Hitler que Staline' (better Hitler than Stalin). Chamberlain may not have obtained peace in his time, but he obtained it for a vital year, a point sometimes overlooked when assessing his term in office.

Later that year Ironside was appointed GCB (Knight Grand Cross of the Order of the Bath).

After the German occupation of the Sudetenland the burgeoning empire of Admiral Canaris, head of the *Abwehr* absorbed the *Deutsche Kompanie* and the *Sudetendeutsche Freikorps*, and merged them into a new formation with an innocent sounding name, *BauLehr-Kompanie zbV 800* (No. 800 Special Purpose Construction Training Company). It was later to become famous as part of *Abwehr Abteilung II – Sondereinsatze, Sabotage und Brandenburgerverbande*; that is, Special Missions, Sabotage and Brandenburg Units. The name derived from its base at Brandenburg-am-Havel, near Berlin.

At the War Office the terms of reference for Study No. 8 *Investigation of the Possibilities for Guerrilla Activities* were completed shortly after Munich, and probably benefited from information gleaned by Ironside in Germany. Between 14 and 28 October, when he started to prepare to move to Gibraltar, he probably helped draft the terms of reference for the study, and possibly nominated the researcher, who was to start work in December, and suggested the names of other officers for an expanded GS (R). The officer selected to carry out the research was Lieutenant Colonel J.F.C. Holland, Royal Engineers. During the Great War he had served in France, first as a Sapper, then as an RFC Observer, and afterwards experienced the Irish War of Independence, and political agitation in India. His official brief was supplemented by another, highly secret one, to work with Grand in producing the clandestine warfare report for the War and Foreign Offices.

The Foreign Office, or at least the SIS, did not wait for the report but moved ahead, appointing a retired naval officer, Commander Stephen Langley, to work with Grand on sabotage techniques and devices. The War Office also started recruiting and in January 1939 Major Colin Gubbins, Royal Artillery, joined GS (R). During the Great War he served in France and North Russia, then, like Holland, in Ireland, and on the turbulent North-West Frontier of India. He spoke French and Russian, and had been Ironside's ADC in North Russia. At GS (R) he was given the task of sifting the information gleaned by Holland during research for Study No. 7, and preparing guidelines for clandestine warfare operations.

The pace of work in GS(R) accelerated when Hitler started to flex his political and military muscles. In February 1939 he invited General Franco to join Germany, Italy and Japan in the Anti-Comintern Pact, an apparent precursor to joining the 'Axis of Steel'. In March Germany occupied Bohemia and Moravia, which made a European war almost inevitable. The efficient and innovative Skoda arsenal, railway and motor vehicle manufacturing complex at Pilsen, Bohemia, passed into the acquisitive hands of the Goering brothers, Herman and Albert. Slovakia declared itself to be an independent nation, and later joined the Axis. On 23 March German forces occupied Memelland, created at Versailles out of a distant corner of East Prussia. It was based on the ancient, free and Hanseatic port of Memel, the most northerly ice-free port on the southern Baltic coast. It, therefore, could import Swedish ore year-round as it had good rail links with Pilsen and Brno, site of a huge small-arms factory and also, via the eastern Dolomites, with Italian industrial centres – useful if the British ever blockaded the Baltic. Memel would also be handy for a war with Russia as the east-west road and railway routes through Poland were poor. The ever-resourceful Poles set about recruiting 3,000 discharged soldiers of the defunct Czechoslovak Army, into the Czech Legion, a useful addition to the Polish forces. The Legion included a number of Jews, some of whom eventually served with British Special Forces, including the SAS in North Africa and Europe.

Hitler's next move was against another Versailles creation, the Danzig Corridor, separating Germany and East Prussia. He demanded the return of Danzig to Germany, (apart from anything else it was the nearest port to Oxelosund) but the Poles rejected the claim and obtained French and British guarantees of support in case of German aggression.

Special Operations

Holland and Grand's report was released on 20 March. It covered possible operations in four areas:

First, the stillborn 'Little Entente', comprising the former

Czechoslovakia, Yugoslavia and Romania, nations bordering aggressive, neo-fascist Hungary, and in turn surrounded by Axis, fascist or communist nations.

Second, occupied territory such as Austria (some thought few Austrians welcomed the *Anschluss*) and Germany (it was thought many Germans hated Hitler and National Socialism).

Third, and more realistically, the Italian-occupied Libya and Abyssinia, both with active resistance movements.

Fourth, nations bordering Germany, Lithuania (touching Memel and East Prussia), Denmark and Holland.

The report recommended forming two bodies, one civil (SIS) and the other military, to handle sabotage, *coup de main*, guerrilla and propaganda operations. The SIS unit would be based on Section IX under Grand; the other, an Army formation headed by Holland; both were to be ready by mid-summer. That allowed only sixteen weeks for recruiting and training agents, developing sabotage material, and establishing support groups and safe houses near the target areas and conducting reconnaissance; those were early and naive days.

The report was seen by the Acting Head of the SIS, Stewart Menzies, then by Brigadier W.E. van Cutsem, the Deputy DMI, and finally by the DMO, General R.H. Dewing. The last two briefed the CIGS, and on 22 March they interviewed Grand. Everything was accepted, pending approval by Lord Halifax, the Foreign Secretary. The following day the paper was discussed by Lord Halifax, the CIGS, Menzies, Sir Alexander Cadogan (the Permanent Under Secretary at the Foreign Office), and Grand. Final approval was forthcoming; the priority target was to be Romanian oil supplies, and strict security was to be observed at all times. The question of funding for both bodies was to be handled by the Foreign Secretary. Section IX became D Section (allegedly D stood for 'Destruction'); and then part of Special Operations Executive; its brief history must unfortunately be told elsewhere.

On 3 April, the GS(R) concept of operations was approved by the DCIGS, and confirmed by the CIGS on 13 April. It was to be based on an enlarged and renamed GS (R) and would have three tasks:

First, to study guerrilla methods and produce guides to irregular warfare in various territories.

Second, to develop simple means of sabotaging marine and rail systems and to develop production and distribution systems for these weapons.

Third, to develop and initiate recruitment and training methods, and an operational infrastructure capable of rapid deployment.

The new body, D/M Section, came into being the day of the meeting with the CIGS. (Work seems to have started a day or two before then; Holland, like Grand, was a thruster.) Thereafter things moved quickly. To ensure cooperation, although they had different roles and masters, the two sections were housed in Caxton Street, Westminster. D/M Section was funded from the Secret Vote, but the section was not part of, and did not report to, SIS. It was technically part of the Directorate of Military Intelligence, and Holland was accountable to the DCIGS, by way of the DDMI. Later, inevitably, there was overlap between the two sections, leading to confusion and tension but these were growing pains, not conflict. They led to a formal distinction of their roles: the military dealt with activities in enemy occupied territory and benign neutral nations which could be discussed with the governments, exiled or resident, of those states; SIS dealt with matters which could not be so discussed.

Holland and Gubbins started recruiting. Major Millis Jefferis RE arrived to deal with sabotage. He received a quick briefing from Holland and thereafter spent much of his time at the government explosives laboratories at Fort Halstead, near Sevenoaks, or the Woolwich Arsenal proving grounds, frequently accompanied by Commander Langley. Major F.T. Davies, Grenadier Guards, compiled a register of service personnel with skills, experience or knowledge which might prove useful, and helped Holland find likely candidates. These included Captain Bill Stirling, Scots Guards, Major Norman Crockatt, Royal Scots, and Lieutenant Colonel L.V. Blacker, Royal Artillery, a Great War veteran who had served in Russia with the 3rd Turkestan Rifles, and in India where he had been one of the aircrew on the first flight over Mount Everest. He was a prolific inventor, specializing in unusual weapons, and worked well with Jefferis and Langley, Holland, Gubbins and Davis, joined at times by Grand and Lieutenant

24

Colonel Michael Chidson, a long-serving member of SIS, to discuss ways and means and ponder over manning charts, maps and equipment scales. Colin Gubbins concentrated on doctrine, building on research carried out for Study No. 8, and assisted Jefferis with drafting guidelines for demolitions. The manuals; the *Art of Guerrilla Warfare,* the *Partisan Leader's Handbook,* and *How to Use High Explosives,* were finished in May 1939, and became the bibles of SOE and if not quite that for OSS, then something like 'Letters to Corinthians'.

In May 1939 Colin Gubbins visited Poland, Latvia, Lithuania, Estonia and Romania, all possible hosts or customers for teams from D/M or D Section. The Polish authorities were the most receptive to offers of help, less so to requests about bases. They also revealed some of their work on codes and code breaking, including unravelling the secrets of the Enigma encoding and decoding system, and provided information on German, Lithuanian and Soviet clandestine operations in frontier areas. These included the borders of Memelland, Silesia, the Sudetenland, Danzig and Alsace. Information about the last had been gleaned from the *Polonia,* Polish communities in northern France, mainly around Lille. The French were building defences, part of the Maginot Nord line, near Alsace, and apparently *Abteilung II* found it a useful testing ground for spies and agents provocateur, and the Poles (and, possibly, French) for counter-intelligence training!

The *Polonia* dated from Napoleon's Grand Duchy of Warsaw, his Polish 'Red Lancers', and the retreat from Moscow. Over the years the veterans and their families were joined by other Poles in search of work or to escape the vengeance of the Tsarist secret police.

There were other British responses to the Axis threat in 1938. The Territorial Army was doubled, and inevitably diluted; most infantry battalions, artillery and yeomanry regiments, units of supporting arms and services, and brigade and divisional headquarters were cloned to form a reserve force twice the size, in theory, of the original. The RAF raised extra Auxiliary Air Force squadrons to operate anti-aircraft balloons; some of the personnel later found themselves helping train paratroops and secret agents.

The Royal Navy Volunteer Reserve and Royal Marines Reserve also expanded, the latter helped by the innovative centralized training scheme at the RMR Depot, Lympstone, Devon, later to become the RM Commando Training Centre. The role of the Joint Intelligence Committee was enhanced, and it was tasked with setting broad requirements for intelligence collection, assessment and dissemination for SIS, the GCCS, and, in part, for the armed forces intelligence branches. The Chiefs of Staff Committee created the Joint Planning Staff, and also a new research body, the Inter-Services Training and Development Centre. The ISTDC was to study such matters as landing an expeditionary force on hostile shores; Michael Calvert's Hangchow Creek report may indeed have been read. The centre, really only four officers and some clerical staff, was based in Fort Cumberland, Portsmouth, alongside, possibly by intent, another new formation, the Mobile Naval Base Development Organization, manned by the Royal Navy and Royal Marines. Their task was to develop a system of ad hoc formations to defend and operate foreign ports for landing expeditionary forces and for use as Naval forward operating bases.

Despite the creation of the MNBDO, one of ITSDC's first tasks was development of landing craft, started by the Royal Navy at Gallipoli but stopped soon after. The centre developed some landing craft, and elementary handling procedures, which helped the rapid evolution of British raiding forces, amphibious warfare craft, and seaborne assault tactics. In late 1938 the centre was also tasked with assessing all aspects of airborne forces. Poland, France, Germany, Russia, Hungary and Italy were busy in that field and most had raised parachute and assault glider units but Britain had done little. The RAF had established a Parachute Test Unit and a rudimentary training school at Henlow in1923, but it only taught escape drills to aircrew, and was manned by a few volunteer instructors. (It also tested parachutes; the tester stood on the wing of a Vimy bomber, pulled the ripcord and, if the parachute didn't open, hopefully did not let go.)

Staff from the ITSDC intended visiting two French composite airborne infantry and air transport units, one in France, the other in Algeria, in late 1939 but war intervened. The staff would have benefited from a visit to Poland. By late 1938 the Polish government and military authorities realized that war was unavoidable, and made what plans they could, faced as they were with a dual threat; resurgent Germany to the west, and belligerent USSR in the east. An airborne centre had been established near Warsaw to provide basic military parachute training and as the base for a small Special Forces unit, derived from an experimental airborne reconnaissance platoon fielded in the 1938 manoeuvres.

The Special Forces unit was tasked with sabotaging railways and key road bridges to delay an enemy invasion; shades of the German railway sabotage troops of 1914. The forty-strong unit consisted of a commander, deputy and senior NCO, a communications squad, a team of assault pioneers and a covering group of infantry. The three-man communications squad was equipped with a portable radio for contact with HQ and with recovery or re-supply aircraft; it also carried pyrotechnics for signalling to aircraft or friendly ground forces and equipment for tapping telephone wires. The nine-man team of pioneers was armed with two sets of demolition charges, one for destroying stone, concrete or iron bridges or viaducts, and the other for cutting rails. The cutting charges were concealed under the rails and detonated by a pressure fuse actuated by the weight of the main locomotive wheels; the charge was also fitted with an anti-handling device which, once set, detonated the charge if lifted or moved. The cover group was armed with automatic weapons, knives and grenades. Their job was to eliminate sentries or guard posts at bridges, to protect the pioneers when laying their charges, and to cover the withdrawal of the force. The team was apparently to be dropped into east Prussia to derail trains, preferably in tunnels, and destroy railway and road bridges along which a German invading force would travel. Roads in that area were few and not always in good condition.

The British government attempted to prepare for a new form of warfare; foreshadowed by the German air raids on London in 1917 and 1918, and recent events in Spain. There, on 26 April 1937 the *Kondor* Legion had bombed the peaceful Basque market town of Guernica, causing around 1,600 casualties. The town blazed for three days after the air raid.

In London plans were made by all government departments to

disperse certain essential and some non-essential but necessary departments, if war seemed imminent, to avoid loss of key personnel through bombing. The Home Office had estimated that within the first twenty-four hours of the war the *Luftwaffe* could cause 175,000 casualties. Most, it was assumed, would be in London, the key target as it was the political and financial hub of the Empire. Government officials scouted the Home Counties, East Anglia and South Midlands for suitable locations to house large numbers of civil servants and military personnel. Others researched Great War records of similar events and revised rules for requisitioning property, while others started to organize a sort of Irish horse fair where ministries and departments could bid for premises. The organization of the lists of premises and the associated legislation was an excellent example of the British civil service at its best and the 'horse-trading' of it at its worst, as departments jockeyed for the plum sites. These were the better and newer country houses close to towns and mainline railway stations, possibly possessing such essentials as private swimming pools, tennis courts, golf courses, pheasant shoots and trout streams.

Among other ministries affected by the evacuation plans was the Foreign Office, including the SIS, part of the Government Code and Cipher School and D Section. The code and cipher staffs were allocated a country house in rural Buckinghamshire, a couple of hundred yards from a small station on the main London-Rugby railway line. Shortly before war was declared the staff of Bletchley Park was told to expect 'Captain Ridley's Shooting Party'.

Chapter Three

The Phoney War

On 1 September 1939 the armed forces of Germany launched a massive land, air and sea attack on Poland, and two days later Britain declared war on Germany. Even before the formal declaration, government departments had quietly started their mobilization schemes. The armed forces started calling up reservists, and recalling personnel from peacetime appointments. The ISTDC was almost disbanded on the basis that, to quote the words of the then naval representative, Lieutenant Commander L.E.H. Maund, '. . . the Admiralty, and Air Ministry were of the opinion that there would be no combined operations in this war'. Accordingly, the Royal Navy, Royal Marines and Royal Air Force officers and clerks were posted to operational appointments, but the War Office thought carefully and left its officers in place. Civilians and retired officers replaced the military clerks and administrative staff; someone was thinking ahead. In addition, the Centre's hastily written recommendation of establishing a British airborne capability was accepted, and work started, albeit with a low priority. Unbelievably, there was a feeling that, '. . . it'll be over by Christmas', quite apart from the massive amount of work caused by mobilization.

Among the many Supplementary Reserve officers mobilized was Second Lieutenant A.D. Stirling, who returned to Pirbright to complete a young officers' course. He still did not altogether take to life in barracks but recognized the need to master the basics of soldiering and of being an efficient officer if he was to be of use on the battlefield. Bill Stirling returned to the First Battalion Scots Guards in London and served stoically for some months. He occasionally saw his brothers and found they, too, were chaffing at the bit; all very much in keeping the theme of all armies, in every war – 'hurry up and wait'.

Elsewhere in London the first week of September saw D Section and GS(R) moving out of Caxton Street. Many D Section staff disappeared into what later became known as the 'Secret Triangle'. This was more kite-shaped than triangular, and covered an area north of London that housed more than a few secret organizations during the Second World War. It was bounded by a line drawn from Roydon, near Hertford, and ran north to Daventry, across to Peterborough then back to Roydon by way of Bishop's Stortford. The D Section possibly moved into Orwell Grange, in the eponymous village south-west of Cambridge; it had been selected by SIS for use as a dispersal site and later housed SIS teams preparing for secret operations.

The Section now numbered around sixty persons, including fifty agents or potential agents. They appeared to have been full of enthusiasm for their new role, and bursting with ideas. One was to form a group of agents, the word 'unit' was remembered as being taboo due to its military connotations, for *coup de main* operations, such as abducting or assassinating key enemy personnel. The idea took hold, but was not developed by SIS but by SOE, the successor body to GS(R).

D/M Section also changed location, subordination, name and role. It moved into the War Office Main Building in Whitehall to become part of the Directorate of Military Intelligence as section MI(R), responsible for developing irregular forces to support conventional military operations. It had four operational and one intelligence roles:
    i) selection and training of personnel
    ii) planning operations
    iii) development and production of sabotage material
    iv) control of operations if so required by DMO

v) gathering intelligence not available through military
collection systems

(The new name provided reasonable cover; in November 1918 an earlier MI(R) handled military intelligence about territories of the former Russian Empire.)

First Attempts

During that first autumn of the war two small liaison units, one RAF, the other Army, merged and, by chance, developed into one of the least known and most effective units of the war, on either side.

The first of these formations to appear was No. 3 Air Liaison Mission, RAF, formed in late 1939 and commanded by Wing Commander J.M. Fairweather. ALMs had been devised before the war, in part by the staff and students attending the RAF School of Army Cooperation, Old Sarum, to collect battlefield intelligence from Allied Army HQs for transmission to the HQ British Air Forces in France, (BAFF), the Air Component of the BEF. Each ALM consisted of a few officers and airmen, some trucks but no radios; information would pass via the Allied military telephone network as radio and wireless silence was to be imposed once British forces deployed onto the Continent.

The Army liaison unit started life as part of No. 1 Military Mission, the British military representative with the French Army *Grand Quartier General* in Paris. The Mission was over-manned and cumbersome, but included in its ranks some able and vigorous young staff officers, eager for action. Among them was Lieutenant Colonel G.F. Hopkinson, North Staffordshire Regiment, who soon found an outlet for his energies and initiative when he was dispatched as 'military observer' to 3ALM, located at the Belgian GQG.

Fortunately Fairy and Hoppy were kindred spirits and got on famously. They also soon realized that the telephone system was less than perfect, and was probably tapped by enemy agents. Further, the Belgians did not know for sure where some of their own forces were, let alone those of the enemy – and this was during

31

the infamous *Sitzkrieg* when nothing much was moving along the entire Front. The solution was to go forth and find out what was happening, and which unit was where, both enemy and friendly, to ensure that Allied aircrew knew what not to bomb or strafe as well as what could be attacked. To cut an interesting story short, Hoppy and Fairy with the blessing of the BEF and BAFF, formed a battle-field reconnaissance and reporting unit, the Hopkinson Mission. Its role was flexible but it was to patrol the front to identify enemy troop or tank concentrations beyond the range of friendly artillery. Intelligence reports were passed to RAF reporting centres, Air Intelligence Liaison Sections, for transmission to the Allied Central Air Bureau. (The entire inter-Allied reporting system was well thought out, but was a refinement of that used in the Great War and, as in the infamous German onslaught of March 1918, the static system collapsed when attacked by mobile forces.)

The roles supplemented the reconnaissance tasks of Army armoured car regiments and RAF Army Cooperation squadrons, some equipped with Lysander Army Cooperation aircraft. The Lysanders were agile maids-of-work, unjustly derided after Dunkirk but later put to excellent use in support of special operations in France.

The Hopkinson Mission consisted of a tactical headquarters including a Signals Section, a reconnaissance group, a motor-cycle platoon, and a mobile Intelligence Liaison Section. The head-quarters team consisted of Lieutenant Colonel Hopkinson, Wing Commander Fairweather and a small team of officers, NCOs and ORs. The reconnaissance group was provided by the 12th Royal Lancers (Prince of Wales's), and was commanded by Captain John Warre. It had two troops of six Guy armoured cars, each fitted with a No. 11 Wireless Set, with a range of about twenty miles, and armed with a 2-pounder gun and two machine guns. The motor-cyclist platoon was commanded by Lieutenant John Morgan, and was drawn from 2nd Battalion, Queen Victoria's Rifles, a rather smart London Territorial unit. The Intelligence Liaison Section consisted of six Intelligence Corps subalterns and six junior NCOs, all French speakers, and mounted on Norton motorcycles. The Mission could form several reconnaissance teams, each of various combinations of Guys, Intelligence Liaison teams and covering groups of mounted riflemen. The Intelligence Liaison teams briefed RAF intelligence and planning staff at airfields or headquarters. The Signals Section was equipped with No. 11 Sets for working forward to the recce teams, and No. 9 Sets for passing information back to static Air Intelligence Liaison Sections. That rear link was restricted to thirty-five miles of relatively flat terrain; anything beyond that was covered by dispatch riders or the Intelligence Liaison Section.

The 2/QVR had been formed in 1938 when the Territorial Army was doubled in size. It was to be one of a new type of unit, a motorcycle battalion. These were a modern form of the Boer War Mounted Infantry, using motorbikes, some solo and some with sidecars fitted to carry Bren guns, to move around the battle area. These battalions were to operate as part of an armoured division, and were yet another innovative concept developed in the mid-1930s. By summer 1939 the 2/QVR attended annual camp at Beaulieu in the New Forest, training with motorbikes hired from civilian sources. The battalion was mobilized in late August, but did not receive any motorbikes and was sent to guard London Docks against saboteurs. In late November the unit was tasked with providing a mounted platoon for a 'special mission'. Lieutenant Morgan was selected to command the detachment and, with the company commanders, picked forty men for the detachment. These included a young Lance Corporal, John Farrell, who was invited to join the special mission to France as he was young, keen and could speak French and German.

Towards the end of the year the platoon departed for Aldershot where motorbikes, motorcycling equipment and clothing was issued and training commenced in earnest. In early January 1940 the unit was allocated the code name Phantom, and all ranks were issued with sleeve patches consisting of a white capital P embroidered on a black background. The men were told to wear the patches but to say nothing of the role of which they were still blissfully unaware!

In early 1940 the Hopkinson Mission deployed to Valenciennes, between Mons and Cambrai. There it was allocated an additional task, that of reporting the disposition, operations, strength and movement of friendly forces at the battlefront. This it did remarkably well under difficult circumstances. The Mission was caught up in the blitzkrieg, and Hoppy, Fairy and their team did what they could to feed information back up the chain of command.

If the Mission failed to achieve its task in full it was because, to quote John Farrell (in 1959, in the rank of Major, to be a founder-member of 23 SAS Regiment TA), the '. . . recce teams lacked radios other than the short-range No 11 sets in the Guys, and the enemy kept moving'.

The main point about the translation of ALMs into a GHQ reporting unit is that the Army and RAF elements in France were sufficiently flexible in their thinking, and were allowed sufficient latitude by the War Office and the Air Ministry, to raise and deploy special purpose forces, and to let them adapt to circumstances as long as they were meeting a clear and urgent battlefield need.

During the retreat to Dunkirk the unit, more or less intact, ended up at De Panne, Belgium, and was evacuated to Britain as opportunities arose. After rest and refitting it settled into the Richmond Hill Hotel, overlooking Richmond Park, and conducted detailed reconnaissance of southern England in readiness for reporting the progress of a German invasion. While that was going on its role was being assessed and changed. Even as the main body of troops was being recovered from France, the CIGS set up the Bartholomew Committee, to study the lessons learned from the campaign. One outcome, based on the success of Phantom in the retreat, was creation of a unit to bridge the 'awareness void' between the front line and army, army group or theatre headquarters. This was the GHQ Reconnaissance Unit, raised in November 1940 and later to be No. 1 General Headquarters Signals Liaison Regiment. It retained the codename Phantom, and embodied many of the surviving personnel from the Hopkinson Mission; 'surviving', as many were lost at sea while being evacuated from France, when their transport, the SS *Abdiel*, was torpedoed. Among those lost was Wing Commander J.A. Fairweather DFC.

Phantom was part reconnaissance, part communications; its forward sections operated alongside front line units and sometimes ahead of them, observing operations and movements. The sections also monitored radio (speech) and wireless (Morse) traffic at all levels, analysed then synthesized the data into brief reports for rapid, secure transmission to Army or Army Group HQ. General Montgomery noted the work of the original Phantom unit in France, and of its successor in the south of England. A special Middle East Squadron worked for him in the Western Desert, Tunisia, Sicily and Italy. It was initially commanded by Major Brian Forester Morton Franks, an hotelier and pre-war TA officer who also appears later in this book. Hoppy also went to the Mediterranean, as a Major General commanding the 1st Airborne Division and was shot down into the sea on the way to jump into Sicily on Operation Ladbroke. He resumed command of his much-depleted division, and was mortally wounded while advancing just behind the spearhead unit 10th Battalion Parachute Regiment, near Brindisi on the Adriatic coast. He always led from the front.

MI(R) Expands

In the autumn of 1939 the pace of work in the War Office was accelerating. In MI(R) new staff were recruited, briefed and, only sometimes in those early days, trained. Thereafter the new men were deployed overseas or retained in London for staff duties. Among the new recruits was Bill Stirling, who, like David yearned for something more demanding than foot drill and guarding the Bank of England. He found it in MI(R), but who recruited him is unclear; probably Colin Gubbins, networking the 'Tartan Mafia', the influential web of Scottish landed families. Whatever the case, Bill Stirling took to the Special Forces world, and remained in it for more than four years.

The men sent overseas were members of MI(R) Missions. These operated in a wide variety of locations during MI(R)'s brief existence. In September 1939 No. 4 Military Mission went to Poland, and later No. 102 Military Mission operated in enemy territory in Libya, raising the Senussi against the Italians. Personnel from that Mission commuted between Egypt and the hills of Cyreniaca by Long Range Desert Group truck, sometimes in company with one Vladimir Peniakoff, later to found No.1 Long Range Demolition Squadron, better known as Popski's Private Army. Other missions went as far afield as South America, various parts of Africa, Asia and Australia.

Several missions or teams went to Romania during August 1939, and two generated ideas for units of what later would be called Special Forces. One involved disguised Royal Navy and Royal Marine boarding parties and gun crews on Danube tugs and motor-barges. Some ratings were deployed but were 'blown' by *Abwehr* agents, and the scheme was abandoned. The other plan, soon adopted and adapted by Colin Gubbins for use elsewhere, involved a floating demolition team, cruising the Black Sea on a merchant ship awaiting the call to action. The plan involved an MI(R) team under a Major Young and a Field Company of the Royal Engineers (100 all ranks) from Egypt, intended to conduct scorched earth operations in the Romanian oilfields. Nothing came of either idea, but not for lack of trying. The Foreign Office, prompted by the ambassadors in the Balkans, appears to have stopped the maritime demolition squadron idea.

Another MI(R) attempt at raising a special operations unit took place in Poland. On 25 August Colin Gubbins set out for Poland with the hastily assembled No. 4 Military Mission which included Captain Peter Wilkinson, Royal Fusiliers, later to be a leading figure in SOE. The Mission arrived on 3 September, forty-eight hours after the start of the German invasion, and did not linger, but stayed long enough to try to raise a unit for guerrilla warfare; an idea obviously thought out beforehand.

The Poles had their own ideas about special operations and had also given thought to stay-behind parties and underground movements including the Home Army; 150 years of occupation by the Austrians, Germans and Russians had honed their survival instincts to a fine edge. The MI(R) team attempted to recruit men from the Czech Legion, but first the German onslaught, then a Russian one on 17 September, swept away the plans and the Mission. The Mission escaped via Romania, as did many Poles and some of the Czech Legion; most went to France where the Czechs set about re-forming the Legion while the Poles set about raising units from the Polonia. The Polonia and their Monika resistance works later became well known to Colin Gubbins and Wilkinson.

In London the need for an irregular warfare force and training centre was accepted by the DCIGS, and someone, possibly Colin Gubbins, suggested Lovats Scouts as both Special Forces and instructors. This was a unique Territorial Army unit, technically Yeomanry but in 1939 two battalions of mounted infantry scouts. The unit was raised in 1899 by Simon Joseph Fraser, 16th Lord Lovat, to provide the British Army in South Africa with a much-needed mobile reconnaissance force. Afterwards the Scouts were retained, first as a unit of the Imperial Yeomanry, then as mounted infantry, and in the Great War as foot infantry. The battalions were decimated at Gallipoli, before the value of expert observers ('good men with a glass', to quote old Highland newspaper advertisements), and marksmen was appreciated on the Western Front. Another Lovats Scouts unit was raised for service in France and Flanders – the now forgotten Lovats Scouts Sharpshooters. One section, No. 4, served in Italy, where the clear air and superb vistas were ideal for getting the best out of the units' skilled observers. The Lovats Scouts remained in being after the Great War and, in 1939, were mobilized at their Regimental Headquarters near Inverness. They were still there in October, training with their hardy hill ponies, and longing for action. MI(R) felt, correctly, that the Scouts would make perfect trainers of guerrillas and partisans, at home or overseas, and would, in many cases, make excellent guerrilla fighters themselves. The Scouts were mainly recruited from hill shepherds and outdoorsmen who were inured to hardship, having spent their days ranging mountain, moor and peat bog in Scotland's capricious weather; 'if you canna see the hills its raining, if you can then its gaen to rain'. They had the added bonus of Gaelic-speaking signallers – natural code-talkers – the *Abwehr* having few men fluent in that language.

An approach to the Scouts about forming a Training Wing for MI(R), and possibly D Section, was made, informally, to the Scouts RHQ, but it appears to have become entangled in regimental politics. The then commanding officer reportedly did not want to have the Regiment fragmented, as had happened in the Great War, but members of the Lovat family serving with the Scouts wanted to follow the secret paths to war.

The idea was not pursued, and the Scouts went to guard the Faeroe Islands – a task for which they were also ideally suited. The cause of special warfare was still served obliquely, by the Scouts, as a few months after the MI(R) idea was rejected one of the most vigorous of the Fraser (Lovat) clan left the 'family' regiment to join a new formation, the Commandos, along with some fine hill men.

Scots Guards on Skis

Shortly after those abortive attempts to raise an irregular force, national or expatriate, there was another short-lived but better-known attempt, this time for service in the silent, snow-filled forests of Finland.

The USSR-German Non-Aggression Pact did nothing to reduce the suspicion each state felt for the other. Shortly after Germany invaded Poland the USSR, without much trouble, occupied Estonia, Latvia, Lithuania, the eastern provinces of Poland and the Romanian trans-Danubian provinces of Bessarabia and Bukovina. Then, in order to protect the key naval base at Leningrad (St Petersburg) and to ensure unhindered access to that city via the narrow Gulf of Finland, they over-reached themselves. The Russians did not trust the Finns; it was only twenty years since they had sought German help to escape Russian dominance. Stalin tried to pressurize the Finns into relinquishing the strategically important border region of Western Karelia, and some islands in the Gulf of Finland, all vital to the seaward defence of Leningrad. The Finns had no intention of being again part of Russia, under any pretext or guise, and declined to part with as much as a single hectare of territory. In December 1939 the Red Army invaded Finland, but the Finns fought back viciously. The Winter War became a nightmare as armoured units floundered in massive snowdrifts, and the advance ground to a halt. The halt became a re-adjustment of lines, then a withdrawal which became a retreat and finally a rout. By late January 1940 the campaign had reached stalemate.

The French and British decided to send an expeditionary force to help the Finns and in London the Cabinet directed the War Office to find troops, equipment and weapons. There was no shortage of problems, not the least finding troops, let alone any trained for winter warfare. The French had *Chasseurs Alpins*, trained and equipped for year-round operations in the Alps, Vosges, Jura and Pyrenees, but the British Army had never needed mountain troops. How a new and unusual formation was to be raised in the early stages of a massive build-up of arms and armies in France was not considered. By a stroke of good fortune there was a precedent to obtaining winter clothing in a hurry, and a supply of suitable items in an Ordnance Depot in Scotland. Both dated from the last year of the First World War when the British Army was sent to the assistance of hard-pressed allies Italy, in November 1917, then the White, or anti-Communist, Russians in 1918. The GOC British Expeditionary Force (Italy), General Sir Henry Plumer, one of Britain's better generals, passed the task of equipping his men for winter warfare in the Dolomites to the DQMG. He simply sent a request up the supply chain to GHQ in France, who in turn passed it to the War Office in London. Without appearing to bat an eyelid the supply staff obtained, or had manufactured, the necessary equipment. Parkas, fur hats, snow hoods designed to button onto Army great coats, long fleecy mittens flexible enough to permit weapon-handling, hose-tops (footless over-socks), fur-lined boots, sleeping bags, ice axes, Alpenstocks, tinted glasses, crampons, and insulated food containers. This minor miracle was achieved due to pre-1914 interest in Arctic and Antarctic exploration, coupled with enthusiasm among the moneyed classes for winter sports and mountaineering in the Alps, Dolomites and Pyrenees. Consequently most large London shops, such as the Army and Navy Stores, and Selfridges, and their provincial equivalents, had useful items tucked away against the return of happier days. Also, manufacturers of arctic and alpine sports wear quickly responded to requests from the supply staff. By the end of February 1918 10,000 sets of winter clothing were in the hands of the BEF (I) – at the tail end of the Dolomite winter, but still useful, and no one knew the war would soon, suddenly, end that year.

After the Armistice (4 November in Italy) usable or un-issued items were returned to Britain, where some were sent to Murmansk for the British contingent in the North Russia Expeditionary Force. In Russia the Italian Front material was augmented by items designed for the War Office by Sir Ernest Shackleton, the Antarctic explorer, who served with the NREF as an instructor in Arctic living and survival. When Murmansk was evacuated in 1919 much of the equipment was removed to Scotland and placed in store. There it lay, inspected and counted annually, for twenty years. In early 1940 some unsung clerk with a good memory, in the War Office, remembered the store of winter clothing and boots, and they were withdrawn for use, in some cases for the third time. Some were found again in 1950 for the Korean War, and others were still in a Scottish depot in the early 1970s.

One idea to be explored with the Finnish, Swedish and Norwegian governments, the last two alarmed at the thought of a Soviet presence along the Gulf of Bothnia, and near the North Cape, was passage through their (neutral) territory for the ski-force. One Allied idea was to have it accompanied by 'Force Avonmouth', several infantry brigades, to be dropped off one by one at key locations along the winter ore route, at places such as Narvik, Kiruna, Gallivare and Lulea. That, it was hoped, would prevent the Germans and Italians, if they entered the war and sent some Alpini north, from garrisoning them to control the ore fields, railways and ports.

Back in London MI(R) was tasked with preparing a deception plan for the Finnish expedition, and set to with its, by now customary, gusto. A plan was devised, but was not required as diplomatic clearance for passage of British troops through neutral Norway and Sweden was not forthcoming. However, the traumas of attempting to coordinate the views and quibbles of the Foreign Office, the three service ministries and their military charges, led to the creation in September 1940 of the Inter-Service Security Board. It was charged with producing or having oversight over all deception plans, including security of these plans, such as the allocation of operational and exercise codenames. No codename could be allocated to an operation by any subordinate body, in any service, including the secret ones, other than from a list generated by the

ISSB. Lists were allocated to individual services, and from there cascaded to operational headquarters and units. When the US entered the war the Joint Chiefs of Staff conformed to that system, albeit with their own lists which were cross-checked with British/Allied ones to avoid duplication. The code names were selected to avoid reflecting the origin, nature or extent of an operation, nor provide an indication of the forces involved, and were to avoid trivialization of operations by using facetious, vulgar or humorous words. The lists were made up of words with common themes, and devised so as to avoid repetition. During the Second World War lists of code names were based on themes such as professions (Acrobat, Salesman), fish (Pencilfish, Halibut), men's names (Andy, Hugh, Godfrey), chemicals (Novocaine, Veganin), makes of car (Dodge, Willys), adjectives or similar words (Titanic, Fortitude), American places (Omaha, Elmira, Utah), and so on. Later, from the 1980s, for British operations, names were selected by computer from a list. This all stemmed from the work of MI(R) for the Finnish expeditionary force.

At the same time as the clothing issue was being raised the question of cross-country movement of troops was examined. Skis were the only solution. Rather than train an existing infantry unit to ski, the DMO sensibly decided to raise a unit of skiers. Apart from any other consideration, in the winter of 1939–40 the British Army did not have a fully manned, trained and fighting-fit infantry battalion to spare, and had very few that exactly matched that description. The new unit had to have a parent regiment or corps but there was no precedent in the British Army for raising a battalion or brigade of skiers.

In January someone decided to raise the unit as a battalion of Foot Guards as the Brigade could provide administrative and training support for the new unit while imparting its high standards of fitness, discipline and weapon-handling. More important, there was to hand a Guards officer who not only had recent experience of commanding an infantry battalion but was also a winter sports expert. There was also a senior major with some operational experience available who could also ski. The new unit was designated Fifth (Supplementary Reserve) Battalion, Scots Guards, and was under the command of Lieutenant Colonel J.S. Coats, Coldstream Guards; the second in command was Major Bryan Mayfield, Scots Guards. Mayfield had served at the front in the closing months of the First World War, and then in Palestine during the now almost forgotten internal security campaign which raged between 1936 and 1939, and where he learned a number of lessons which he put to good use later.

In January 1940 the Director of Recruiting circulated an appeal for skiers, not just to the Regular and Territorial Armies but also to the other services and to embassies around the world. It met with an immediate and enthusiastic response from 600 or so officers, 200 NCOs and ORs, and the same number of civilians. The latter responded from every corner of the world, wherever embassy staff unearthed someone with what appeared to be relevant experience. Among the service recruits were Lieutenants Bill Stirling, Ralf Farrant, Alexander Scratchley, David Stacey, and Guardsman John Royle.

Accommodation for the new battalion was found at Quebec Barracks, Bordon, Hampshire, and true to expectation the Brigade of Guards produced, apparently effortlessly, personnel to man a skeleton Battalion Headquarters and HQ Company. An advance party was dispatched to Bordon late in January to take over the accommodation, barrack stores and the few vehicles allocated to the battalion, and to start acquiring food and the other necessities of life for 1,000 men. Some of the Great War arctic clothing was issued to the Battalion Quartermaster – not much, just a few parkas, boots and hoods – the rest was to be issued later. The volunteers started to arrive in early February, summoned to Bordon by telegram. Speed was vital, as the battalion was to move overseas by 1 March. Lieutenant Colonel Coats or Major Mayfield interviewed each volunteer as soon as possible after arrival. Among the newcomers were a large number of officers, many of whom came from commanding companies in infantry battalions serving in Northern France with the BEF. Others came from cavalry squadrons, artillery or engineer regiments, or from supporting arms and services; they may have been expert skiers but were of little use to an infantry unit. The main problem was the obvious imbalance between officers and troops. The battalion had to begin with the same establishment as any other; Battalion Headquarters, a Headquarters company with three platoons of specialists, and four rifle companies, later increased to five rifle companies when there was a welcome influx of trained Guardsmen from the Guards Brigade Depot at Pirbright, who, of course, could not ski. There was immediately a surplus of officers, as only six majors and six captains were required for the companies, and nineteen subalterns to fill the assistant adjutant and platoon commander's appointments. Once these had been filled the remaining officers were invited either to relinquish their commissions on a temporary basis and remain with the Battalion as non-commissioned officers or private soldiers, or to return to their units. Many decided not to stay, assuming correctly that they would be more use to the war effort fulfilling the role for which they had been trained than serving in the ranks of a ski-battalion. Those who remained carried out their NCO or Guardsman roles with enthusiasm, and were better regimental officers for the experience. The only problems encountered were by those filling the demanding role of Company Quartermaster Sergeant Major, over which a tactful blank will be drawn, but the temporary CQMSs learnt a lot, very quickly, sometimes painfully, and they, too, were better for the experience.

The Battalion was formed, equipped after a fashion and, armed only with rifles and pistols, moved to France, not to join the BEF in the *Sitzkrieg* among the mist and mud of Flanders, but to the crystal clear air and glittering snow fields of the Alps. It went to Chamonix, the famous, if almost deserted, winter sports resort and also the depot and training centre of the *Chasseurs Alpins*. The only troops in the depot were mobilized Territorials who, for some reason, were not allowed to make use of the ski slopes but the instructors were delighted to help the British. The Battalion's seasoned skiers and the French instructors were impressed by the rapidity with which the ordinary Guardsmen became proficient; most had never seen skis before, nor much in the way of snow or mountains, but thrived on the exercise, fresh air and the exhilaration of skiing. Less successful were the early attempts by this odd collection of officers, officer-NCOs, officer-soldiers and soldier-soldiers to look after themselves. Of cooks there were almost none, so everyone solved the messing problem by using restaurants and cafes. They were welcomed with open arms, literally in many cases, by the proprietors, and the many young (and not so young) ladies who had made the annual trek to the snowfields in search of sun, snow and stimulating conversation with fit, healthy men.

Irrespective of whatever else happened during that brief idyll in the snows, two things transpired which influenced the development of British Special Forces. First, many officers realized for the first time how competent and adaptable ordinary soldiers can be, given good instructors, stimulating training, a real challenge and active, positive encouragement. Secondly, in the cafes, bars, apartments and dining rooms of Chamonix this eclectic collection of young, and some not-so-young, men (Brian Mayfield was approaching forty, old for an infantryman) talked about war; most people in the unit had seen, and endured albeit briefly, the problems of poor equipment, humdrum training, mindless discipline and adherence to sometimes stupid orders. They were horrified at the apparent inexorable degeneration of the Sitzkrieg into a reprise of the Somme, Passchendaele and Loos; places where their fathers and uncles had lost limbs, life or sanity, while leading young men, akin to the skiing guardsmen, to their deaths just to gain a few yards of fetid mud. All present had heard older men speak of the horrors of the Western Front, and the insidious hopelessness which infected so many men; the feeling that there was no alternative to slogging forward into machine-gun fire, uncut wire and artillery barrages until killed or mutilated. There had to be a better way of fighting a war and during those few days in Chamonix a number of ideas started to take shape in the restless and vigorous minds of men in the ranks of the Fifth Battalion, Scots Guards. It is worth noting that at Chamonix there was a wide mixing of ranks and many soldiers found themselves eating and drinking with officers on an equal basis, discussing the pros and cons of life, war and preparations for war. It was a powerful learning experience for many, and not just the officers. Michael Calvert likened the atmosphere to that of a Renaissance university; constant, intense, wide-ranging debate, and a relentless questioning of orthodoxy.

The story of this unusual battalion ended in anti-climax. The collapse of Finnish resistance in March 1940 nullified the need for an Allied expeditionary force. The battalion was recalled and sent to Gourock, a trooping port in the west of Scotland, to join the multi-national North-West Expeditionary Force for operations in (neutral) Norway. The battalion found itself on a damp Scottish quayside awaiting embarkation onto a troopship. As they waited the skiers watched another unit embarking, some clutching large brown garments and long white floppy boots; parkas and muk-luks (over-boots), dating from 1918 and resurrected for service in a Norwegian spring. A number of the soldiers encumbered with polar gear were wearing kilts; members of the Liverpool Scottish, a Territorial Army battalion affiliated to the Queen's Own Cameron Highlanders. They were off to Norway as part of another new formation, an independent company, one of the first real British Special Forces, raised by MI(R) after the disappointment over the Lovats Scouts.

The North-West Expeditionary Force did not sail at that time. Loading was first suspended, then ordered to cease and the stores unloaded; Norwegian neutrality was not to be challenged. 5 Scots Guards were recalled to Bordon, and disbanded. A few days later the NWEF was reactivated, and thrust into Norway. Such is war.

Swedish Ore

The reason for raising Independent Companies to support the NWEF was the famous Swedish iron ore. In those days the upper reaches of the Gulf of Bothnia were closed by ice between October and May, when the ore moved west by electric powered trains to Narvik, where it was loaded onto the re-positioned bulk carriers. The last twenty miles of the line descended around 500 metres through nineteen tunnels, and across dozens of bridges over mountain gullies; all tempting targets for sabotage, as was the hydroelectric generating station providing power for the railway engines. Any prolonged interruption to the ore traffic would have a serious effect on the Axis armament industries, as both Germany and Italy had few domestic sources. Ore carriers sailing offshore would be open to attack by surface ships, submarines and aircraft unless the Germans seized the few airfields along the Norwegian coast, and ports for naval operations. The ore carriers could use the Leads, a seaway running inside the long archipelago of islands down the Norwegian coast. The seaway was studded with navigation aids; lighthouses, buoys and beacons, prime targets for saboteurs, and could also be rendered useless by mining, which is what the Allies had in mind. They also intending neutralizing Narvik as a port, and the railways running south through central Norway linking the ore mines to Oslo, in case the ore traffic was diverted. Hence the North West Expeditionary Force, consisting of five British brigades, the *Corps Expéditionnaire Français en Scandinavie* which included a Polish brigade and the *Chasseurs du Nord*.

The NWEF was supported by six MI(R) formations. These were, in order of departure date:

i)   2 April; four Liaison Officers were dispatched to Narvik, Trondheim, Stavanger and Bergen, selected earlier for disembarking 'Force Avonmouth', the defence brigades for the iron-ore sites.

(The Germans invaded Norway on 7 April, and captured Narvik in a brilliant *coup de main* on 9 April. The leading elements of the NWEF sailed from Scapa Flow on 12 April, and included an MNBDO group, including a Royal Marine guard force with light anti-aircraft batteries and searchlight units.)

ii) 13 April; an Expeditionary Force Liaison Officer at the port of Namsos, Captain Peter Fleming, and Sergeants Bryant and Berrif, Royal Signals, to establish communications with the NWEF convoy.

iii) 16 April; No. 13 Military Mission to the Norwegian GHQ. Major A.W. Brown MC, RTR, Captain R.B. Redhead, 12/Lancers, and an interpreter, Sergeant Peter Dahl RAPC, a Norwegian hotelier who had been working in England and who joined up when the war appeared to be heading for his homeland.

iv) 19 April; a two-man demolition support team, Major Jefferis and Sergeant J. Brown RE.

v)   23 April; Operation Knife, a six-man sabotage and guerrilla warfare team dispatched to central Norway once it became clear the Germans were going to be fighting in the north, but supplied from southern ports by road and rail.

vi) 1 May; Scissorforce, the code name for 2,000 troops in five special units plus a headquarters, all commanded by the recently promoted Lieutenant Colonel Colin Gubbins.

The first five operations either failed to reach Norway or were unable to achieve much before the German invasion swept them back to Britain. However, the Military Mission had some wild adventures after joining the retreating GHQ at Oyer, in the Gudbrandsdalen. The officers joined a Norwegian attempt to impede German traffic lower down the valley. The plan involved pincer attacks by ski-patrols on the road near Faaberg, where traffic stacked up at some road and railway bridges. This bold effort was only partly successful, but the two British officers learned some valuable lessons which were put to use later. The question of contact with the Operation Knife force does not seem to have been raised due to problems of communication, and in any case the Knife team did not reach Norway. Captain Redhead and some of the Norwegians collected British stragglers and harassed the enemy in the Gudbrandsdalen before withdrawing to Sweden. Major Brown produced a recruit, Captain Martin Linge, a Norwegian reserve officer who had been attached to 13 M Mission from the Norwegian GHQ. He was evacuated with the bulk of the NWEF, arriving in Britain determined to continue the fight with the Germans from overseas. Sergeant Dahl also returned to Britain and joined forces with Captain Linge in a new national unit, the Norwegian Independent Company. (Peter Dahl later joined SOE.)

Operation Knife was to conduct operations around the Sognefjord and in the wild country beyond the Jotenheim glacier. It was intended that it would work with unspecified Norwegians to destroy road and rail bridges far up the Sognefjord, some as far inland as Faaberg, once the Norwegian rearguard was clear of the area. The road and railway linked Oslo with Trondheim, and other ports in the north, including Lulea. If the road and railway bridges around Faaberg were demolished a German invasion force would be either halted, giving the Allied forces time to prepare a defence line, or forced to resort to movement by sea, exposing the ships to British submarine, surface ship and air attacks. Also, iron ore from Lulea could not be moved to southern ports by rail. It was a bold attempt, and indicative of the desperate measures attempted early in the war.

The Independent Companies

The Norwegian Independent Company was originally to be a mirror image of the special units in Scissorforce. When the NWEF was reactivated in early April, MI(R) had only a short time in which to raise Special Forces to accompany the main body. A plan had been drafted earlier and it was moved swiftly through the War Office bureaucracy, only four days from start to finish. On 15 April a signal went to the six Army regional commands in Britain, announcing that each was to raise two Special Infantry Companies. Each company was to be manned by 289 volunteers from Territorial Army divisions; Regular Army formations were not approached at that time. The response was overwhelming; five divisions immediately raised one company each. In reality each was a 'company group', as they included pioneers, engineers, signallers and other support troops. MI(R) envisaged that each company would be based on a merchant ship, preferably a cross-Channel ferry, as they would be issued with light vehicles. No. 1 Independent Company was organized by 52nd (Lowland) Division in five days and sent to the Royal Navy base at Rosyth in Scotland, where the NWEF flotilla was assembling. It was quickly joined by Nos. 2–5, recruited from 9th (Scottish), 54th (East Anglia), 55th (West Lancashire) and 1st London Division respectively. By 25 April these five companies, plus some light anti-aircraft guns for local air defence, were formed into Scissorforce. The staff included some Indian Army officers with mountain warfare experience, caught by the outbreak of war while in Britain on home leave. The Force was to be based on ships, hopefully ferries, in fjords around Mosjöen, Mo-i-Rana and Bodö in northern Norway, tasked with destroying German supply lines in central Norway.

The ships carrying Scissorforce sailed from Rosyth between 4 and 9 May and duly deployed into the Norwegian fjords, but the speed of the German advance created an urgent demand for conventional soldiers, and for commanding officers, and on 18 May Colin Gubbins was suddenly appointed to command 24 (Guards) Brigade. The leaderless companies were briefly engaged in some disappointing and confused fighting before being evacuated in early June, and sent on leave, future unknown. They were not however disbanded, but re-assembled in Scotland, in the general area of Fort William, in the Western Highlands. Their training was about to start.

The NWEF fought a brief, confused and complex campaign under difficult circumstances. It was not a total disaster; the Germans lost many warships and highly trained men, neither of which was easily replaced. The Allies learned several lessons from the campaign, including the need for really fit troops and a theatre commander with authority over all Allied forces and supported by an integrated headquarters where naval, land and air operations were co-ordinated and controlled. The need for air supremacy was learned yet again, and it was found that the RAF had lost its army cooperation skills, hard-earned over France, Flanders and the Venetian Plain. Finally, there was a definite requirement for small, self-contained teams to carry out *coup de main*, sabotage and scorched earth operations. Some officers were found wanting, and others found their feet on the ladder of promotion. These included Colin Gubbins, and the commander of the British land forces, General Bernard Paget, of whom more later.

The Independent Companies were an interesting experiment. Their experiences in Norway led to better training, especially fitness training, for subsequent Special Forces, so all was not lost. They foreshadowed several later Allied Special Forces; there is a definite flavour of Special Boat Squadron/Service about the Norwegian deployment. An MI(R) Mission, No. 104, helped the Australian Army raise twelve Independent Companies, also originally to be ship borne, which became commando companies and served with distinction in New Guinea and East Timor, amongst other places.

In November 1940 most of the Independent Companies were formed into five Special Service Battalions, which were later subdivided into Nos. 1–9 Commandos. No. 10 (Inter-Allied) Commando contained several independent troops manned by men from occupied nations of Europe.

It is interesting to note that in late 1943, when the planning and preparations for Overlord were moving into high gear, someone saw a requirement for Independent Parachute Companies and (for the Mediterranean Theatre) Independent Parachute Platoons. The Director of Staff Duties was put to the trouble of preparing the appropriate War Establishments, 1/240/2 and NA II/413/1; each section in the Platoon was to be equipped with a Boyes anti-tank rifle.

There was one bright spark of initiative to lighten Allied gloom after the exodus from Norway, and the unravelling of the static front in France and Belgium. The German Army invaded the Netherlands on 9 May, and the invasion forces included an airborne force landed by Heinkel seaplanes on the Maas River in the heart of Rotterdam, to seize key points and assets. The Dutch government appealed to the British for help and, among other things, a warship was sent to evacuate the Crown Princess and other members of the Royal Family. The British, or at least MI(R), sent Major Davies to Amsterdam where, just ahead of an *Abwehr* team bound on the same errand, he removed a large consignment of financial assets and took them to London, the new seat of the House of Orange and the *Staten General*, the Dutch government. It was a piece of cheeky privateering which enraged the senior Nazis but which amused the Brandenburgers who claimed it was a coup worthy of themselves.

Chapter Four

Special Training Schools

While the men of the Independent Companies were enjoying their leave MI(R) assessed the problems the volunteers for Scissorforce encountered in Norway. These included lack of fitness, poor stamina, limited ability to cross rough country in small groups or as individuals and general lack of confidence when in operating in wilderness areas. There was also a marked inability to sleep rough and live without access to a cookhouse, field kitchen or kitchen trailer, and there was no experience (apart from former Boy Scouts) of setting up base camp in the wild. Few of the volunteers had any experience of seamanship in large vessels, fewer still of handling small boats and even less of landing on rocky terrain or even beaches in any seas, heavy or flat calm. On the other hand, Gubbins and the other regular Army officers had been impressed by the enthusiasm and high spirits of the men, especially those from the Liverpool and London TA units, and their universal determination to be good soldiers. The volunteers were aware that they were an elite group, selected for a special mission, and had been to the wars and in some cases been under effective enemy fire so were in some respects battle-tested. They were also acutely aware of their deficiencies, particularly the lack of cohesion in their units and sub-units, which was hardly surprising after only a few weeks together, but were determined to do better.

Equipment Deficiencies

MI(R) staff and experts from the Small Arms School Corps (SASC), a very small elite group which was little known outside the infantry, scrutinized the weapons available for special operations. There were obvious failings, such as lack of a short-range, rapid-fire, hard-hitting gun for house-clearing, street fighting and close-quarter combat in woodland and scrub. Adequate supplies of the American Thomson sub-machine gun, which fired a .45-inch round, and its companion weapon, the .45 Colt automatic pistol, a 'man-stopper' introduced following bitter US experience in the Philippines in the early 1900s, were not yet to hand. A few 9mm Parabellum MP18 sub-machine guns had been captured in Norway from German mountain troops. The MP18 was developed in 1917 by Hugo Schmeisser for the Bergman small arms company and entered service with German storm-troops during the German offensives of spring 1918. The captured weapons, a modified version of the original, were admired by all who handled them. The Admiralty copied the design for naval boarding parties, but the Army found the Lanchester, as it was called, too complicated for rapid production, and liable to jam in muddy or dusty conditions. The SASC staff recommended another new weapon firing the same ammunition and with similar characteristics to the Bergman, and in 1941 the Army and SOE received the first Sten guns. (STEN – Designers Shephard and Turpin, made at the ENfield Royal Small Arms Factory.) Resistance movements across Europe were issued with thousands of Stens, and the story of training civilians how to use them safely would make interesting reading, as throughout their service, in all marks and versions, Sten guns needed careful, competent handling to prevent accidents.

There was also an obvious need for weapons for attacking convoys or machine-gun posts. There was such a weapon to hand in British armouries, the much-derided Boyes anti-tank rifle, a fearsome 5-foot, .55-inch (13mm) bore weapon. It was almost useless against medium tanks as it could only penetrate fifteen millimetres of 30° armour plate at 100 yards, or twelve and a half millimetres at 500 yards, but was devastating against soft-skinned vehicles. (It could also star or shatter the tank drivers', gunners' and commanders' vision blocks, and be used for long-range sniping against tank commanders driving 'head out'. It was seldom used that way.) Boyes rifles were later issued in large numbers to French Resistance and Maquis groups; one document notes 550 being delivered by air into France in the months before D-Day. A similar weapon is now finding favour in some NATO, and other armies, as a platoon-level sniping system.

The standard of battle shooting, especially at fleeting targets, was poor, mainly because it had rarely received any attention, as mostly all that was taught was massed, aimed infantry rifle fire derived from the Boer and Great Wars. The shooting and weapon handling of many Territorial Army units was poor due to lack of time and money for ammunition, and limited access to ranges. In some units for much of the time, ammunition and effort available was devoted to training teams for prestigious events, such as the world's premier shooting competition, the annual Imperial Meeting at Bisley, organized by the National Rifle Association. Territorial units not deployed in France received little practice, again due to lack of time, weapons, ammunition and ranges, and because Regular Army formations received priority as they would probably see action first.

In spring 1940 the bulk of the Territorial Army was not fully trained; only to be expected after less than eight months of disjointed and inadequate tuition while carrying out home defence war roles. For the Independent Companies other, obvious, problems included lack of any training for their new role, scarcity of training manuals for turning British infantry soldiers into guerrillas, and lack of a school or training centre for that task. However, during the Norwegian campaign, plans prepared a few weeks earlier by MI(R) for training facilities were brought rapidly to fruition, urged on by the sudden, speedy creation of the Independent Companies.

Training Needs

While these lessons were being recorded and assessed, preparations were underway for the opening of a guerrilla warfare school. With wholehearted support from the Directorate of Military Training,

MI(R) had established a training branch centred on the MI Wing for training guerrilla leaders and paramilitary staff (sabotage agents). The Wing was to operate a School for Irregular Warfare, comprising the Special Training Centre for Independent Companies and other small units, and a separate (but preferably adjacent) school for agents. This project was authorized on 7 May 1940, and funds allocated by 9 May. By a piece of good fortune, a classic case of a silver lining to a storm cloud, and independent of the work in London, a group of MI(R) officers had been planning for such an event, and had found what they thought were ideal premises. This group comprised the disappointed (but lucky) members of Operation Knife, the sabotage and guerrilla warfare team dispatched by submarine to Norway.

The Knife team consisted of Major Bryan Mayfield (commander), Major John Gavin RE (demolitions), Captains Bill Stirling, Ralf Farrant and Peter Kemp, and Lieutenant David Stacey; veterans of 5SG. The team assembled at Rosyth with a large consignment of demolition charges, small arms and ammunition, and started for Norway on HM Submarine *Truant*, but the boat was detected, attacked and damaged, and returned to Rosyth. Once ashore Bill Stirling contacted MI(R), and was told that due to the rapid German advance in Norway the operation was cancelled, and the team should lie-up somewhere with a telephone. The naval authorities wanted nothing to do with army people armed with explosives, arms and ammunition and to get rid of them agreed to supply transport for a short journey. Bill Stirling used it to take the team a few miles west to Keir, the family estate located on the southern edge of the Highlands, close to Dunblane and Stirling.

The team enjoyed a few days hill-walking, and during the long spring evenings reflected on their amateurish attempts to establish a sabotage, raiding and guerrilla force in a foreign land, and on the trials and tribulations of 5SG. These discussions led to designing an ideal training centre for toughening volunteers, teaching them close-quarter combat, rock climbing and boat handling, all for seaborne raids. The team refined their ideas in terms of terrain, facilities and premises and, thanks in no small way to Bill Stirling, identified suitable sites from among the dozens of shooting and fishing lodges in the Highlands, lying largely unused in that first year of the war. Discreet enquiries were made among family and friends; the Tartan Mafia at work again. Through the good offices of the 17th Lord Lovat, otherwise Lieutenant Simon Fraser, serving with the Lovat Scouts, cousin to the Stirling brothers (their mother was a Fraser), a suitable location was found. It was the Inverailort estate lying a few miles south of the fishing and ferry port of Mallaig, on the remote west coast of the Highlands of Scotland. It was easily (by the standards of the time) accessible from London by overnight trains; the castle was less than a mile from the railway station. The chosen spot was a sporting estate owned by a widow, Mrs Cameron Head, a relative of the Frasers'. Mrs Head lived in Inverailort Castle; really a shooting lodge dating from the 1890s. The castle sits on a rocky shelf above the River Ailort, a few yards from where it enters Loch Ailort, a long, deep, sea loch leading to the Sound of Arisaig. The Lochailort estate covered a vast area of mountain, moorland and flood, virtually useless for anything but sport or training soldiers. The estate had everything needed for a Special Forces' training school; accommodation, staff, remoteness and rough terrain. There was a tiny village and a railway station with a small goods yard, good connections (for that era) by road and rail with central Scotland and London. There were many offshore islands and remote peninsulas for practising raids or setting up base camps, and no shortage of food and whisky; legal, illegal and illicit, it was grand country for secreting a still, or so it is said.

The team contacted Jo Holland, and found their ideas coincided. The creation of the MI Wing School at Lochailort was approved immediately, and the process of requisitioning the estate was set in train through Scottish Command and Inverness-shire County Council. Bryan Mayfield was appointed Commandant, and promoted Lieutenant Colonel. Bill Stirling, Ralf Farrant and Peter Fleming were also promoted; Farrant became Deputy Commandant and Stirling Chief Instructor. Other instructors included Major Martin Lindsay and Captains Peter Fleming, Freddie Spencer Chapman and Charles Scott, all holders of the Polar Medal, and later to be leading figures in SOE operations. The syllabus was to be based, more or less, on *Art of Guerrilla Warfare*, the *Partisan Leader's Handbook,* and *How to Use High*

Explosives. The School administration team was headed by the adjutant, Captain Alexander Scratchley, a former winner of the Grand National and member of 5SG. His right-hand man was the regimental sergeant major, another former member of 5SG, Warrant Officer Class One John Royle. Before the war he had been through Sandhurst then commissioned into the Highland Light Infantry and was posted to India, along with a certain Lieutenant David Niven. Once in India Royle fell from grace; one version has him thumping his commanding officer while 'with the drink taken', another claims he borrowed beyond his means from Sikh money-lenders and was hounded to the disgrace of his regiment. Whatever the truth of the matter, he was cashiered and returned to Britain in disgrace. At the outbreak of war he enlisted in the ranks, answered the call for skiers and arrived one day at Lochailort as a guardsman before appearing on parade next day as the RSM – the Tartan Mafia at work yet again.

Bill Stirling also obtained the services of brother David, who was delighted to exchange the gloom of wartime London and Pirbright for the mountains and sea-lochs of the 'rough ground', the area of near-wilderness encompassing Morar, Moidart and Ardna-murchan, once a refuge of those on the run from the law. David joined the Schools' Fieldcraft Wing and worked under, and argued with, his recently promoted cousin, Captain Simon Fraser, who had escaped the Lovats Scouts' foray to the Faeroes and was Chief Fieldcraft Instructor. The Scouts also provided three other Fieldcraft Instructors, Sergeants Chisholm, Davidson and Maclennan, previously ghillies (Gaelic; 'sportsman's attendant') on highland estates. After being mobilized in 1939 they had been trained at the SASC Centre, Hythe, as weapons instructors and snipers. At Lochailort they were joined by three locally enlisted instructors, also ghillies, all fitter than men half their age, and seem-ingly tireless on hill and moor. The full team, cousins, sergeants and ghillies, put their considerable energy, skills and enthusiasm to good use, helping teach townsmen all about stealthy movement across country (and through burns and rivers) by day and by night, in every kind of weather.

One of their specialties was to ambush trains bringing a new intake of trainees as it was slowing for the curve into Lochailort

56

Station. Loud explosions, smoke, screams, Bren guns firing live ammunition (safety regulations were different then, and the LMGs in the hands of experts) and yells of 'Dismount, Dismount' sent soldiers (and officers) scurrying for cover, grabbing their kit. They were then harried across country to the Castle, including negotiating the river if not in spate; a quick way to sort out the sheep from the goats.

Shooting was also in the hands of experts, and was both innovative and exciting. The first instructor was WO1 Peter 'Wally' Wallbridge, SASC. He had been the senior instructor at the BEF School of Sniping in France where Sergeant MacLennan had been one of his assistant instructors, and had put his skills to good use during the retreat before being ordered home as being too valuable to be lost in action. Wally started his service in the Rifle Brigade but as he was fascinated with weapons and shooting transferred to the SASC in 1931. He was an outstanding shot, winner of the King's Medal at the 1938 Imperial Meeting, and a member of the British Army Shooting VII. He was an outstanding instructor and while at Lochailort was responsible for improving the standards of rifle and light machine-gun shooting in just about every student (and many of the staff).

Enter Fairbairn and Sykes

Fairbairn and Sykes had returned to Britain in 1939, just before war broke out. (Many ex-Shanghai hands, especially bachelors, continued to live in China or Hong Kong after retiring.) The duo approached the War Office, seeking useful employment, or possibly steered by Harry Steptoe and SIS. Their appearance in London just when two organizations were setting up training centres and requiring the services of probably the best close-combat instructors in the world is too much of a coincidence. They were rapidly enlisted and commissioned in the General Service Corps, a useful holding body for agents and experts who had to be made officers but without needing to be dedicated to one corps or regiment. They were quickly promoted to captains, obtained uniforms, and posted to the Special Training Centre. Before leaving for Lochailort they went to the Army Physical Training Corps Training

School at Aldershot to demonstrate their unarmed combat techniques to the staff and senior students, who were duly impressed. Some of the officers, many of them ex-warrant officers with extensive overseas service, already knew about the SMP Training Wing, and one or two had sat, or more likely landed head first, at the feet of Fairbairn, Sykes and O'Neil in the police gymnasium. After the demonstration, and a long and animated debate between the professionally-enthralled APTC men and the duo, the School Commandant asked if one of his staff could join them at Lochailort, as the STC establishment for four PTIs was about to be filled. One of the audience, Company Sergeant Major Benjamin Chapman, asked if he could go; when Fairbairn left the STC in 1941 Ben Chapman was appointed Chief Instructor, Unarmed Combat Wing.

Fairbairn and Sykes arrived at Lochailort in July 1940 and reportedly got on very well with Wally and the other instructors, each recognizing in the others, experts in their fields. Sykes and Wally developed a remarkable sniping range, including targets inside and around some dummy buildings. Fairbairn worked with the physical training staff, teaching them not only unarmed combat but use of formal and informal weapons. These ranged from steel helmets to ropes, matchboxes and bayonets. It was immediately obvious that the then current Army bayonet was useless for trench and house clearing so the resourceful duo set to work. They replicated, then improved, on the work carried out by Nikolai Solntseff and produced the world-famous Fairbairn-Sykes Fighting Knives; a series of ferocious but efficient edged weapons mainly manufactured by the Wilkinson Sword Company, London. The series covered at least eight models; the best known and most widely used being the No. 2 Fighting Knife; the archetypal dagger or poniard.

As the tempo of converting Lochailort into an Army training centre increased, the STC started advising the companies of the dates of courses. The first course, for men from Nos. 6 and 7 Independent Companies, commenced on 3 June, four weeks after authorization and funding was approved. During the summer of 1940 the Independent Companies progressively moved into the area around Fort William to prepare for training at the STC. No. 11 Company moved there from the south coast having taken part in what was hailed at the time as being the first raid on occupied France.

In fact it was at least the third raid. The first appears to have been organized by D Section and the second by an MI(R) team. The D Section one took place in the Sognefjord area between 25 May and 18 June, and involved a group of thirteen untrained but enthusiastic agents, all fluent in Norwegian. They sailed from the Shetland Isles in a Danish fishing boat, converted to carry arms, ammunition and demolition gear, and fitted with machine guns on concealed mountings to provide a limited self-defence capability. The expedition had interesting adventures among the unsuspecting Germans, and a two-man team sabotaged some industrial and infrastructure targets before returning home. The raid produced three recruits for the Norwegian exile forces, and provided valuable experience of sea access to, and establishing a base in, the fjords. On the operational side the two men learned much about selecting targets from the ground level (no air photographs), close target reconnaissance, and placing charges in the twilight of a Norwegian summer.

The MI(R) raid also took place in June, and involved three officers landed near Boulogne by 'fast launch' during the low moon period. Their missions were:

i)   to investigate German defences, bases and camps
ii) to recover British evaders or escapers
iii) to assess the scope for forming guerrilla forces

The team survived in occupied territory for nearly eight days, returning empty-handed (and blistered after rowing a small boat across the Channel) but with much useful detail about life in occupied France. The incursion, it was hardly a raid, also provided useful information about movement to and from the Continent by sea.

Most sources quote the first raid on enemy territory as a commando raid on the night of 24 June. A commando raid did take place then, but as noted above, it was not the first.

In July 1940, after the dust of Dunkirk had settled, the idea of strike forces, hornets rather than mosquitoes, occurred to several people, but most importantly, to Winston Churchill. In a minute of 4 June 1940, he wrote:

> What are the ideas of Commander-in-Chief Home Forces about Storm Troops? We have always set our faces against this idea, but the Germans certainly gained in the last war by adopting it, and this time it has been a leading cause of their victory. There ought to be at least twenty thousand Storm Troops or 'Leopards' drawn from existing units, ready to spring at the throat of any small landing or descents. These officers and men should be armed with the latest equipment, Tommy guns, grenades, etc, and should be given great facilities in motor cycles and armoured cars.

Note that there was no mention of raiding the enemy-held coast for the minute. That, however, did not deter the more aggressive spirits in the Army.

The C.-in-C. Home Forces passed the minute to the Director of Military Operations, who in turn passed it to Lieutenant Colonel Dudley Clarke, a South African-born Gunner. He treated the matter with urgency, acumen and imagination, sensibly ignoring the apparent defensive implications of the wording. In the space of an evening he drafted an outline for raiding forces, for operations anywhere, at home in the event of an invasion or enemy incursion, or on the coasts of Europe. He would probably have known about the Independent Companies, and realized that their intended role in support of a conventional expeditionary force was only separated from a raiding one in the mind. He based his ideas in part on the Boer raiding parties described in *Kommando*, about which he heard so much when young. The resulting paper about raising, training and deploying commandos passed upwards to the desk of Churchill, who approved. He issued orders that the coasts of occupied Europe were to endure '. . . a reign of terror', leaving the shores '. . . littered with German corpses'. Dudley Clarke was promoted, placed in charge of a new section, MO9 Raiding Forces (Military), and ordered to mount a cross-Channel raid 'as soon as possible'. Possibly sour grapes from DMO following the D Section and MI(R) events, security was not too strong about such matters in those early days, according to veterans of the inter-departmental wars and skirmishes of the time.

The first MO9 raid took place only nineteen days later, on 24 June, when four raiding parties, a total of 115 all ranks, were transported across the Channel in high speed Royal Navy motor boats to the coast near Boulogne. The mission of each party was to assess the strength and location of German defences and attempt to capture enemy personnel for interrogation; implicitly this was also to remind the enemy that the British Army may have been knocked down, but not 'out'. The raid was a public relations triumph, trumpeted widely in the press and radio of national, Empire and neutral states. In reality it was not much of a triumph, but it did provide a valuable understanding of the requirements for future ventures. These included better weapon training, thorough fitness, all-terrain agility and stamina, seamanship for raiders, confidence in moving at night in unfamiliar territory, and good discipline – all the subject of the MI(R) syllabus. The Navy also learned much about landing on an unfamiliar shore at night, navigation, fitness and stamina for small boat crews, and silent running when close to enemy defences.

The Independent Companies gradually worked their way through the STC. One Company in turn was based at another shooting lodge a few (Commandos) miles over the hills from Lochailort. This was the STC Holding Unit at Achnacarry Estate and Castle, another part of the Fraser fiefdom, and later world-famous as the Commando Basic Training Centre.

Special Training Centre

At Lochailort the main building, a large rambling house, not a castle in the conventional sense, housed the STC headquarters, some of the classrooms, and the Officers' Mess. The NCOs and administrative staff lived in other estate buildings, including a smaller lodge, Glenshian House, a few hundred yards away overlooking the River Ailort. The students lived in tents, damp and cold in winter, damp and cool in summer, with the added discomfort of the West Highland midge, a tiny insect with a nasty bite.

The estate immediately around the castle soon sprouted a wide variety of training and exercise areas, including assault courses and

61

shooting galleries and ranges. These included conventional 25-yard small-arms ranges, some with pop-up targets, and longer range ones for training snipers. These included a 'battle village' for practising close quarter shooting with semi-automatic pistols and revolvers. This complex range was designed by Bill Sykes and was based on the Shanghai Mystery House. The 'village' was built between the Castle and Glenshian Lodge, close against some high rocky ground. The battle village had half-a-dozen houses, made of timber (no stone – ricochets), and lay at the foot of a low but steep hill. At the top of the slope a soldier stood beside a set of levers, somewhat like those in an old-fashioned railway signal-box. The houses were fully furnished and fully occupied by dummy enemy soldiers. Whenever a pistol-carrying student moved within range of the dummy the soldier pulled a lever, causing a dummy German to appear from nowhere. Other refinements were bottles and chairs propelled at the students' heads. Few men who passed through the STC did not become good snap-shots, with an accompanying boost to their self-confidence.

Lochailort had, and still has a station on the railway line from Glasgow to Mallaig, by way of Fort William and Roy Bridge. Close to each school the line crossed viaducts and plunged straight into tunnels; popular sites for agents and small groups to practise sabotage raids. Their exercises were enlivened by the local Home Guard and Army Cadet Forces who frequently provided a vigorous and resourceful guard force, and acted as guerrillas for agents to organize, train and lead on raids. In addition to Home Guard duties many of the locals found employment with the STC and the other secret warfare sites in the area. There was little work for older estate workers and ghillies during the war, and many of these older but remarkably fit men (and some women) carried out numerous tasks in the various training sites in the Highlands. They released soldiers for other duties, notwithstanding that War establishments for many of these locations usually noted, 'All staff of this establishment except instructors may be of low medical category'.

At one stage the STC administered two other special training establishments, a sailing and boat-handling school, and a training base for guerrilla (resistance) organizers. The school for teaching 'seamanship for raiding purposes' was based at Col Durlin, near Acharacle, a few miles south of Lochailort. It spawned another, even smaller, sailing school, for SOE. This was at Tarbert, a tiny community, a clachan, north of Lochailort; used to train agents and *coup de main* parties in boat handling. It was associated with what became known as the Arisaig Schools, based on another idea of Holland and Gubbins.

Arisaig

The other part of the School for Irregular Warfare, trained agents as leaders of guerrilla forces. The syllabus was similar to one being set up by D Section but with greater emphasis on raising guerrilla groups. In fact the initial syllabus was similar in many respects to that of the STC. It included weapon training, covering Allied, neutral and enemy items, demolitions, insertion and extraction of people and materials by boat, close target reconnaissance and tuition and practice in intelligence collection. This school was based in the tiny community of Borrodale, but is better known from the name of the main premises, Arisaig House; the village of Arisaig lies three miles to the west. Arisaig House was used briefly by MI(R) as a basic training school for agents, and its syllabus, itself derived from that of the STC, was used later for Special Operations Executive, and possibly the Secret Intelligence Service, MI9 and the Psychological Warfare Executive, for preliminary training of field operatives. The Office of Strategic Services (OSS) certainly used it as a foundation, and also the schemes of work used at the other Special Training Schools (STS). The STS in that area were based in shooting and fishing lodges, and were used throughout the war by SOE, and other organizations.

Their story really only touches slightly on Special Forces, in so far as some Americans and French SF troops trained there in 1944, and Colonel Sir David Stirling is buried in Rhubana Churchyard, overlooking Loch Morar. The church was built with funds donated by his father, on ground owned by his mother as a member of the Fraser family. It overlooks the loch, the deepest in Britain (1,000+ feet), and linked to the Atlantic by the shortest river in Britain, the Morar. The loch has a monster, Morag, shy but not silent who, during the war, was much disturbed by foreigners practising demolitions on various piers around the shores. The railway stations and the many bridges and viaducts on the railway line between Fort William and Mallaig were used for demolition training, as were salmon pools – unofficially. In those days Lochailort station boasted a sheep and cattle dock which also doubled as a vehicle unloading stage, connected to the main line by a short siding; the points were frequently used by STC instructors at the start of demolition courses, under the interested gaze of sheep or cattle, and small boys and girls.

The STC Lochailort staff devised an arm patch, a pouncing eagle, with outstretched claws, on a quartered shield. Many were surreptitiously acquired from the QM stores by trainees, and stitched onto their battledress blouses on the train back south; a sort of battle honour or early commando-style qualification badge, and hard-earned. (Some of the local girls made good money by wielding needle and thread on these trains.) The patch, with different colours is now worn by 16 Airmobile Brigade; the STC staff and graduates would approve.

The STC and the Arisaig School had barely started training when the MI(R) vision of Special Forces was turned upside-down with the formation of SOE.

SOE

Around the time that the MO9 appeared on the scene the rather confused array of British organizations dealing with irregular warfare was shaken, sifted and re-arranged. The SIS was tasked only with intelligence collection, either HUMINT or COMINT, and (ostensibly) lost its offensive role and arm. D Section was transferred to a new secret service, the Special Operations Executive. The War Office was also deprived of any major responsibility for irregular warfare, and in autumn of 1940 most MI(R) personnel were also transferred to SOE, and the short-lived branch research section was disbanded. Other secret services were formed, MI8, the Radio Security Service, to deal with radio interception, and MI9 to handle all aspects of Prisoners of War, and (to put the matter loosely) processing arrivals into British territory, or interrogation.

That second task eventually produced yet another secret service, MI19, the interrogation service. (MI8 was later absorbed by GCCS, and the designation was transferred to another role.) If that wasn't enough, in September MI10 was formed to handle deception, although that designation was later applied to the intelligence section dealing with enemy weapons and equipment. The development and handling of deception passed to part of the Inter Services Security Board.

SOE was responsible for a wide range of activity, all designed to help 'set Europe ablaze', in Churchill's words. Among the 'box of matches' would be small teams for 'butcher and bolt' operations, the forerunners in some ways of today's Spetsnaz, SAS and other Special Forces around the world.

Small Scale Raiding Force

This had been raised by DCO and SOE following some early raids on targets outside the scope of commandos, which in any case were just being formed. The first raids were made by Free French Paratroops, raised in Britain at the instigation of Captain Georges Roger Pierre Bergé. Georges Bergé graduated from the French Infantry School and in 1937 applied to join the fledgling *Infanterie de l'Air*. He served briefly with *601 Compagnie d' Infanterie de l'Air* at Rheims but a prolonged bout of ill-health forced him to change his plans. In 1939, once again fit for active service he was posted to 13 Infantry Regiment, just as war was declared. He was subsequently wounded three times, and recuperated in his parent's home in Mimazan, south-west of Bordeaux. There he and his father, a veteran of the Great War and a leading light in the local branch of the *Ancien Combattant de la Grande Guerre*, heard Marshal Pétain's radio announcement of the Armistice. Father and son were revolted by this, and determined to continue the struggle against the Germans. Bergé senior stayed in Gascony, and was an early and enthusiastic resistant. George made his way to Dunkirk and gained passage to the UK on a Polish merchant ship with some British soldiers. He eventually arrived at a provisional camp for French servicemen outside Plymouth, housing the survivors of the CEFN, newly returned from Narvik. Georges foresaw the value of airborne forces in liberating France, something about which he had no doubts whatever, and travelled to London to meet General de Gaulle. The General asked Georges to present his plan on no more than one page, which was done and accepted by a note in the margin in de Gaulle's unmistakable handwriting, '. . . d'accord'. By General Order No. 765 dated 29 September 1940, *Capitaine* Georges Bergé was authorized to raise a unit of paratroops, to be known as *1ᵉ Compagnie d'Infanterie de l'Air* (1CIA).

By the end of December 1940 the first section from the unit had completed their parachute training at Ringway and started field exercises in earnest. At the same time Bergé and a small team of officers, plus a representative of the French counter-intelligence department, interviewed potential recruits from other Free French army, air force and marine units. They also interviewed French and French Colonial émigrés reaching the UK from around the world, after each had been screened by the British and French counter-intelligence services at the 'Royal Victorian Patriotic Asylum for the Orphan Daughters of Soldiers and Sailors killed in the Crimean War', otherwise known as the Royal Patriotic School, Hampstead. In February 1941 the 1CIA moved into the orbit of SOE. That organization wanted to mount some *coup de main* operations in France, as much to demonstrate its value to the UK government, those Allies who had been made aware of its existence, and to its enemies and critics in Whitehall, of which there were several. SOE attempted to recruit a team of Frenchmen, but failed, so turned to the Free French, who volunteered the 1CIA. At that time it was little more than a weak platoon (twenty-one men) in strength, so it was decided that rather than use the whole unit, which was still recruiting, they would use one small section, thought to have been eight men. Officially known as 1e Section, 1CIA, it was detached from the unit and moved into a large country house in Hampshire.

The section's new home was Inchmerry House, known to SOE as STS 38, and set in a secluded part of the New Forest near the estuary of the Beaulieu River. Inchmerry was one of a cluster of a dozen or so Stately 'Omes of England in and around the Beaulieu estate, owned by the Montague family. (Inchmerry was owned by the Rothschilds.) Some of these houses were later combined into Group B, comprising STS 31 to 37, some with several houses (33a, 34a, etc). This collection of houses was close to the Solent and the English Channel, handy for a quick sea-passage when 'fair stood the wind for France' from nearby seaplane, submarine and MTB bases. It was also close to airfields, such as RAF Tangmere, the departure field for Lysander flights to France, and to RAF Tarrant Rushton, later in the war an important base for Special Duties (SD) squadrons.

The Inchmerry Estate had been requisitioned from the Rothschild family at the outbreak of war, and was used continuously by various secret services between February 1941 and 1945. The estate lies on the west bank of the River Hamble, close to the Solent, and in those days consisted of around 100 acres of woods, water-meadows and farmland. Inchmerry House was spacious, comfortable (by paratroop standards), fitted with several bathrooms and good kitchen and pantry facilities. The main hall was reportedly converted into a gymnasium, and the heated (at least in peacetime) swimming pool was also used for fitness training. It had an enclosed quadrangle-like area at the rear, which was ideal for unarmed combat, and the occasional session of foot drill. The estate was excellent for fieldcraft and training in minor tactics, and a number of field firing ranges were built, as well as a small compound of 'mystery-houses'. The estate made an ideal operational base for a small amphibious or airborne strike force. It was originally to be the Preliminary School for Free French agents, but instead became the depot for the 1CIA and its Special Forces offshoot. The estate was also used by the Small Scale Raiding Force (SSRF), also known as 62 Commando, the strong-arm/*coup de main* section of part of SOE and then briefly, in May 1943, by the first members of the Polish Bardsea Teams, described later. (Just to confuse things Inchmerry House appears on one list of SOE establishments as STS 62d, STS 62 and 62a-d; all seemed to have hosted SSRF at one time or another, hence the unit cover title – or maybe it was vice-versa!)

Operations Savannah and Josephine

These were part of a series of *coup de main* operations that led, in part, to the formation of the SSRF. Operation Savannah A enjoyed some success, if not quite as it was intended. It involved Bergé and four colleagues, Lieutenant Marcel Petit-Laurent, Adjutant Jean Forman, Sergeant Joel Le Tac, and Corporal Jean Renaud. The aim was to assassinate aircrew manning a *Luftwaffe* pathfinder-type unit *Kampfgeschwader 100*, while travelling by bus between their billets and the De Meucon air station, Vannes, Brittany.

At that time *KG100* was operating Heinkel He111 bombers fitted with a version of the *X-Gerat* beam-guidance blind bombing system. Aircraft from the unit were leading heavy night raids that were causing disturbing casualties and damage to industrial centres in Britain. The team was dropped into Brittany on the night of 14 March, but Bergé cancelled the mission when Resistance sources monitoring the bus movements reported that they had ceased as the aircrews were now travelling by car at random times and differing routes.

The team split up and attempted to return to Britain. Bergé, Forman and Le Tac headed for Bordeaux to await exfiltration by British submarine; ever resourceful they helped establish a Resistance circuit while lying-up near the Bergé home. On 4 April they made their way to St Gilles Croix de Vie, a small fishing port near the mouth of the Gironde estuary. After dark they went to a rendezvous (RV) on the shore to await collection by three canoes paddled by Lieutenant Geoffrey Appleyard and two colleagues from the Special Boat Section. They had arrived in HM Submarine *Tigris*, conducting a routine patrol collecting SIS reports and delivering items for various organizations, frequently the packages were left in un-baited lobster pots for collection by fishermen. Bad weather and heavy seas meant that only Bergé and Forman were recovered, mainly through the courage and persistence of Geoffrey Appleyard, who earned the DSO for his efforts. Sergeant Le Tac remained in the Bordeaux area; Petit-Laurent and Renaud were to try to reach the UK via Spain.

Savannah B was to be the assassination of U-boat crews travelling by bus from their luxurious (compared with a submarine) shore billets to Brest and Lorient prior to sailing against Allied convoys. This operation was not mounted, but one SOE document indicates that there was an air operation under that code name consisting of one man, one container and two pigeons which was mounted during the night of 15 March 1941. It may have been a reconnaissance mission to confirm the feasibility of the outline plan which, like other assassination attempts, would have provoked fierce reprisals.

Operation Josephine A was also to assassinate aircrew from *Kampfgruppe 40*, based at Bordeaux-Merignac airfield. The unit was operating Focke-Wulf 200C Kondor maritime patrol aircraft used for very long-range anti-shipping operations. These started in August 1940, and were one-way flights over the Bay of Biscay, around the west coasts of Ireland and Scotland, and terminating at Trondheim; a reciprocal course was flown a couple of days later. In the first two months of operations Kondors allegedly sank 90,000 tons of shipping, and 363,000 tons by February 1941; Winston Churchill referred to them as the 'Scourge of the Atlantic', hence the SOE mission. It too was cancelled.

The second mission, Josephine B, was also an early part of the Battle of the Atlantic. It was intended to disrupt maintenance of the growing German and Italian submarine fleet at Bordeaux by sabotaging the large power station at Pressac which supplied electricity to the German naval base. The power station had been the subject of several bombing raids by RAF Bomber Command, a force that in spring 1941 had yet to perfect its precision bombing techniques. The air attacks were not only inaccurate but counter-productive as collateral damage to French property and persons provided the German and Vichy propaganda machines with useful material, and upset de Gaulle. The Joint Intelligence Committee (JIC) and Joint Planning Staff (JPS) turned to SOE where it was decided, presumably at a very high level, to use a *coup de main* party to sabotage the plant.

SOE, the Bureau Central Renseignements et d'Action (BCRA) and several Resistance circuits within western France cooperated to identify the best means of attacking the power station, and to help the saboteurs. It was decided to destroy the casings of some powerful transformers with specially designed explosive charges, carried and placed by a four-man team. Three men from 1CIA were selected for the mission, Jean Forman, recently promoted to Warrant Officer, and Sergeants Pierre Cabard and André Vannier. They were trained by SOE at STS 17, the Industrial Sabotage Training School at Brickondenbury. They were parachuted into France on the night of 10–11 May to join Sergeant Le Tac. The mission was a success in so far as the power station was put out of action for some time, but that merely alerted the Germans to the need to create alternative, and well-guarded, energy systems for key establishments. However, they also were so enraged by the success of the sabotage team that the French guards at the power station at the time of the raid were shot for incompetence or collusion. The 1CIA team returned safely to the UK.

As a result of the success of Josephine B, and of the recovery of Bergé and Forman, in June 1941 the 1CIA formed a new sub-unit, referred to as the Special Parachute Company in some SOE papers, and also as D Troop of 62 Commando. This small French force was manned in part by men who had taken part in Savannah A and Josephine B. It was struck off the strength of 1CIA and became part of the BCRA, the Free French equivalent of SOE. Thereafter it may have operated at times as part of, or under the mantle of, the SSRF, a unit the history of which is difficult to fathom.

Chapter Five

Something New

By June 1944 the only large Allied units in the west with prolonged experience of offensive operations behind enemy lines were 1st, and, to a lesser extent, 2nd Special Air Service Regiments. (The Long Range Desert Group was primarily an observation unit, with a secondary role as a transport service for other units and agencies, and occasionally, but very effectively, it conducted offensive operations.)

Both SAS regiments had endured much in their brief histories, and this chapter covers some issues of their formative months that affected operations beyond the Mediterranean theatre.

During the early years of the war the minds of many officers produced numerous plans for raiding forces – teams of fit, thoroughly-trained men – but it took two young 'hostilities-only' Guards officers to turn the ideas into reality. Lieutenants David Stirling and John (Jock) Lewes would, however, have emphasized that their efforts were nothing without the active involvement of many other men, of all ranks. Both subalterns shared a conviction that well-planned precise attacks against targets carefully selected to support specific military objectives of senior commanders of all three services and of the theatre commander, could influence events out of all proportion to the size of the raiding force. They also recognized that such operations could only supplement, not supplant, conventional military operations.

In North Africa there were two obvious targets; POL (petrol, oil and lubricants) and aircraft. Without fuel there would be no tanks on the battlefield. The German *Panzerkampfwagen III*, for example, used about two litres of fuel for every kilometre of off-road driving in Central Europe, and considerably more in the desert. No aircraft would mean no reconnaissance flights for anti-shipping strikes against convoys relieving Malta, that critically important Allied air and sea base in the middle of the Sicilian Narrows, a piece of sea across which Axis supplies and reinforcements for North Africa had to pass. Both sides in North Africa were dependent on seaborne supplies of POL, especially the Axis, so the obvious targets for raiding were POL handling equipment at docks, inland dumps, airfield tanks and refuelling equipment. The Allies were more successful at general raiding than the Axis, but as there are few English language accounts of enemy operations, their number and effectiveness are mainly, but not completely, matters for conjecture. There is (or was – the people concerned are now deceased) anecdotal evidence that such raids took place, and some collateral evidence in the shape of special Italian raiding vehicles. In the 1950s Italian veterans spoke of such raids on Allied supply lines, using special vehicles designed in 1940 for the Italian Army, the Fiat AS37 and AS42, (AS – *Africa Settentrionale* – North African). They were superb vehicles, much sought-after by German and British forces. Fleet Air Arm pilots of 815 Squadron obtained several of the latter when serving in the desert, flying Fairey Albacore and Swordfish torpedo bombers to drop bombs on Rommel's forces, and at times to help re-supply LRDG patrols.

A thorough trawl of the War Diaries of British and Commonwealth rear echelon transport and supply formations, and Royal Army Service Corps POL units, or of Desert Air Force station and squadron/unit Forms 540, the RAF equivalent of War Diaries, may reveal the extent of these incursions. However, the British appear to have been first into the field.

A New Way of Raiding

In spring 1941 Stirling and Lewes were serving in Egypt with the remnants of 'Layforce', an ill-fated and short-lived Special Service Brigade. It consisted of a headquarters and five fighting units, three

British and two Middle-East Commandos, the latter manned by Palestinians, Jews, Muslims and Maronite Christians, some serving amicably together in sub-units. (A third ME Commando was deployed in the Sudan for operations against Italian forces in Eritrea and Abyssinia.) Layforce included in its ranks a number of other officers who were to make a major contribution to the development of British Special Forces, including Lieutenants Blair Mayne (1 SAS), David Sutherland (SBS), and Ian Collins (GSO1, SAS), and Major Bill Stirling (2 SAS). For a brief period there were four Stirling brothers in Egypt; Bill, David, Hugh, killed near Sidi Barrani on 19 April 1941, and Peter, a diplomat.

During its brief existence Layforce mounted several seaborne raids, all conducted with vigour but enjoying little success through official indifference, lack of lightweight weapons for neutralizing ships, armoured vehicles, or parked aircraft, and no suitable means of moving men and materials in and out of enemy territory. None of these problems deterred Lewes, who attempted to solve the problem of post-raid exfiltration by training a small group of Layforce personnel in long-distance cross-country marches. These involved water and ration discipline, improving individuals' attitude to, and powers of, endurance, learning day and night navigation, and careful concealment of daytime hides. During these marches and related exercises, he encouraged everyone to think about, and discuss, all aspects of their training and recent operational experiences, good, bad and indifferent, and to discuss new techniques. All now commonplace in many armed forces, that was almost heresy in British Army units at that time as many officers held rigid attitudes about the ability or even the necessity, let alone the desirability, of other ranks 'thinking'. In addition to training, Lewes worked with Captain Bill Crumper, a long-serving Sapper, to devise a simple means of destroying aircraft, oil dumps and 'soft-skin' vehicles. Their efforts produced the 2lb/1kg 'Lewes Bomb', a light metal container holding a mixture of used machine oil and thermite explosive, detonated by a 'time-pencil', a simple delayed fuse. The bomb was designed to destroy aircraft but proved equally effective against POL container dumps and vital airfield support vehicles such as heavy-duty cranes (for lifting aircraft or changing aero-engines), petrol bowsers and mobile oxygen-making plants.

Parachutes and Parachuting

The problem of infiltration into enemy territory seemed solved when the RAF allowed the Layforce group use of some aircrew parachutes. Their provenance has never been identified; possibly they were destined for India where a parachute force, first proposed in September 1940, was taking shape. However, the first Indian Army personnel, three British officers, only started parachute and general air landing training at Ringway in May 1941 so it is unlikely parachutes, always in short supply in the early years of the war, would have been dispatched to India before anyone was ready to use them. They may have been aircrew parachutes not taken into stock by any RAF station in the Middle East, which seems odd, as RAF suppliers, like Army quartermasters, are acquisitive by nature. Alternatively the parachutes may have been intended to add authenticity to a phantom airborne formation devised by Lieutenant Colonel Dudley Clarke, by then in Egypt directing A Force, the deception branch of GHQ Middle East. The RAF also provided use of an airfield, aircrew and aircraft, obsolete, stately Vickers Valencia bombers, and equally slow Bristol Bombay bomber-transports, relegated to delivering mail, spare parts and beer to remote landing grounds.

The first jumps did not go well. Neither the aircrew nor the men from Layforce knew anything about parachuting, and everything was 'by guess and by God'. The first descents were made at too low an altitude for the canopies to fully deploy, which is how the tall and well-built David Stirling damaged his back and ended up in hospital. Later there were two deaths caused by problems relating to the rings attaching the rudimentary static lines to the makeshift tethering rig inside the Bombay.

Over the years the RAF staff at the then Parachute Training Squadron at RAF Ringway have been blamed, if only by implication, for not responding to a signal requesting advice about the use of parachutes in an aircraft not fitted with proper tethering wires. The PTS allegedly knew about the problem encountered in Egypt, but probably did not know parachuting was underway there, and may not have received the signal sent from RAF Kabrit, where the lethal parachute jumps were made. It should also be mentioned in this context that exits from the Valencia and the Bombay were by a side door, unlike the rear turret, then hole in the floor, of the Whitleys used at the PTS. Also, in the first SAS descents the men dived out of the aircraft head first, much like *Luftwaffe* paratroops; a dangerous technique with aircrew parachutes, a point possibly not explained to Ringway. All wireless traffic between the Middle East and Britain was coded and of such volume that the signal may have been misdirected, albeit temporarily. It was, after all, dealing with an RAF matter but had been raised by an Army formation, and could have gone to either the War Office or Air Ministry. Within the latter it would probably have been delivered to the Army Liaison section, still preoccupied with such anti-invasion matters as air to ground cooperation and bombing of invasion beaches. And probably no one in either ministry knew immediately where it should be re-directed. Anyone who knows anything about RAF specialists such as PJIs and officers and NCOs of the Engineering Branch knows that even in those early days they would have responded immediately if there was a risk of a fatality or even injury; it is time those unfair aspersions were quashed.

Once the problem had been solved parachuting resumed, led by Jock Lewes. David Stirling, still confined to hospital, refined the ideas he, Lewes and other members of Layforce, not all officers, had discussed for long-range raiding. He produced a short hand-written paper which noted that the fighting in North Africa was confined to a very long and narrow coastal strip making the enemy lines of communication not only extended but also open to attack from both the seaward and landward flanks. Any such attack should be made by small teams trained to operate by night, and infiltrated by air, sea or land. The teams should be part of a small unit answering directly to the theatre commander for the sake of simplicity, speed of reaction to orders, and for security which, in Egypt, was lax. Anti-armour operations, i.e. POL supplies, were to be a key target. In view of the Axis air superiority in the Western Desert, airfields were the next priority as the thirty-five or so Italian ones mainly lay beyond the range of RAF bombers. Finally, the unit should be administratively independent, to avoid delays in procuring the necessary specialist equipment and training facilities.

Once discharged from hospital he presented the paper to the Deputy C.-in-C. GHQ Middle East, General Sir Neil Ritchie, in a piece of well-recorded opportunism. (The fact that General Ritchie knew the Stirlings and their estate from pre-war grouse shoots helped; the Tartan Mafia once again.) The paper was accepted by General Auchinleck, the C.-in-C., and in July1941 GHQ ME authorized Stirling (and Lewes) to raise and deploy a small raiding unit as quickly as possible. The unit required a formal title or name, but it is doubtful if David Stirling or any of the original members cared what it was to be called. Dudley Clarke seized the opportunity to magnify his phantom airborne force named from the, by then defunct, first British Army parachute unit, 11th Special Air Service Battalion. He had invented K Detachment, 1 SAS Brigade, and had dummy paratroops dropped near Axis prisoner of war camps in the Nile Delta, while dummy gliders were strewn around Egyptian airfields for high-altitude *Luftwaffe* Ju86P reconnaissance aircraft to photograph. Clarke proposed, and Stirling accepted, that the new unit should seem to be part of a larger force, and L Detachment, 1 Special Air Service Brigade, came into being. It was formally on strength of GHQ as L Detachment, 1 SAS Brigade on 28 August 1941, but had in fact been in existence, as a cadre and recruiting team, for some weeks before that date.

The command, control and administrative arrangements for the new unit were simple; orders did not pass through any intervening command echelons, and it was also administered without recourse to the numerous tiers of the military hierarchy. These positions of trust were not abused by the unit, which made life very much easier and simpler for all concerned. It should be borne in mind that David Stirling and his colleagues were very junior hostilities-only officers, basically civilians in uniform, yet were dealing directly with experienced, highly trained and very senior professional soldiers. An interesting situation, and one which gave more than one Regular Army officer food for thought.

First Strike

In the autumn of 1941 General Auchinleck and General Ritchie, who was about to assume command of the newly-designated

Eighth Army, were in the final throes of planning a major offensive, Operation Crusader. Both Generals were concerned about the threat from *Luftwaffe* ground attack aircraft, including the infamous Stukas. Air Marshal Cunningham, commanding the recently formed Western Desert Air Force, was equally concerned that Axis fighters would destroy his new ground attack squadrons equipped with slow Hurricanes and Tomahawks, and his fighters, RAF Hurricanes and Fleet Air Arm Martlets. Therefore the first SAS mission was to neutralize enemy aircraft on airfields around Tmimi and Gazala, in Cyreniaca, west of Tobruk, during the night before D-Day for Crusader, 18 November. Almost the entire trained strength of qualified parachutists from L Detachment was to be used or as many as could be carried in the available aircraft, and for whom parachutes could be found. They would be parachuted in five parties onto blind DZs anything up to twenty miles from the target areas, and move overnight to the immediate vicinity of the airfields. They would find hides for observing the airfields on D-1 Day, and then attack the aircraft dispersal areas during the night before the battle.

The night drop was a disaster due to bad weather and lack of experience by the aircrew and the SAS. Two-thirds of the SAS troops were injured or captured, and the RAF lost two of its scarce Bombay bomber-transports. One was captured intact with its crew and SAS team, after getting lost and landing on a German-manned airfield by mistake; in those days night navigation was not much practised by RAF aircrew. It should also be borne in mind that this was only the second British parachute operation of the war. The first was Operation Colossus, also an SAS operation, but conducted by 11 SAS, later to become 1st Battalion Parachute Regiment, and mounted from Malta; all three onto blind DZs. The survivors of Colossus had hardly been able to send back reports on the problems of finding, then parachuting onto blind DZs and there was no information for the SAS and RAF staff in Egypt.

The Tmimi-Gazala operation achieved results, possibly eighteen or nineteen aircraft destroyed, but enough to prove the point, and both Stirling and Auchinleck pressed ahead. Another result was a higher priority being given to weather reports from the LRDG and some thought was given to having certain elements of the SIS – the so-called 'Field Parties' – do the same thing. Later the Americans went one better and trained meteorologists in OSS skills, including Morse code, and deployed them into France and the Balkans. Parachuting, as a means of insertion, was discarded by the SAS, but was retained for confidence building and in case circumstances changed. Apart from any other reason, there were very few parachutes available for training where they could be recovered and re-used and the RAF could not spare any more of their scarce transports for training or operations. The SAS went to battle with the help of the LRDG, and of some captured Lancia lorries, equipped by the previous owners for desert travel. They were useful load-carriers, and would serve the unit well until something better arrived in the shape of the Jeep.

In November 1941, a second raid on Italian airfields, mounted from hides reached with the help of the LRDG, resulted in the destruction of around ninety aircraft and thirty airfield support vehicles. One fringe benefit of the first raids for the Eighth Army was that the Axis forces in North Africa removed infantry battalions from fighting divisions to guard *all* airfields and landing grounds and had to use scarce defence stores, barbed wire, mines and concrete to erect defences around airfields and static installations such as vehicle workshops.

The following month Sirte and Tamet airfields were raided, and twenty-seven aircraft, three airfield support vehicles, two trailers of aircraft engine parts and some scattered POL dumps were destroyed. There were other raids on the airfields at Agedabia, El Agheila and Nofilia: few of these raids were carried out without casualties.

The most serious loss to the fledgling force occurred on the morning of 31 December 1941, when Jock Lewes was mortally wounded by cannon fire from an Me110. The fighter was one of a pair conducting a low-level sweep of the open ground near Nofilia; one doing the sweep, the other flying top-cover and checking for vehicle tracks. The pilot of the lower aircraft spotted the Lancia lorries of the SAS team, and circled round to get into position for a strafing run, one of several, as the troops bailed out of the Lancias which were too obvious a target. Lewes was hit and died almost immediately. He was buried in the desert; one loss of many the SAS was to suffer in the war. His impact on the development of the SAS, and on the training regimes, now in widespread use throughout the world by many Special Forces, commando and parachute units, has only recently been acknowledged. He evolved a system of developing stamina, navigational skills and self-confidence in 'ordinary' soldiers through long cross-country marches, especially at night; water discipline (not water depriv-ation); night training in weapon handling; shooting; simple vehicle repairs; selecting and setting up hides and careful reconnaissance and planning. His greatest legacy, however, is that the system he helped create survived and flourished without him.

The death of Jock Lewes highlighted the serious threat to LRDG, SAS and PPA patrols from low, slow aircraft, and the need for anti-aircraft guns similar to those fitted to the Fiat AS vehicles of the Italian desert patrols. These vehicles operated in groups of four; two were fitted with three medium or heavy machine guns (crew's choice), one with a Solothurn 20mm AA and anti-armour cannon, and the fourth with machine guns and a single Breda 47mm anti-tank gun; a light, accurate and useful weapon. Allied aircraft also caused several casualties to various raiding forces, as there was at that time neither workable ground to air radio, nor any recognition panels; both came later.

Contested Command and Control

In theory the new unit should have been part of the Directorate of Combined Operations, nominally responsible for raiding forces (at least in Britain), but the SAS was never under operational command or control of that formation. It was, however, allocated space on the DCO site at Kabrit, at the southern end of the Great Salt Lake, part of the Suez Canal system. Another organization, G(R), was also interested in acquiring the SAS. G(R) was the military design-ation for the Directorate of Special Operations of the Middle East branch of SOE. (The designation G(R) remained in use after the original section in London became MI(R); it is not clear from surviving records when the Middle East G(R) was established.)

G(R) was ostensibly part of the ME GHQ Directorate of Military Operations, headed by Brigadier J.F.M. Whiteley. At one stage G(R) was the intermediary for orders issued by GOC Western Desert Force (later the Eighth Army) to the Long Range Desert Group, but it also had some small operational units, as did SIS, under the guise of the Inter-Services Liaison Department, 'Field Parties'.

In October 1941, just a few weeks after L Detachment was formed, the first of several attempts was made to absorb it into a larger formation. This was a reasonable attempt by the Directorate of Staff Duties at ME GHQ to bring some rationale and structure to the burgeoning Special Forces across the Middle East theatre. DSD proposed that a Middle East Commando should be formed from the remains of Layforce, the third ME Commando (No. 51), L Detachment, and the Special Boat Section. The new unit would be grouped with the LRDG and some small units based at Geneifa, near Kabrit, and referred to vaguely as Depot G(R), the triumvirate to be controlled by G(R). The proposal was administratively neat, but operationally clumsy and fortunately withered away after two sections of the ME GHQ Directorate of Military Operations, G(Ops) and G(R), could not agree on who should control the SBS. However, another bid for rationalization surfaced a few weeks later, and again L Detachment managed to avoid being absorbed in an ME Commando. This was formed in January 1942 at Geneifa, and consisted of the Depot G(R) units, 51 Commando, and the SBS. It was to be commanded by Lieutenant Colonel J.M. Graham, Scots Greys, and to have an HQ plus five British 'squadrons', plus depot and training staff. However, it was not a GHQ unit, but part of the Ministry of Economic Warfare Mission to the Middle East, or SOE, and was controlled by the Directorate of Special Operations, under Colonel T.S. Airey. Colin Gubbins' ideas for a group of Independent Companies for both 'Butcher' and 'Bolt' operations, and for shipborne operations in the eastern Mediterranean seemed to be coming to fruition. This was heightened when the new unit was empowered, but not initially authorized, to raise additional squadrons or troops possibly manned, as with the LRDG, by Empire forces, including Canadians for use in the Caucasus. Also considered were squadrons of

80

Frenchmen, Greeks, Yugoslavs, Poles and Czechs; GHQ ME was responsible for a huge area, and its borders touched many nations. This G(R) unit, ME Commando, later to become 1 Special Service Battalion, included at one time or another the SBS element of Layforce; a mixed squadron of Arabs from all over the Levant and Spaniards, including Jews. It also had other Jewish troops, some fluent in German, being former members of the Czech Legion and now serving in the Special Interrogation Group. The SIG was commanded by a Captain Buck, formerly of the Indian Army, 3/Punjabis, who was invited to transfer to the British Army while on home leave when war broke out.

Another oddity which was nearly incorporated into the ME Commando at a later stage was the Iraq Parachute Company, raised from Assyrian and Kurdish volunteers serving in the RAF Iraq Levies. It was a fine unit, RAF not Army, and later made an operational drop in the Aegean in support of some LRDG operations.

G(R) retained its base at Geneifa, near Kabrit, so knew what its near neighbour, the SAS was doing, and never seems to have lost its desire to absorb L Detachment.

Slack Security

Security was certainly lax in and around ME GHQ, a situation made worse later when a Colonel Bonner Feller appeared in Cairo as President Roosevelt's special military observer, officially the Military Attaché. At the direction of Winston Churchill Colonel Feller had open access to secret information, and probably had ways of finding it out anyway, being a natural politician. He regularly reported back to Washington much of the Allied plans for operations in the Western Desert, including some Top Secret information, but his signals were being read by Axis COMINT teams. This created problems for the Allies. The worst example for the SAS, and for the Royal Navy and many merchant seamen, occurred in June 1942 when the siege of Malta was at its height, and the island was short of everything, especially POL and food. The War Cabinet in London agreed to an Admiralty plan to mount two fast relief convoys simultaneously from Egypt and the Atlantic,

81

Operations Vigorous (Alexandria) and Harpoon (Gibraltar). As part of the Allied counter-air preparations GHQ ME ordered the SAS, and the SBS, not at that time part of the Regiment, to raid airfields used by bombers, German Ju88s and Italian SM79s, capable of anti-shipping operations and Me110s operating as long-range escort fighters. The SAS planned raids against six airfields in North Africa (Operations 10A and 10B – operational code-names came later), while the SBS tackled three airfields on Crete, all within the period 9–14 June. The main effort was to be the night of 13–14 June, when the convoys would be getting close to the critical zone just outside the operating range of Malta-based fighters but within that of the Me110s. The dutiful Feller reported everything to Washington in State Department Cable #11119, dated 11 June 1942. It included the sentence:

ON NIGHTS OF JUNE 12TH JUNE 13TH BRITISH SABOTAGE UNITS PLAN SIMULTANEOUS STICKER (sic) BOMB ATTACKS AGAINST AIRCRAFT ON NINE AXIS AIRDROMES. PLANS TO REACH OBJECTIVES BY PARACHUTES AND LONG RANGE DESERT PATROL.

The signal was one of thousands of Allied and neutral diplomatic items intercepted and deciphered by two Axis versions of Bletchley Park. One was near Rome, Italian operated but with the inform-ation (usually) shared with the Germans. The other was at Lauf an der Pegnitz, in Bavaria. The Lauf station was one of twenty or so *Feste Nachrichten-Aufklarungsstellen* (static intelligence recon-naissance posts) of the German Military Cryptographic Bureau, strung out in a long skein between the Canary Islands and East Prussia. The Lauf station concentrated on short wave diplomatic radio traffic, and had built up a formidable expertise at intercep-tion and deciphering many codes, including those of the US State Department. Despite the successful interception and deciphering of #11119, the information does not appear to have been dissemi-nated sufficiently widely or quickly enough for the Axis to strengthen the defences of all except one airfield, Barce. Five Free French paratroopers, lead by Lieutenant Jacquier, attempted to raid the airfield but found it well-guarded. The surrounding area was patrolled by armoured cars manned by skilful, alert and suspicious crews.

Whatever happened on land as a result of the interception pales when compared with the carnage at sea. Between 14–16 June the Harpoon convoy was under almost continuous attack by aircraft, surface vessels including E-boats, and German and Italian submarines; only two cargo ships reached Malta. The other convoy, MW11, incurred serious losses, four out of eleven merchantmen sunk and three damaged, before turning back to Egypt in the face of a large Italian force of surface ships. The SAS and SBS teams destroyed thirty-three enemy aircraft (six on Crete), possibly thirty aero-engines, several ground support vehicles, including almost irreplaceable mobile cranes, and a large quantity of POL. The losses amounted to fifteen SAS men missing and two wounded, while the two Cretan raiding parties, each of six men, suffered one Frenchman killed, and three, including Capitaine Bergé, captured. Whether or not thirty-three aircraft would have completed the destruction of the merchant ships in both convoys (the escorting Allied warships were not so important) is immaterial, enough of the western convoy got through to help Malta survive a little longer.

Canoes

These raids involved the SBS, one of several units or sub-units to bear that set of initials during the Second World War. This particular SBS had originally been part of Layforce. It was a tiny amphibious warfare team, No. 1 Special Boat Section, raised by Roger 'Jumbo' Courtney, a larger than life man who before the war had been a gold prospector and big-game hunter in East Africa, and a sergeant in the Palestine Police. He was also an enthusiastic canoeist, who before the war had once paddled alone down the Nile from Khartoum to Cairo, and later honeymooned in a canoe (the marriage survived the experience). Courtney became enamoured with one particular make of canoe, the *Folbot*. This fine little craft was designed by a fellow enthusiast called Jack Kissner, who is believed to have worked at one time for the Klepper organization in

Germany, designers of the *Faltboot* (folding boat). The Klepper, first made in 1907, was a small kayak-style canoe that could, as the name implies, be folded for carrying on public transport and in cars. In 1930 Kissner designed and started making and selling lightweight folding kayaks under the trade-name *Folbot*, but the rise of the Nazis forced him to emigrate to London. There he met Courtney, and sold him a *Folbot*.

At the outbreak of war Courtney joined the King's Royal Rifle Corps but found his way into No.8 Commando. Some of his fellow commandos had served in Norway with the Independent Companies and their experiences and frustrations led Courtney to propose the formation of a small canoe-borne reconnaissance and raiding force, to operate either in conjunction with a Commando or as an independent unit. The canoe force could be based on a mother ship, something akin to the Independent Companies in Norway, or operate from hides in enemy territory, or be carried to the scene of action by MTBs or submarines. The force would use folding canoes, either off-the-shelf *Folbots* or developments to improve their sea-worthiness and load carrying. The idea was accepted, after some telling demonstrations in the Firth of Clyde, and an experimental *Folbot* Troop was formed within No. 8 Commando. The aim was to test the concept, develop the equipment, and train the men. If all went well each Commando unit would have a *Folbot* Troop added to its establishment, but that did not come to pass.

Early in 1941 the *Folbot* Troop, its parent unit, with Nos. 7 and 11 Commandos and some headquarters and support staff, were formed into Z Force and deployed to the Middle East. The force travelled in three Glen-class fast (17 knots) merchantmen converted into Assault Ships, Transport (AST) by fitting them with large davits for launching landing craft. Once in the Middle East Z Force became Layforce and came under temporary control of the Directorate of Combined Operations. As there was no immediate role for the SBS it found itself at the Combined Training Centre at Kabrit where it was based in a tented camp next to HMS *Saunders*, the Middle East amphibious warfare-training centre. The SBS being soldiers and very odd ones indeed – Pongos with boats – were looked at askance by the Senior Service. They, poor souls, were not amused at operating landing craft (vessels deliberately run ashore, anathema to any proper naval person) on a canal in the middle of a desert (but were mollified by living on houseboats). The Troop was eventually billeted in tents next to the CTC's Royal Engineer detachment, but made good use of the naval facilities. Courtney set the men to work, concentrating on general physical fitness and long distance paddling. As the SBS 'depot' was just over a low headland from the SAS base, they soon made contact.

Overstretch

In September 1942, GHQ ME was conducting operations over an area stretching from Gibraltar to Iran by way of Corsica, Sardinia, Italy, the Adriatic, Greece and the Aegean, Crete, Cyprus and the entire Levantine and North African coast; wonderful raiding grounds and full of targets. A number of raiding forces had been raised, some more useful than others. SOE in Cairo was in some disarray, and did not enjoy the wholehearted confidence of either the C.-in-C. Middle East, or of some of HM Ambassadors in the theatre. Its Augean stable was eventually cleaned in August 1942. That cleansing took place following the panic in Cairo caused by Rommel's last lunge at the Nile, and thereafter G(R) lost much of its admittedly limited strong-arm and reconnaissance elements. The SAS-SBS put the seaborne base concept to use in their own way, aided by the disreputable looking but efficient little sailing craft of the Levant Schooner Flotilla. It should be noted that G(R) was quite separate from G(RF), General Staff Section (Raiding Forces), part of the Directorate of Military Operations, GHQ Middle East Land Forces, described below.

By spring 1943 L Detachment had grown from the size of a small infantry company into a large multi-national formation, complete with a new designation. 1 Special Air Service Regiment consisted of a headquarters and five operational elements. These were L and M Detachments, each of two squadrons (A & B, C & D), a *Folbot* (canoe) Section, a squadron of French paratroops (under the irrepressible Bergé) and one of Greek officers and men. The latter were determined to take the war to the enemy to help free their homeland and had raised, for only the third time in history, the

Helios Lokos, the Sacred Squadron, traditionally formed by Greeks in times of mortal danger. On his right breast each man in the SAS Sacred Squadron wore a brass badge embellished with the ancient Greek exhortation to soldiers departing for the wars – Return victorious or dead.

The 1 SAS Regiment had some other resolute warriors in its ranks. There was a remnant of the Special Interrogation Group; after a large and ill-fated Tobruk raid of September 1942 there were very few of these German-speaking, or in one or two cases, ethnic-Germans or Sudeten Czechs left. Around a dozen found a home of sorts within the Regiment. One or two certainly profited from the experience; they served with distinction in the Israeli Army, and many continued to serve with the Regiment until the end of the war. Captain Buck was killed in 1946 in an air crash while returning to the Operation Nimrod team in Germany from his home in Somerset. Also present were some extremely tough Spaniards, a few were Jewish former members of the *Tercio Espanol de Extranjeros,* the Spanish Foreign Legion. After the Civil War they were no longer politically acceptable in Franco's African colonies but were determined to fight Fascism somewhere. Some were non-Jewish, anti-Franco Spanish veterans of the Civil War and a few, Jewish and Gentile, were from the 135 Spaniards trained by SOE, many for Operations Sconce and Sprinkler, *coup de main* parties intended to attack any Germans attempting to seize Gibraltar and Tangier. A very few then joined the French Foreign Legion, and went through the same process of assimilation then rejection followed by ejection. Others found themselves in Syria after Dunkirk, and after the Allied invasion were discharged from the Legion and became French citizens. They joined the Free French, then Bergé's paratroops, then their 'real' Spanish comrades in the SAS. These Spaniards were reportedly ready to do battle with anyone, anytime, anywhere, preferably in Spanish territory and with Germans, Italians or *Falangistas,* (members of the Falange, the Phalanx of Spain, a para-military movement for young men). The Spaniards were incorporated into the Regiment in case it was required to operate in Spanish North and West Africa, or around, on or from the Balearic and Canary Islands, possibly against the German wireless interception station.

David Stirling had a wide vision of war, and in early 1943, only a few months after the Battle of El Alamein, just as Stalingrad was about to be won by the Russians, and German and Italian forces in North Africa surrendered, the fighting could be carried on anywhere.

The SAS had its own base, in a corner of the Combined Operations estate at Kabrit. The Regimental base had various administrative and support sections, such as a large Light Aid Detachment (LAD), for vehicle modifications and maintenance; some of the REME fitters stayed with the Regiment until it was (mostly) disbanded in 1946. There was also a Parachute Training Section, originally consisting of Captain Waugh, sent specifically to L Detachment in November 1941 after the fatal accidents. Three more instructors, two Army and one RAF, arrived at Kabrit in April 1942, and No. 4 Parachute Training School, RAF, was opened in early May at Kabrit airfield. (It later moved to Ramat David, Palestine, as the Kabrit DZ lay on the opposite side of the Suez Canal to the airfield and was very hard and rocky; the hot, up-welling desert air did not make for good basic parachute training.)

When General Alexander replaced Auchinleck, and Montgomery replaced Ritchie, both initially approved the existing tasking arrangement, except that at times operational command of the SAS was delegated to GOC Eighth Army. Montgomery made good use of the SAS (also of Phantom, LRDG and Popski) despite jocularly saying of its leader, 'The Boy David (Stirling) is mad. Quite, quite mad. However in war there is often a place for mad people.' Jocularity from Monty, and use of the word 'boy', was a sign of high esteem.

In July 1942 GHQ ME began a review of its concept of clandestine warfare operations by all irregular forces and organizations. These included the LRDG, the SAS, the remnants of the ME Commando, the SBS, the Senussi-manned and (mainly) British officered Libyan Arab Force, the Special Operations portion of G(R), the various parts of the ISLD including its version of MI9 and, courtesy of the Navy, access to the Levant Schooner Flotilla, and other maritime elements. The DMO, at that time, Brigadier

George Davy was a keen advocate of the Long Range Desert Group and Special Air Service. As those units were the main military-controlled special warfare units, they were called to a conference in Cairo to decide the best means of coordinating their operations at GHQ level. Representatives of ISLD and G(R) were also present, the latter probably being Colonel Airey. The result was agreement on coordination and roles between the four main players. All operations would be planned and controlled at GHQ by section G(RF) of the Director of Military Operations. The Long Range Desert Group would be responsible for long-range reconnaissance and some sabotage and raiding, and for transporting personnel from other organizations into the enemy rear areas. ISLD was to conduct reconnaissance, i.e. intelligence, areas unspecified, but at the behest of GHQ or of the Joint Intelligence Committee in London. G(R) would not conduct intelligence gathering. The SAS would conduct sabotage (covert raiding) and *coup de main* attacks (overt raiding) against rear area or battlefield targets. Both it and G(R) were not to conduct reconnaissance, but to note matters likely to be of interest to the Director of Military Intelligence and other Special Forces organizations and report them to GHQ. That meant for the first time the SAS would be provided with wireless sets and signallers that needed vehicles, workshops and REME staff which meant a revised War Establishment. In addition, the orphans of the SBS were to join L Detachment.

Fresh Fields

By September 1942 GHQ had completed its review. L Detachment, 1 SAS Brigade gained a new, broader and clearer mandate, more precise targeting, and a new War Establishment, and became 1 Special Air Service Regiment. This only confirmed what had happened by chance of war, and was good administrative house-keeping by the Director of Staff Duties. The unit was to remain under the direct control of GHQ, but command of all or part of it could be delegated to another body as operational circumstances dictated (a foretaste of operations in Algeria). One change was that the Commanding Officer, 1 SAS reported through G(RF) as mentioned above, and no longer had, in theory, direct contact with

GOC Eighth Army or the C.-in-C. ME. Irrespective of that sensible adjustment, made to relieve the top commanders of too many contacts, Alexander and Montgomery kept in touch with David Stirling, and were well aware of the Regiment's capabilities against 'deep' targets.

G(RF) was set up in September 1942 to rationalize control of the plethora of raiding forces within the Middle East Theatre, which was enormous and about to be enlarged in scope, if not in scale, due to Operation Torch, the Allied landings in North Africa. Soon there would be no more North African operations, but access to Italy, the Balkans and the Aegean. The problem was going to be finding suitable strategic targets for the SAS and a role of any sort for the LRDG. The Levant Schooner Flotilla was doing much of the LRDG role in the Aegean, so the unit voted by many desert veterans, and other people, as the one in which they would have liked to serve, was faced with a void. The SAS, too, would have to find new energies and suitable outlets for them. Throughout its time in the Western Desert all operations mounted by the SAS were directed by the theatre commander, (C.-in-C. Middle East) or, when specifically delegated, by the GOC Western Desert Force, later the Eighth Army. There were no intervening layers of head-quarters or formation, as was to happen in Algeria for operations in Sicily and Italy and in Britain for Overlord, which caused un-necessary delays and problems. Moreover the North African campaign provided scope for using raiding forces against targets of strategic importance and rarely, if ever, against tactical ones. It was to be different in Normandy, Flanders, Belgium and Germany; there were no strategic targets capable of being raided by Special Forces.

The achievements of the SAS were reported to the War Office in official dispatches, operational analyses and other reports, and by less formal memos, notes and letters. The Joint Planning Staff were therefore aware of the role of the Regiment, and of other Special Forces in North Africa. The JPS was responsible for formulating outline plans to meet contingencies or for proposed Allied offensives. It was decided to add an SAS unit to the Order of Battle of the First Army, the British element of Operation

Torch. There was a problem about raising such a unit at short notice; Torch was planned, mounted and took place all within ninety days. 2 SAS was to be raised after the landings to conduct offensive operations in enemy rear areas ahead of US and British forces advancing eastwards, and would link up with 1 SAS. When it was announced that 2 SAS would be commanded by Bill Stirling, wags in the GHQ ME quipped that 'SAS' meant 'Stirling and Stirling'.

In 1941 Lieutenant Colonel W.J. Stirling is recorded as being the Commandant of a group of SOE training schools, STS 62, 62a and 62d, in the West of England, used at times by the Small Scale Raiding Force. This intrepid group had been raised by SOE for 'butcher and bolt' operations, allegedly at the instigation of Lord Mountbatten when Director of Combined Operations. The units' first members were associated with Operation Postmaster, a cutting-out mission to the Spanish colony of Fernando Po, an island off the coast of central Africa. This took place in January 1942, and the account of it reads like something written by John Buchan or Ian Fleming. The SSRF does not appear to have been used for 'butcher and bolt' operations as such, due to the political and humanitarian problems of reprisals, such as the massacre at Lidice in Czechoslovakia. This was retribution for the horrible death, allegedly due to blood poisoning caused by grenade splinters in his spleen, of Reinhardt Heydrich, *Reichskommissar* of Bohemia and Moravia, as a result of Operation Anthropoid, an SOE sponsored mission. In April 1943 the SSRF was transferred from SOE to the Directorate of Combined Operations and became No. 62 Commando, yet at the same time also appearing as Military Operations 1 Special Projects (MO1 SP), an SOE designation in some files. The DCO did not have a role for the unit, but the call for a second SAS Regiment for Operation Torch saved the personnel from returning to mainstream soldiering.

Brothers, Yes – Cousins, No

One of the stipulations laid down by the War Office when agreeing to the formation of an SAS unit for the First Army was that, '. . . the

Commander must be someone who would co-operate whole-heartedly with Commander First SAS Regiment'. Bill Stirling appears to have been the first nomination for the Commanding Officer of 2 SAS, but someone in authority preferred Lieutenant Colonel Lord Lovat, CO of No. 4 Commando which was to provide the nucleus of 2 SAS. However, a letter dated 20 January 1943 addressed to Major General J.C. Haydon at Headquarters Combined Operations by someone identifiable only as 'Antony' makes a telling point:

'. . . although they (Lovat and David Stirling) are cousins . . . (they) do not always see to eye. It would mess up the whole thing up if the two commanders of these two forces fought and you may wish to reconsider the question of sending Bill Stirling.'

The matter *was* reconsidered, and Bill Stirling was appointed Commanding Officer, 2 Special Air Service Regiment, and travelled to Algeria with a nucleus of fifty volunteers. Fifteen came from the SSRF, including Geoffrey Appleyard who became second in command of 2 SAS, six more from the No. 2 Special Boat Section and twenty-nine from No. 4 Commando. The unit was slowly expanded by volunteers from No. 1 Commando, Nos. 7–10 troops were manned by US Army soldiers trained at Achnacarry, and from 1 (British) Airborne Brigade. A small group from 1 SAS was posted-in to act as instructors and patrol leaders.

Captured

David Stirling knew about the formation of the new regiment, which seemed to herald the realization of his ambition, a group of SAS regiments, capable of operating anywhere from Norway to New Guinea, Morocco to Manchuria, in mountains, desert, snow-fields, jungle or islands. The final ME Commando was formed with that in mind, but was disbanded after some raids on Axis supply columns after Alamein. On 3 January 1943 the Director of Military Operations for the Eighth Army issued Operational Instruction No. 6/1943, directing, among other things, that Lieutenant Colonel

A.D. Stirling was to travel overland to Tunisia where he was to come under command of HQ First Army. He was to take with him a detachment of eight patrols, establish a base in the broken country near Gabes on the Gulf of Sirte and raid enemy lines of communication. (Over the years there has been some criticism of David Stirling's overland journey to Algeria; Operational Instruction 6 reveals that it was not his decision.)

Although not mentioned in the orders, after establishing the base and handing over command of the detachment to another officer, David was going to Allied Forces Headquarters (AFHQ) to discuss the formation of 2 SAS and the role of both SAS units, and possibly the SBS, in North Africa until the capitulation of the Axis forces. Other topics to be discussed included the subsequent role, and the command and control arrangements and plans, for what would be an SAS Brigade in all but name. These plans might include the invasion of Sicily, and raids against enemy garrisons and radar stations on islands in the western Mediterranean capable of housing landing grounds, or submarine and Motor Torpedo Boats' bases covering Allied sea and air routes to Sicily and Italy. And there was the whole of the Aegean and Adriatic seas to be considered, as AFHQ would cover all of the area once the fief of GHQ ME. There was also the question of possible operations in Italy, the Balkans, Greece, and even Austria and the Caucasus, with the consequent need for mountain warfare training, including skiing. After these discussions he was going to return to the UK for about five weeks' leave and to see Jock Lewes's family and those of other SAS men killed in North Africa. Thereafter he was going to discuss with COSSAC the role of an SAS formation in the invasion and liberation of western Europe before returning to Algeria and Allied Forces HQ. How the SAS Brigade was to be divided between the Mediterranean and Overlord, and who was to command its units in each theatre, would also have to be clarified. He was going to be busy.

David Stirling left Egypt in late December 1942, leading a small convoy of supply trucks and jeeps. By nightfall on 23 January it was west of Gabes, and laid up for the night in a wadi. Meanwhile, the Germans, plagued by SAS and Long Range Desert Group patrols, had brought an experienced motorized anti-partisan parachute unit to North Africa to hunt them down. During this unit's first desert exercise, a simple cordon-and-search of a wadi, they hit the jackpot; Lieutenant Colonel Arthur David Stirling and many of the detachment were captured. The ecstatic German Army telegram advising Field Marshal Rommel of the capture is in the Liddell Hart Collection, housed in King's College, London.

Ironically, while David was motoring towards Tunisia a staff officer from COSSAC was travelling to North Africa to discuss the role of the SAS in Overlord. David Stirling's capture was a devastating blow to the development of the SAS concept of operations, and it nearly spelled the end of the regiment. 1 SAS lost their leader and a number of highly experienced non-commissioned officers and troopers. They were also deprived of a voice at GHQ ME and Allied Forces HQ that was to have unfortunate results in the short term for the Regiment.

After the surrender of Axis forces 1 SAS returned to the Nile Delta and became part of a new formation, Raiding Forces Middle East, command by a Brigadier Turnbull. 1 SAS was first dismembered, and then disbanded. The reason for this piece of organizational butchery remains shrouded in mystery. Personnel were RTU'd or transferred into some new units – the Raiding Support Regiment (RSR), the Special Boat Squadron (SBS), the Special Raiding Squadron (SRS) and Special Forces (ME). There was a certain degree of logic in the roles of the three new units, but no one seems to have considered the longer term requirement for units capable of operating for prolonged periods behind enemy lines. A few months later AFHQ, by its own admission, was in dire need of such units.

The War Establishment for the last unit reveals it to have been for an SAS type unit with three operational squadrons, each of three troops, with three sections each with three jeeps. The RSR was devised by Combined Operations in the UK, developed in the Middle East, and served mainly in the Adriatic theatre. Its War Establishment (ME VI/1313/1) allowed for a headquarters and five batteries, one with 75mm mountain guns, one with German 20mm Solothurn anti-aircraft guns, one with Italian 47mm anti-tank guns, one with Vickers .303 medium machine guns and one with 3-inch mortars.

The SRS bore the closest resemblance to 1 SAS, but only consisted of a squadron headquarters and three troops, about 150 all ranks in total. It was sometimes referred to as Special Raiding Squadron, 1 Special Air Service Regiment, but officially that regiment had been disbanded. That fact later led to a bureaucratic hiccup which upset a certain Lieutenant Colonel Blair Mayne.

2 SAS gradually came into being and started training for airborne and amphibious operations and was blooded in both during Operation Husky, the invasion of Sicily on 9–10 July 1943. In addition to amphibious landings 2 SAS carried out several parachute operations, none successful and marred by accidents. The first was Operation Chestnut, a three-phase operation, initially to consist of submarine landings on the north-east coast of Sicily followed by the air insertion of a follow up force and a supply drop. It was suddenly cancelled in mid-June, then reinstated as an airborne operation, cancelled again, despite being intended to divert attention from an airdrop on 9–10 July, the first operational descent for the US 82nd Airborne Division and which was severely disrupted due to strong winds. The airdrop was to be part of the assault by General George Patton's Seventh US Army, but in the event stiff resistance held up Patton's force, and he called for a second airdrop to reinforce his central sector. On 11 July the aircraft carrying the follow up airborne force approached the Landing Zone just after a *Luftwaffe* raid, and US anti-aircraft fire shot down or scattered thirty-seven out of 144 C47 transport aircraft. The Chestnut plan was reinstated on 12 July, and was to utilize almost one (under strength) squadron from 2 SAS. Chestnut 1 – two twelve-man teams, Team Pink (OC Captain Pinkney), and Team Brig (OC Captain Bridgeman-Evans) to be dropped into two blind Dropping Zones to the north of the beleaguered central sector by two RAF Armstrong-Whitworth Albermarles of 296 Squadron, flying from Tunisia. Chestnut 2 was a follow-up force of three twelve-man teams to be dropped on the next night, with Teams Pink and Brig acting as pathfinders, setting out a DZ, operating marker lights, Eureka beacons 'radios', possibly S-phones. Chestnut 3 was to be a supply drop to the Team Brig DZ. However, most of the DZ equipment was lost or damaged in the Chestnut 1 drop, as well as many of Team Brig's weapons, supplies and radios.

In addition, Team Pink landed close to the town of Randazzo, alerting the Italian garrison. Without Eureka or S-phones the teams could not receive the follow-up teams, although the supplies were dropped. Both teams made their way to Allied lines and safety. However, Chestnut 1 involved a double tragedy. It was not only the first operational drop for 2 SAS but also for 296 Squadron's Albermarles. In recognition of this double first the Squadron's CO, Wing Commander P.J. May, flew one of the aircraft, with Major Geoffrey Appleyard acting as an assistant dispatcher. The drop completed, the Albermarle turned for home – and was never seen again.

Chapter Six

A Grand Alliance

In 1939 the war in Europe came as no surprise to President Roosevelt and many senior American diplomats and businessmen in Washington. Their first question was not if, but when, it would break out, how long it would last, and whether America would become involved. They also recognized that the United Kingdom was the pivot on which war would swing, and quietly established service liaison teams in London. The US Army, and the US Army Air Corps (later Force), sent observers to London in late 1939 tasked with keeping abreast of developments in weapons, tactics, engineering, and what could now be called the battle-management of land and air campaigns. Later, in 1940, the US Navy sent Rear Admiral Robert Ghormley to London with two main tasks. First, to discuss with his Royal Navy counterpart co-operation if the United States entered the war and secondly, to develop the US Navy end of a conduit between the two Navies, exchanging information on naval operations including control of merchant shipping.

These low key but effective arrangements led to an agreement between the two governments to exchange military missions; in Washington the British Joint Staff Mission represented the British Chiefs of Staff Committee, with a similar US body in London. The dual system worked well and led to two formal conferences on possible combined strategy between the two nations, and their allies, in the event of America entering the war. Events in Hawaii on December 1941, and Germany's declaration of war on the

United States of America, changed many things. Thereafter there was open, close and useful dialogue and cooperation between the two nations, and their armed forces. Not always agreement, but cooperation.

Intelligence Agency

In 1939 America did not have an integrated command system or much of a mechanism for formal cooperation between the two armed services in wartime – like the Japanese 'system', described earlier. The days of the Joint Chiefs of Staff and their Chairman were yet to come, as was the building of the Pentagon, and a national intelligence service – but that was about to change. During the early stages of the war President Roosevelt decided that the United States should have a foreign intelligence service. There was no precedent for such an organization in America. During the American Civil War, the US Army, the President and Congress depended to a great extent on the services of the Pinkerton Detective Agency, who were better at catching train-robbers than collecting military information about the Army of Northern Virginia. As late as 1940 the armed services were ambivalent about the need for military or naval intelligence branches or departments. They took the view that any officer could handle such information, and that only line officers were best equipped to know what information was needed, and relevant, for operational use.

There may not have been an intelligence service, but there was a large and steady flow of political and military information to the State Department supplied, as a matter of routine, by embassy staff around the world, including defence attachés. There was also a very large amount of economic information acquired daily by international financial, business and industrial organizations, much of it containing significant amounts of intelligence about Axis political and military intentions, capabilities or deficiencies. Much, if not all, of that information was regarded by each of the recipients as 'commercial in confidence' not to be shared lightly, if at all. Within the government there was no central collection agency to which that information might have been passed. There was apparently little interest by the State Department or the armed services in seeking help from the business world, despite it intermeshing more closely with the administration, that is Congress and the House of Representatives, than in most other nations at that time, with the exception of Germany.

A further complication was the antipathy between the US Army and Navy. Apart from any other differences during the 1920s and 30s they had had to fight for every dollar in their modest budgets, each one allocated at the expense of the other service. Their intelligence services were modest, and not manned by professional intelligence officers as such. The Military Intelligence Division consisted of twenty-three service personnel and about fifty civil servants, scattered across the Washington DC area in four buildings; a tiny department for a huge task. On the other hand, many of those small bands of long-serving civil servants were dedicated, able and willing, if rarely given scope to display their talents before the war. (The backbone of most intelligence services is a core of industrious, dedicated civil servants working away behind the scenes; their work is invaluable but rarely acknowledged.) America fortunately possessed a counter-intelligence service, the powerful Federal Bureau of Investigation. The Director of the FBI, J. Edgar Hoover, and the British government, in the shape of William Stephenson, the Canadian head of the British Security Coordination Commission in New York, had made contact early in 1940 and established a good working relationship. That was followed later in the year by the appearance in London of a certain Colonel William J. Donovan.

Wild Bill Donovan

Donovan was vaguely known to be a Presidential adviser-at-large. He was a man-mountain, whose propensity for wheeling and dealing earned him the nickname of Wild Bill. Donovan was tough, smart and worldly-wise. During the Great War he earned the Congressional Medal of Honor while serving with the 165th Infantry Regiment, lineal descendants of the 69th 'Fighting Irish' New York Infantry Regiment and heroes of the Civil War. During the 1920s and 30s he made a fortune on Wall Street as an anti-trust lawyer, and was head-hunted by President Roosevelt when the war began.

In December 1940 Donovan arrived in London after a European tour. He had come to complete his education, so to speak, on the murkier side of war; intelligence, subversion, clandestine operations and propaganda. At the direction of Winston Churchill he was given a guided tour and detailed explanations, warts and all, of the British secret state. This appears to have included contact with Stewart Menzies, Head of the SIS, who probably reflected aloud about the desirability of but one intelligence service to cover intelligence collection, analysis and distribution, and clandestine warfare. Donovan also received a thorough briefing on the SOE, PWE and MI9, and was given a tour of selection and training centres, wireless stations and experimental establishments, including a visit to the Loch Morar area with Colin Gubbins. He found in Colin Gubbins a kindred spirit; both had a touch of the buccaneer or border reiver, and they got on well. Donovan was escorted on the tour by David Boyle, ostensibly a stockbroker but, in reality, a contact man and fixer in and around Society, Whitehall and the City; he was close to the Royal family, and helped make his American guest's tour as informative and interesting as possible.

Donovan was shown much, learned a lot, and went away convinced that the British would fight to the end, come what may. He returned to Washington and reported to the President. Whether or not Menzies had planted the idea in his mind, Donovan could see little sense in having three separate organizations for handling intelligence, clandestine operations and propaganda. Early in the summer of 1941 Roosevelt signed a presidential order creating the office of the Coordinator of Information, and later Head of the Office of Strategic Services, both posts filled by Donovan. Roosevelt had found the right man for the job; 'Wild Bill' relished a challenge and tackled his new post with energy and enthusiasm. He acquired a small staff from various sources and throughout the summer and autumn of 1941 they evolved a concept of operations for the new agency. In November Donovan sent one of his staff officers to the UK to study the organization, training and operational methods of SOE, and sent others to STS 103, Camp X, at Whitby, outside Oshawa, east of Toronto. The COI/OSS men and women went as students, then instructors, but at all times to exchange ideas and share problems and experiences. Donovan also engineered the secondment of US Army Rangers to Achnacarry, then to commando units and Rangers later took part in cross-Channel raids.

In late October 1941 OSS established a training section under Lieutenant Colonel Garland Williams, former director of the New York Bureau of Narcotics; he was an inspired choice. He quickly acquired a team of instructors from police forces and the armed services including the Marines, who had got wind of something tough and wanted some of the action. The US Department of the Interior obtained training areas to a specification prepared by Donovan and Williams; forest, scrub and farmland, thinly populated, existing accommodation, easy access to rivers, swamps and the sea, near army or navy bases for services, supplies and medical facilities, and close to Washington with its corridors and dining rooms full of power-brokers. The department quickly found four sites. One was in Prince William County, in the Tidewater area of rural Virginia, some thirty miles south-west of Washington. The Tidewater area surrounds Chesapeake Bay and is drained by four rivers famous in American history, the James, York, Rappahannock and Potomac. The OSS site had an interesting history. It encompassed the Quantico Creek watershed, nowadays a fragile eco-system slowly recovering from centuries of abuse and neglect. As part of President Roosevelt's New Deal that helped drag America out of the Depression, the Federal Emergency Relief Administration initiated many recreational projects, and wanted to create an exemplary recreational area for state and local governments on a site near Washington. The agency obtained 15,000 acres of 'agriculturally sub marginal' land near Quantico, and built five 'Cabin Camps', clusters of rough but comfortable frontier-style log huts, to house staff working on the project. The area, Prince William Forest, was requisitioned for the OSS in 1941, and became Areas A and C. It was close to the USMC base at Quantico, and had good connections with Washington by railway and roads. The cabins were popular with the OSS trainees, and made for quick and powerful team building.

Area B was set among the Catoctin Mountains in Maryland, foothills of the Appalachian range, and consisted of upland forest scattered across hundreds of acres of rocky slopes and rugged hills, west of the small city of Thurmont. The Catoctin area lay about seventy miles north of Washington, and close to the rich farmlands around Manchester, York and Gettysburg, in southern Pennsylvania. From the 1890s it had been a popular summer holiday area for wealthy families from Washington, Baltimore and Philadelphia so enjoyed good road and rail links to the outside world. The area, like A, was also divided into two sections; B-2 was Camp Albert C. Ritchie, a pre-war Maryland National Guard training camp. B-1 had been a private hunting ground, complete with a fine lodge, before the Depression ruined the owner, and it became a Recreational Demonstration Area. The WPA manicured the forest, improved trails, cleared rivers and ponds, and upgraded access from main roads and the railway depot at Thurmont. The area also contained recreational camps for federal employees, and in 1941 some were requisitioned for the OSS. B-2 was leased by the Federal government from the state of Maryland for $1 per year while the war lasted, and became simply Camp Ritchie, home of the Military Intelligence Training Center. Another area was acquired for use by President Roosevelt who did not enjoy good health. He was not only almost completely paralyzed from the waist down through poliomyelitis, but also suffered from severe sinusitis, and found muggy Washington summers trying. When he could not escape to his cool and airy home, Hyde Park, on the banks of the Hudson River, north of New York, he cruised Chesapeake Bay on the Presidential yacht, the USS *Potomac*. In 1942 the US Secret Service, which is responsible for guarding the president, vice president and their families, became worried about Roosevelt's continued use of the USS *Potomac* in the face of U-boats prowling the Atlantic coast, close to a deep trench leading far into Chesapeake Bay. The hunting ground and lodge was adopted as a presidential retreat. Roosevelt named it Shangri-la after the perfect city set in the Himalayas featured in one of his favourite books, the best-selling novel *Lost Horizons* by James Hilton. President Roosevelt died in April 1945 and, in 1953, President Eisenhower changed the name to that of his grandson; it is world-famous as Camp David.

Quantico Creek and the Potomac River and the wider reaches of Chesapeake Bay were ideal for teaching seamanship; about the only thing they could not provide was surf. Fortunately the Atlantic beaches of the Carolinas were close by, complete with plenty of US Coast Guard Lifeboat Stations and Beach Patrols, manned by extremely tough men with years of practical experience of launching surf boats to aid stricken ships, swimmers or leisure craft. (As no large naval or coastguard ships were involved the prowling U-boats could be ignored.) The facilities were similar to those at Dawlish, the Devon equivalent, itself noted for heavy surf and a rugged, year-round training regime. The USCG surfboats were double prowed, and almost identical to the dories used at Dawlish. The British ones were built by a firm of yacht builders in Southampton to a design derived from West African surf boats, the brainchild of Captain William Armstrong, ex-Merchant Navy and the Chief Instructor of Navigation and Seamanship at Dawlish.

The OSS training staff had benefited from, and in some ways improved on, the British experience of infiltrating and extracting agents and other personnel by sea. The OSS used another stretch of sub marginal farmland near Quantico, but on the opposite side of the Potomac. This was Area D, along Chickamuxen Creek, near Doncaster, southern Maryland. It was used for instruction in all aspects of handling small boats, and practising minor amphibious warfare tactics such as sabotaging docks and ships. It was used by the OSS Maritime Unit, which had an interesting war and in some ways was an ancestor of the present day US Navy SEALs. Among other things the MU acquired PT boats and crews for running agents and material across the Channel and throughout the Mediterranean – but that is another story, and belongs to the post-Overlord days. There was also a Maritime Operational Group, another remarkable unit that also deserves a book to itself, and which leads this one to the OGs.

Before these areas were ready the OSS also obtained use, by means unspecified, of a splendid training site almost within the city limits of Washington. This was Area F, the Congressional Country Club, at Potomac, Bethesda, Maryland, close to the then brand-new US National Naval Medical Center. Full use was made of every part of the CCC; golf course, grounds, premises (the plush club-house was used as a mess hall) and nearby areas including the Potomac River, the Chesapeake and Ohio Canal and railway sidings. The training was thorough and demanding, and sometimes involved trainees in visits to the NNMC, sometimes after they tried too hard to tackle Bill Fairbairn, who arrived at the invitation of Bill Donovan, who had met him at Lochailort. Bill Fairbairn was joined by Pat O'Neil in 1943, and with other unarmed combat and shooting instructors they made training tough and varied for many OSS men, including a new formation, the Operational Groups.

The Operational Groups have been compared with the Jedburgh teams and with the SAS but were, in fact, unique. They predated the former and not quite the latter, with whom they later came to share some roles.

Operational Groups

In 1941 America faced war in two hemispheres, and with inadequate and poorly equipped armed forces. Both of these issues could be, and were, solved with typical American flair, energy and ingenuity, but it took time. Among many other things Roosevelt and the JCS realized when the war in Europe started that if America became embroiled it would take at least a year to raise and equip an army, air corps and naval/marine force able to meet the Germans on anything like equal terms. In the interim there would be almost nothing the US armed forces could do in the way of offensive action. Donovan's original proposals included one idea, deploying agents to organize guerrilla forces in occupied territory. The agents would be assisted by small groups of weapons instructors, medical staff, demolition experts, escorts and 'door-kickers'. These groups, it was argued, could be recruited in America from first or second-generation immigrants from the occupied nations. Donovan and his team developed the idea into a firm proposal, and after some bureaucratic shuffling of papers and objections by the die-hards in the War Department, it was accepted. The specification covered probable operational theatres and within them possible deployment areas, likely targets; command, control, communications; a provisional establishment with personnel specifications, and notes on recruitment, selection and training. Each team would control several activities, intelligence collection, operations, research and analysis, and administration within its designated area of operation. Within a theatre of operations there would be an OOS Station which would include an OSS Operational Branch detachment which would, in turn, contain one or more Area OG Staff Teams controlling several Field Service Headquarters, each responsible for the administration and pre-deployment training of two OGs. An FSHQ consisted of five officers and twenty-three SNCOs and sergeants, six of whom were wireless operators. All of the FSHQ were supposed to be fully trained OG members, and could be used as reinforcements and battle-casualty replacements. The OGs were to be manned by uniformed members of the US Army, preferably natives or first generation immigrants from the operational area. They were to be trained in land, sea and air insertion and extraction techniques, and had three tactical functions: sabotage in enemy and enemy-occupied territory; support and supply of resistance groups, and assisting guerrilla operations. The original intention was for each OG to consist of a commander and deputy commander and two operational teams, each with a commander and two squads; in all thirty-eight men. The squads would have eight men, four riflemen, a machine-gunner and a loader, a wireless operator, and a medical assistant. (Other sources give thirty-four men, three riflemen.) In reality the composition of OGs changed in each theatre to match the load-capacity of aircraft available for parachuting; and in Europe one OG deployed with just two men, the commander and a wireless operator, demonstrating the flexibility of the organization.

Later the role of the OGs was refined; they were to be capable of conducting *coup de main* operations; raids on airfields, HQs, barracks, supply dumps, and ambushes. They could also help resistance groups in conducting partisan warfare, *coup de main* operations and in conducting 'counter-scorch' operations; i.e. preventing the enemy from destroying high-value economic or military installations such as lock gates, railway or road bridges, power stations, fuel dumps or food depots. The OGs were also to be capable of providing small teams of junior leaders, weapons and demolitions instructors, signallers and medical orderlies to act as 'operational nuclei' for resistance organizations in occupied territory.

On 23 December 1942 the JCS issued Directive 155/4D requiring the OSS to conduct guerrilla warfare in enemy, and enemy occupied, territory and to raise a force to support insurgent movements. Recruiting teams could now openly canvass on posts and at training areas for volunteers who spoke a foreign language and expressed a willingness to perform hazardous duties. The OSS recruited its paramilitary agents from the Army and Navy although the US Marine Corps manned one small, seven-man OG in Britain; it deployed into France as Mission Union II.

Colonel Donovan, never one to let the grass grow under his feet, had pre-empted formal approval and by mid-April contacted several formations and units. He and his staff were seeking vigorous, tough and self-reliant men with some experience of fighting. Real fighting from choice, preferably with guns and in formal combat, not sticking-up neighbourhood taverns or conducting back-country feuds over bootleg liquor distribution rights, and with experience of using explosives; but in most cases not too many questions were asked. The OSS also sought men with wireless or telegraph experience, such as Western Union or merchant marine operators, and others with knowledge of field medicine, such as timber camp 'medics', a term covering anyone from fully-trained paramedics to assistant cooks. Apart from any other attributes, it was essential that OGs sent to resistance circuits should be able to speak the local language; not to pass as natives but to be able to conduct training and planning sessions without interpreters. That led to the formation of OGs recruited from natives, and first or second generation immigrants from Germany, Greece, Italy, France, Yugoslavia and Norway, and attempts to raise Austrian and Danish ones. The first to be raised was the NORSOG, the Norwegian Special Operations Group, formed at Area F in July 1943. It had an unusual and complicated pedigree, even for an OG, and it was mainly about Scandinavian iron ore for Germany.

Norway – Again

The previous year the War Department, in a move unrelated to OSS, raised an infantry battalion manned by ethnic Norwegians for Operation Plough, an ambitious (and unfulfilled) plan to disrupt the iron-ore supplies. Although all Army formations based in the continental US were canvassed for Norwegian-American recruits much effort was expended in Minnesota, traditionally settled by Scandinavians. The 99th Parachute Infantry Battalion (Ski) (Separate) was activated on August 1942 at Camp Ripley, Minnesota, and soon found some interesting problems. Its role as an independent airborne winter warfare unit was unique, and apart from speaking Norwegian it was hoped that all applicants would be proficient skiers. But these two qualifications were rarely present in the 99th Infantry. Not all Norwegians in Norway can ski, and Minnesota is not exactly over endowed with mountains. Further, hard-working farmers and businessmen are too busy for winter sports, and, unless it could be avoided did not go out of doors in the searing winters of the American mid-west (minus 60 degrees in Minnesota, on one occasion). As to language, the recruits came from many different backgrounds and if their families spoke Norwegian it could have been with a marked Trondelag or Telemark accent, mutually incomprehensible to any but natives, and laced with American words or phrases unfamiliar in the home-land. Yet another complication was changes to Norwegian introduced in the 1930s and which never really found their way to the mid-West. However, sufficient recruits were found to man a battalion of around 1,000 men, including an extra large medical platoon of thirty-six men.

In autumn 1942 the battalion moved west to Camp Hale, near Denver, Colorado, for mountain and winter warfare training. The civilian ski instructors had no experience of training soldiers, the US Army did not have any experience in mountain or Arctic operations, and the snowfall was late that year. Common sense prevailed, and the troops were first taught how to move through mountains on foot, carrying everything they needed for the day. These marches graduated to overnight stops, with everyone sleeping in rough shelters built from whatever could be found, but with advice from forest guards, game wardens, and hunters. Longer trips were introduced, and then pack-mules, with all their interesting ways. The battalion learned how to cross mountain ranges fully equipped, first simple transits, then tactically, then against a simulated enemy. That was followed by rock-climbing, crossing mountains the hard way. The training became even more arduous with the first fall of snow, and those who couldn't ski soon

1. Hitler and the Armistice railway carriage in the Fôret de Compiègne, 1940.

Private Collection

2. Fort la Turra.   *Private Collection*

TWIN ENGINE RECONNAISSANCE AIRCRAFT "SAVOIA-POMILIO 4" WITH 540HP

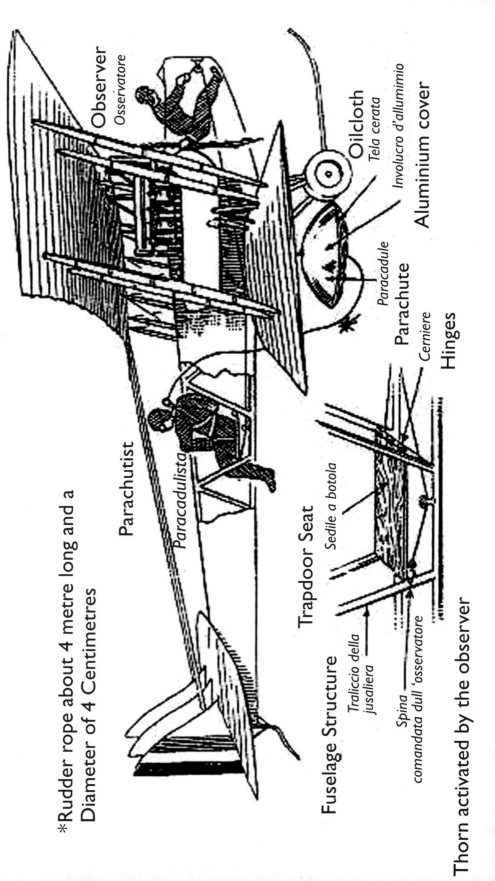

Observer
Osservatore

Oilcloth
Tela cerata

Aluminium cover
Involucro d'allumimio

Paracadule

Parachute

Hinges
Cerniere

Parachutist
Paracadulista

Trapdoor Seat
Sedile a botola

Fuselage Structure

Traliccio della
jusaliera

Spina
comandata dull 'osservatore

*Rudder rope about 4 metre long and a
Diameter of 4 Centimetres

Thorn activated by the observer

4. British troops in Norway being looked after by a farmer (extreme left) and his wife during the Norwegian campaign.
Private Collection

5. Inverailort Castle, late 1990s.

Highland Photos

6. The Western Highlands. One of the railway viaducts used for sabotage training in the Loch Ailort area. *Highland Photos*

7. Loch Ailort station in the late 1990s, showing 'Ambush Bend' and the remains of the cattle dock (ramp and white gate on right). *Highland Photos*

8. The Cairngorm Mountains; a wartime training area for Allied mountain troops and the NORSOG
SCOTAVIA Images

9. OSS Area H; container packing station and agent holding zone at Holmewood Hall near Peterborough.
Tom Ensminger

10. Area T, Harrington air station. Lieutenant Colonel Serge Obolensky, hatless, centre, with RAF dispatchers and parachute riggers prior to a mission.   *Tom Ensminger*

11. Eureka Beacon – demonstration layout, possibly at Somersham practice field.   *Louis Meulstee*

12. Rebecca fitted on C47 aircraft. 1 – receiving aerial, 2 – transmitting aerials.

Louis Meulstee

13. US C47 aircraft about to 'snatch' a CG4 Hadrian glider.

Tom Ensminger

14. Armed jeeps of a French SAS squadron. *Tom Ensminger*

15. Stuart-Turner Pumps Ltd. solid-fuel steam boiler and spare hearth ring which used anything from coal to wood chips and dried cow-dung. *Stuart-Turner Ltd.*

16. German troops
    loading a
    Nebelwerfer rocket
    launcher.
    Private Collection

17. Arthur Lyon & Co. Ltd., steam driven battery charging set. *Stuart-Turner Ltd.*

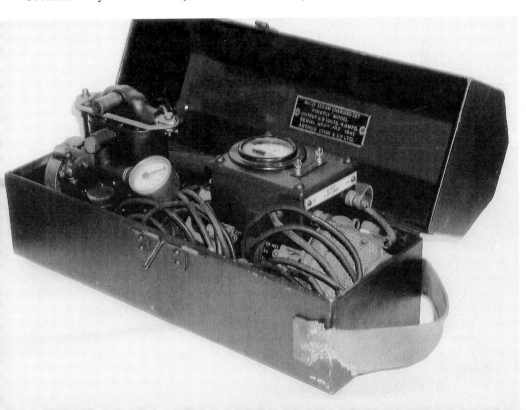

18. Brockhall Manor and parkland near Weedon, Northamptonshire in the 1990s.

Captain P. B. Smith

19. Jedburgh wireless set.

Louis Meulstee

20. An SOE 'suitcase' wireless and hand generator.

Louis Meulstee

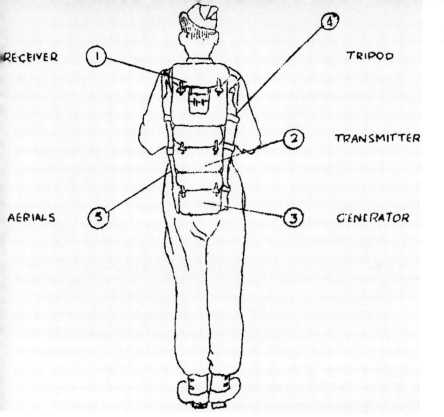

RECEIVER ①

④ TRIPOD

② TRANSMITTER

AERIALS ③

③ GENERATOR

22. RAF pigeon
parachuting
system.
Mrs Doreen Smith

23. Area T – Dispatchers and riggers getting ready for practice descents. Note British style airborne forces helmet and flash-eliminator blanking plates on .50 inch Browning machine guns in tail turret.

Tom Ensminger

24. B-24 Liberator, Carpetbagger version, showing port side. Rebecca aerial, shrouded Browning .50 inch machine-gun muzzles and

25. RAF Tempsford commemoration corner.　　　　　　　　　　*Bruce Blanche*

26. RAF Tempsford, Gibraltar Farm barn at sunset.　　　　　　*Bruce Blanche*

TEMPSFORD AIRFIELD
GIBRALTAR FARM

ERECTED TO COMMEMORATE THE BRAVE DEEDS
OF THE MEN AND WOMEN OF EVERY NATIONALITY
WHO FLEW FROM THIS WARTIME AIRFIELD TO THE

FORCES OF THE RESISTANCE

IN FRANCE, NORWAY, HOLLAND.
AND OTHER COUNTRIES

DURING THE YEARS 1942 TO 1945

THE EQUIPMENT FOR THEIR DANGEROUS MISSIONS
WAS ISSUED TO THEM FROM THIS BARN

could. Ski-ing led to ice climbing, carrying skis, followed by ski-movement across snowfields nearly 15,000 feet above sea level. The 99th remained at Camp Hale into the summer of 1943, getting fit, tough and bored. Fortunately in April 1943 the OSS started recruiting for OGs in earnest, and the 99th was an obvious candidate, and provided many of the first hundred or so members of the NORSOG.

Lacking experience in special operations, Garland Williams largely based the training of the OGs on that of the British commandos, and appointed Major Serge Obolensky to head the training programme. Obolensky had served on the Eastern Front as an Imperial Russian cavalry officer during the Great War, then emigrated to America and became vice president of a hotel chain based in New York. He proved to be a capable and responsible trainer, and then an outstanding leader of OGs in action.

Part of the course included infiltration techniques (parachuting at Fort Benning, maritime training in and around Chesapeake Bay and the Atlantic coast), and learning how to organize, train and lead locally-recruited dissidents. The first OG recruits were processed and trained at Area F, followed by field training at Area A. The syllabus included close quarter combat, industrial sabotage, fieldcraft, demolition and advanced weapon handling. Much of the latter was conducted by a hard-bitten, long-service US Army sergeant, one of the first of the new breed of soldiers, a US Army Ranger, then, as now, an elite force. He had trained in the UK, passing the basic commando course and had been trained as a commando instructor. Much of the training at Quantico and Catoctin took place at night, and bad weather was not allowed to interfere with instruction, range-work or exercises; the philosophy was '. . . the Krauts don't goof-off in rain or snow so neither do we'. Few recruits complained; they enjoyed the life, especially in the log cabins at Quantico and Catoctin that most preferred to the usual spartan and draughty wooden barracks of military bases.

Over There

In late November 1943 the ninety-eight strong NORSOG departed the US on a troopship bound for the UK under the command of

Major Harold Larsen. The troopship docked at Liverpool. Immediately after disembarking the unit travelled north by train to the (modest) British equivalent of Camp Hale; the British Army mountain warfare training centre. This was near Aviemore in the upper valley of the River Spey and at the foot of the Cairngorm Mountains. Apart from the 52nd Lowland Division and some other British units Strathspey was the base of the exiled Norwegian Army, three Mountain Infantry companies and a Special Forces unit. The former were the reconnaissance units for 52nd Lowland Division and mountain and arctic warfare training and demonstration teams. The Special Forces unit is sometimes referred to as NORIC 1 (sometimes mistakenly presented as 'NORICI'), the Norwegian Independent Parachute Company, No. 1 Norwegian Independent Company, F Kompagnie, and K Kompagnie, but is best known as Kompagnie Linge. This was an SOE controlled force (the independent company concept never really died out in the Second World War), named after Martin Linge, killed early in the war while taking part in a raid on his occupied homeland.

The NORSOG was initially accommodated in Rothiemurchus Forest, at STS 26c, Forest Lodge, near Loch Morlich. It was only a temporary home as a purpose-built training centre was being prepared for the unit. This lay a few miles west of Aviemore as the crow flies, but nearly forty by road, and not very good ones at that, even by the standards of wartime rural Scotland. This training centre was being built in a remote glen, selected by Major Frederick Cromwell, former head of the OSS Scandinavian Section in London with help from SOE and the Commando Centre at Achnacarry. Major Cromwell wanted a base in terrain similar to where the NORSOG was intended to operate. OSS also wanted one designed to meet the unit's needs, not some hand-me-down from SOE or the British Army. Money was not a problem so Major Cromwell got exactly what he wanted. The site finally chosen was a mountain glen, complete with a stone-built castle, a smaller hunting lodge and a deer forest. (In Scotland a deer forest is a vast expanse of barren mountainside and open moorland, usually devoid of woodland; 'forest' is used in the medieval sense, signifying a place of deer, not a place of trees.)

On 17 January 1944 the NORSOG and a team of US Army

support staff moved north, then south-west, by road to a long, shallow upland valley, Stratherrick, east of Loch Ness. In the middle of the strath is the tiny community of White Bridge, then little more than some houses and farms scattered around the bridge over the River Fechlin. This drains Loch Killin, lying a few miles to the south in the mouth of Glen Fechlin, site of the NORSOG base. (The river is now famous for white-water sports, and the loch as home of the Haddy Char, a species of fish found nowhere else in the world; like Arctic Char they make good eating, and somehow survived the Americans attempts at fishing with grenades and plastic explosive.) The glen is very like parts of Norway, and is surrounded by a wilderness of moors and hills. It is only around 2,000 yards wide at the most, and the hills on each side rise abruptly for 1,500 feet from the floor of the glen. The head of the glen is star-shaped, four glens meeting in a hollow which in those days housed Stronelairig Lodge (castle on some older maps and in official OSS documents). Further down the glen lay Killin House and Garrogie Lodge. In pre-war days all three were used by sporting parties; shooting grouse in August and red deer in the autumn. The estate belonged to the ubiquitous Frasers, but is now in other hands. The area is still wild and lonesome, and a distinct change from the wooded hills of Virginia and Maryland. It is a splendid place for toughening troops, as the NORSOG found, the hard way. They may never have come to love it, but appreciated its training value.

Neither the Lodge nor Killin House (Garrogie was not used by the NORSOG) were really suitable for housing troops in winter, as the heating and domestic arrangements were primitive. The Lodge was not large enough for the troops, but the OSS could spend hundreds of thousand of dollars unvouchered, and millions more vouchered. Supplies of cut timber, nails, roofing felt and the like appeared as if by magic, as did catering equipment suitable for feeding hungry soldiers; the vestiges of the cookhouse and of some large soup boilers could still be found at the start of the twenty-first century. The estate gamekeeper stayed on at the Lodge and acted as custodian on behalf of the owners, and had an interesting, if demanding, few months.

Being resourceful and properly organized, the detachment's

quartermasters did their best and settled into the village of White Bridge; the unit headquarters and administrative staff were installed in a large building, now defunct, opposite the White Bridge Hotel, the local, very comfortable, watering hole, much appreciated by the NORSOG. In 2002 a local resident, Ian MacCaskill, remembers them well; Major Larsen arranged for one of his drivers to take Ian and his fellow scholars to and from school in Fort Augustus each day as part of a routine supply and mail dispatch/collection run.

The NORSOG not only built accommodation, they also erected some ingenious training facilities. These included a gallery range for zeroing their Garands and BARs, and for general marksmanship. A special sniper range was built, after the fashion of Lochailort; Captain Fairbairn had taught some of the OGs at Area F, after all. NORSOG also built an assault, or confidence-building course, with some hair-raising features incorporating the River Killin (that portion of the Fechlin upstream from the loch). Pony tracks winding up into the high tops, built to allow deer carcases to be brought off the hill by horseback, were improved to allow access to the snowfields and for speed marches. A simulated village was constructed, a larger version of the one at Lochailort, based on Shanghai Mystery House variants built at Quantico and Catoctin. It was used not just for snap shooting but for practicing street fighting, fighting through a village, and ambushing enemy foot and vehicle patrols.

The training regime was severe, with the accent on fitness and survival in hostile terrain. The glen is set in the north-west corner of the Monadhlaith Mountains, an outlying section of the Cairngorm massif, and to this day is relatively unknown to hill walkers. The weather in winter is severe, even in these days of global warming, and records for the winter of 1943–44 show that it was very cold, with much snow, followed by prolonged spells of heavy rain. The training programme included cross-country patrols, map and compass work. There was considerable practice in attacking remote installations, guarded by US administrative staff, Norwegian and British Mountain warfare troops, or local Home Guards. The accent was on swift but careful approach, good CTR and planning, a fast and lethal assault, and a long exit march to a remote RV. Also much practised were shooting, unarmed combat, use of fighting knives and improvised weapons, radio (speech) and wireless (Morse) communications, field first aid, combat survival (bivouacs, snow-shelters, field sanitation), what later became known as FIBUA (Fighting In Built Up Areas). The single track railway line running past Achnacarry to Fort Augustus was used to practise railway demolitions, and the small goods yard of the station in the latter was used to demonstrate the placing of charges in points (turnouts to the Americans) to best effect. There was some discreet instruction in driving coal-fired engines, and more open practice at getting onto, and off, moving trains, by day and night. Surprisingly, no one appears to have been hurt but the local small boys were a major hazard, as they too wanted to be 'commandos' leaping on and off trains. Longer expeditions were made to the railway line running from Fort William to Mallaig, which passed close to the SOE schools around Loch Morar. The NORSOG used some of the schools, also the Army Camouflage Centre at Arisaig, and the Commando Centre at Achnacarry. There were trips to the Moray Firth for practice with landing craft at Nairn, and training with six-man rubber boats at the SOE base at Tarbert Bay, Loch Nevis. This was an out-station of STS 23b Swordland, South Tarbert Bay, Loch Morar, where the NORSOG practised 'naval demolitions', no one appears to have mentioned Morag.

The Carpetbaggers

In early May 1944 the NORSOG moved out of their bleak upland glen (spring comes late in the Highlands) and travelled several hundred miles south to Northamptonshire, in the heart of the leafy English Midlands. They were billeted in one of SOE's stately homes, Brockhall Manor, pronounced Brockle, built in 1603, and purchased in 1609 by a nobleman called Thornton; in 1944 it was still owned by the same family. The house can be seen from the M1 motorway, about four miles south of Watford Gap Services, on the east side, on a gentle slope above a long ornamental lake. The house and its policies lie a few miles from the village of Weedon Bec, and (in 1944) its main employer, the huge, Napoleonic-era Army

Ordnance Depot of Weedon, a handy source of useful items for the ingenious NORSOG supply staff. The owner of the hall, and of much of the village of Brockhall, was Lieutenant Colonel Thomas Thornton. Brockhall was used by SOE between 12 December 1940 and May 1944. It was one of the first stately homes allocated to the new organization, and housed STS 1, one of six SOE Depot Schools providing induction and basic training for prospective agents and wireless operators. Between January 1941 and April 1944 the Commandant was Lieutenant Colonel Thornton, an unusual appointment but a sensible one; there was nothing like an owner as commandant for keeping damage to the premises at a low-level. Brockhall is listed as being relinquished by SOE on 15 May 1944, when it was taken over by OSS; the NORSOG arrived the day after. In early June 1944 two French OGs and a Field Service Headquarters joined NORSOG at Brockhall.

There were several camps containing German and Italian prisoners of war in the area around Brockhall. It is just possible that the NORSOG was located in the hall as an additional ploy within Operation Fortitude North, the deception plan intended to focus Hitler's eyes on Norway as the destination for an invasion, rather than France. However, the main reason for moving the group south was to locate it close to the SOE/OSS air delivery system. This comprised two USAAF squadrons of B-24 Liberators at Station 179, Harrington in Northamptonshire, the RAF and Polish Special Duty units at Tempsford, the important training airfield at Somersham, the SOE/SF air-landing communications training unit at Howby Hall, and the supply packing bases at Holmewood (OSS), Cheddington and Gaynes Hall (SOE, SIS, MI9).

In May 1944 the US squadrons were a relatively recent and very welcome addition to the air assets available to SOE/Special Operations. The RAF SD squadrons, and the small Polish SD flight had been hard pushed to supply the needs of SOE and SIS due to shortage of aircraft, and the limitations on operations imposed by weather and the short 'moon period' of each month. The sensible amalgamation of SOE and OSS produced many benefits, including the unfettered use of two squadrons of long-range Liberators. This helped resolve the thorny issue of shortage of RAF Halifax bombers for dropping agents and supplies into Europe.

The shortage was caused mainly by the intransigent attitude to SD squadrons by the Air Officer Commanding RAF Bomber Command, Air Marshal Arthur Harris. 'Bomber' Harris was devoted to the notion that aerial bombardment could shatter the German will to wage war. Bomber Command at one time was the only Allied force actively taking the war to the German nation, and Air Marshal Harris had much to be proud of with his force. He made every attempt to ensure that as many bombers as possible were available for each mission, a constant struggle as *Luftwaffe* night fighters and flak exacted a heavy toll on each raid. Much has been written about Bomber Harris and his war, not all of it fair. To his credit he personally endorsed the log-books of most of the SD aircrew, a testimony to his breadth of vision, attention to detail and a fierce loyalty for his men.

Operation Carpetbaggers was the second name given to the USAAF SD squadrons, as the first, Sabotage Squadrons, was a little bit indiscreet. The force initially consisted of two squadrons, each (in theory) of twelve aircraft, but aircraft taken out of operational use for modifications and a general shortage of US bombers meant that figure was only slowly achieved in the first months.

The Group Commander was Lieutenant Colonel Clifford J. Heflin, the former commanding officer of the 22nd Anti-Submarine Squadron, which operated B-24s over the Bay of Biscay on long-range, low-level missions against U-boats and in the face of *Luftwaffe* fighters. The combination of precise navigational skills and low-level operations made this squadron and a sister unit, the 4th AS Squadron, the logical choice for the new SD units and, it should be noted, the demonstrated leadership of Clifford Heflin, and the capabilities of his air and ground crews. In November 1943 the two units were taken off ASW operations, de-activated and re-formed as the 36th and 406th Bombardment Squadrons. They moved from Dunkerswell in Devonshire to the Midlands, first to Alconbury and then to Harrington, as the 482nd Bombardment Group (H); 'H' for Heavy. On 10 December 1943 Lieutenant Colonel Clifford J. Heflin was appointed to the position of Air Executive, Special Project, with Major Robert W. Fish as Operations Officer and Captain Edward C. Tresemer as Group Navigation Officer.

Starting in November the B-24s were flown to the US maintenance base at Burtonwood, near Liverpool, and almost taken to bits, then re-assembled but with many changes. The main modifications were the fitting of Rebecca and S-Phone equipment, removal of the forward section of the nose including the gun turret and fitting a replacement with extensive glazing, to improve visibility for the navigator in the low-level phases of missions, replacing the cockpit side windows with bubble canopies to do the same for the pilot and co-pilot, fitting dampers on the engine exhaust to reduce glare, and fitting flash-eliminators to the .5-inch machine guns in the upper and rear turrets. The ball, or ventral, turret was removed and a 'Joe-hole' fitted; a circular exit suitable for dropping agents or packages. The hole was lined with sheet metal, and the area around it was floored with plywood, as were the fuselage sides. The mountings for the waist guns were removed and the gun positions secured and provided with curtains as red lights were fitted in the dispatch area. Droplights, red and green were fitted in that area and their controls installed in the navigator's position. The bomb carriers and release equipment were modified to take the standard SD supply containers, and anchors for parachute static lines fitted close to the Joe-hole, which was fitted with wooden trapdoors with metal hold-backs.

Clifford Heflin and some of his aircrew were attached to RAF Tempsford for familiarization and training in SD operations. Sadly, on 4 November 1943 one of the pilots, Captain A. James Estes, of Kentucky, was posted as 'Missing in Action' while flying as co-pilot in Halifax DT726 of 138 Squadron, on Mission John 13 to DZ Temple, north of Toulon, on the Mediterranean coast. The aircraft was later reported by the resistance to have struck high ground, the Col des Quatre Vios, near Marcols-les-Eaux, in the Ardeche; only the RAF rear-gunner survived the impact. James Estes is buried in the US Rhone Cemetery, Draguignan, north of Toulon.

A few days later, during the night of 10–11 November, Lieutenant Burton W. Gross was killed while acting as co-pilot on a Halifax of 161 Squadron flying to three DZs in north central France.

It was a sombre group that returned to Harrington to make the first of many missions to France, Belgium and Norway. The first missions were flown on 4 January 1944, six aircraft flying from RAF Tempsford, four supplied by the 406th and two by the 36th, all recently arrived from Burtonwood. The six missions did not involve agent-dropping as none of the crews was fully trained for that but each aircraft carried a load of twelve supply containers and eight 'Nickels'; bundles of PWE leaflets. Leaflet dropping over enemy or occupied territory had started in September 1939 and continued until the final weeks of the war in Europe, and the SD squadrons dropped propaganda leaflets (or sometimes bombs) as cover for their other tasks. Five of the aircraft were tasked with dropping supplies to the Wheelwright resistance circuit, based in the south-west of France, in an area bounded by the Atlantic, the Pyrenees and, to the east, the Massif Central. The first three missions were classed as 'completed', i.e. DZ found, recognition letter correct, load dropped. The remainder were not completed for one reason or another.

Some of the NORSOG personnel had learned to parachute in the US, jumping from C-53 Skytroopers or C-47 Dakotas, which meant leaving the aircraft through a side exit. In the UK they had to adapt to the floor exit of the B-24s, Halifaxes and Albermarles. The Liberators had been extensively modified for their new role; the USAAF had fewer inhibitions and better resources than the RAF, whose SD Halifaxes had to remain capable of operating as bombers or minelayers in moonless operating periods. Many, if not all, members of the NORSOG went to one or other of the STS 51 Parachute Schools and qualified for and wore, their SOE wings, as well as their US ones, amongst them Serge Obolensky. Some Carpetbagger air gunners were cross-trained as dispatchers at Ringway, and at parachute training at STS 51 and all of the parachute riggers at Harrington were also sent there. All of the jump-qualified personnel carried out a number of practice descents from the B-24s during routine navigation or landing ground flights, described in the next chapter. These jumps were usually made at Area T (Harrington), Area H, (the OSS container packing depot at Air Station Gratton better known as Holmewood), or at an extemporized DZ/practice landing ground in Fawsley Park, about five miles from Brockhall.

The NORSOG made only a brief visit to Norway, late in the war.

Before then it operated in France, and afterwards some of the personnel carried out missions in China. In 1975 some of the veterans returned to Glen Fechlin, and drank the White Bridge Hotel dry – again. They also went south to Brockhall, and to Harrington, and some found their way to Fawsley Park and Hall, by then rather down at heel. The veterans met one of the few remaining estate workers, who told them a strange story, and not just about the Elephant Man who stayed there once.

While the NORSOG were at Brockhall the father of another estate worker had been walking across the park one night in late May to reach his place of work, a railway signal box on the main line, near Brockhall. He saw a single parachutist descend into the park, of which no trace could be found by the local Home Guard platoon, manned mainly by railway workers. There was no Carpetbagger training mission involving parachuting that night, and in any case they did not use blind DZs for practice jumps. Thereafter, and for some weeks, until well after D-Day, the platoon had to mount a guard every night at the highest point of the park. On the night of 5–6 June 1944 the NORSOG deployed to Harrington to act as ground defence force in case of a German parachute attack to coincide with D-Day. Harrington is the nearest airfield to Brockhall which, as mentioned, had several POW camps in the vicinity. There was a German plot for POWs to break out of their camps and march on London. Coincidences, perhaps.

Chapter Seven

Special Delivery

As mentioned in Chapter Two the Inter-Services Training and Development Centre had been tasked with investigating airborne forces. The subsequent report recommended the formation of a dedicated evaluation, development and training centre for air-landing techniques. This was accepted, and by May 1940 the Central Landing School (CLS) was formed. (In June 1940 the ISTDC was absorbed into the recently formed Directorate of Combined Operations, which initially assumed overall responsibility for the development of airborne forces.) The role of the CLS, which later became the Central Landing Establishment, was to devise techniques and tactics for transporting troops, equipment and vehicles onto the battlefield. The troops could be raiding forces or an all-arms form-ation capable of fighting a conventional battle or denying enemy the use of vital ground until a larger land force arrived on the scene.

RAF Ringway

By May 1940 the War Office and the Air Ministry had selected staff for a development formation, agreed on scales of equipment and procured accommodation at RAF Ringway, on the new orbital road (hence the name) south of Manchester. As the PTS had to share the airfield with other users it is not clear why Ringway was selected; perhaps it was all that was available at a time of massive expansion of all services, and despite Churchill's interest in airborne forces many senior officers felt they were a waste of

117

time. The CLS was allocated six powered aircraft and some small civilian gliders, plus 1,000 aircrew-type parachutes. On 21 June 1940 the CLS was declared operational despite having few parachutes and only one Whitley bomber for dropping parachutists. The unit consisted of a headquarters with sections for supplies, transport, maintenance and administration, and three training and development elements, the Parachute Training Squadron (PTS), the Glider Training Squadron, and the Development Unit. The PTS later became the Parachute Training School, then No. 1 Parachute Training School, RAF; it remained at Ringway until 1947. Between 21 June 1940 and VJ Day, 15 August 1945, it trained hundreds of parachute jump instructors and assistant parachute jump instructors, and thousands of men and women from all services, some secret, of many nations.

Early parachute tests were made onto the open spaces of Tatton Park, close to Ringway, owned by Lord Egerton of the famous Manchester brewing family. He had readily given his consent to the use of his ground and the park was used by the PTS throughout the war. Among other things its lakes were used by SOE and other organizations for water-jumps, an attempt to find a way of making softer landings, and more secure landing sites, for agents. Development work for that idea included the WELBUM waterproof parachute-cum-self-propelled flotation suit, hence the name. The RAF and Army staff at Ringway had realized that parachuting onto a busy airfield was hardly a realistic proposition. The choice of Ringway was unfortunate; it was subject to much fog and rain that restricted the amount of flying which could take place each year. The airfield was also too small to allow for the subsequent expansion of the PTS, which meant that the Glider Training Squadron and some development sections had to move to other locations later in the war.

The first training course was for additional instructors, the forerunners of RAF parachute jump instructors. The first trainees were either drawn from conscripted or voluntarily enlisted pre-war professional stuntmen who specialized in parachuting or RAF Parachute Packers or Physical Training Instructors who had been involved in providing RAF pilots with some elementary instruction in the handling and use of parachutes. All were dedicated and enthusiastic men and laid the foundations of the highly successful RAF involvement with parachuting. The RAF instructors in turn trained a number of Army Physical Training Instructors, whose ranks included one or two more former stuntmen with parachuting experience. On completion of their parachute instructor training these NCOs were qualified to act as unit Assistant Parachute Jump Instructors; a skill and not a trade. They were later authorized to wear a special wing, the normal parachute badge but with APJI within a wreath below the parachute.

Some trained PJIs were provided by Allied forces. Of particular note were Lieutenants Jerzy Gorecki and Stanislaw Kruszewski from the pre-war Military Airborne Centre and School at Bydgoszcz, about 100 miles north-west of Warsaw, where Gorecki had been the Chief Instructor. They were later joined by Lieutenant Jilian Gebolya, from LOPP, a civilian sport parachuting organization. Another instructor appeared later from the Free French forces. His name has not been confirmed, but he is thought to have been an instructor in the pre-war French Air Force airborne task force, the TAP (*Troupes Aero Porte*). This formation consisted of a headquarters and two airborne infantry companies, the *601e et 602e Groupementes d'Infanterie de l'Air*, each with an associated flight of transport aircraft. The *601e* was stationed at Rheims and the *602e* at Algiers-Baraki, in French North Africa. On the outbreak of war the companies were concentrated into one operational unit in central France. On 11 November 1939 the TAP was placed on alert for a possible operational drop onto Walcheren Island at the mouth of the River Scheldt in the Netherlands, later cancelled. At the time of the Franco-German Armistice the TAP unit was in the Loire valley and on 23 June it moved, or some of its personnel did, for North Africa where it was disbanded on 27 July 1940. In August 1940 the Order of Battle of the Free French forces in the UK included the *1e Compagnie d'Infanterie de l'Air*, raised, as mentioned earlier, at the instigation of Captain Bergé; the instructor would have come from this unit.

119

Other Sites

Tatton Park was also used for balloon jumps. These first descents were made by trainee paratroops and were an economical way of training when aviation fuel and aircraft were in short supply. The first jumps were made out of a doorway in the end of the basket, more a large wooden tray with a canvas roof, then a 'Joe-hole' was added as for several years all RAF paratroop transports in Britain were converted bombers, with parachutists exiting through a hole where the ventral gun turret had been located. (After the war the balloon baskets lost their Joe-holes; they were reinstated in the 1950s when the Blackburn Beverley transport aircraft was introduced, with an exit in the floor of the boom.) The majority of parachutists carried out their synthetic (ground, or pre-jump) training at RAF Ringway, the only exceptions being special agents of the various clandestine warfare bodies. The agent groups were referred to by the PTS as 'E Syndicate', and it was segregated from the other students and the service personnel at Ringway. The agents lived and carried out their synthetic training at STS 51, an umbrella designation for three large country houses close to Ringway, all in Cheshire. They were STS 51a, Dunham House, Charcoal Lane, Dunham Massy, Altrincham; STS 51b, Fulshaw Hall, Alderley Road, Wilmslow and STS 51c, York House, Timperley. Every agent from the Allied nations in the UK trained at these sites, then at Ringway, although some Polish and other nations' agents received preliminary fitness and synthetic training in Scotland. STS 51 trained 7,204 persons during the war, including 872 SIS/MI9 agents, 172 French SAS troops, 420 Jedburghs and 520 'Army personnel'. These are thought to have been specialist personnel, such as doctors, from Inter-Allied Missions, members of the British Bardsea team, from Phantom or S Force, mentioned later. All of these persons were probably only going to make one operational descent, if that, so did not require the full PTS training. A number of OSS agents also trained at STS 51. Some of these OSS agents had undergone parachute training in the US but needed to learn about British parachutes and exit techniques as for some months they used RAF aircraft for training and operational missions before

American aircraft were available. One batch of E Syndicates included thirty-seven Russians. These were NKVD agents who were to be dropped into western Germany and the Low Countries by the RAF as part of Operation Pickaxe, one of the few British-Russian cooperative ventures during the Second World War. The NKVD agents travelled to Britain by ship, either on one of the returning Arctic convoys or from the Middle East, and were housed in London before undergoing refresher parachute training by PJIs from Ringway.

Until early 1944 all parachute training for Allied forces and agents was carried out at Ringway, with national PJIs, supplemented by student-interpreters where possible. Later the two US Airborne divisions sent to Britain for Operation Overlord opened Jump Schools as American parachutes, aircraft and their internal fittings were quite different from those used at Ringway. The Poles also formed a parachute school, the Basic Parachute Training Centre, located in the grounds of Largo House, a modest house near the south coast of Fife. The PTC was equipped with a fitness and confidence-building course centred on the *Malpi Gaj*, Monkey Grove. It also had cross-country running and scrambling routes, and synthetic parachute training facilities such as fan-trainers and dummy aircraft fuselages for practising exits, at nearby Lundin Links. The PTC was not used for initial parachuting, that was confined to Ringway, but was used for preliminary training, and for continuation, or refresher, synthetic training for qualified personnel, and with descents at nearby Stravithie airfield, officially No. 26 Satellite Landing Ground, and Crail airfield (HMS *Jackdaw*).

For the record, the Polish authorities awarded 6,252 sets of parachute qualification badges during the war, 5,762 to Poles. Polish officers paid for theirs, but not NCOs and ORs, or Allied personnel, commissioned or otherwise, awarded the badge. Four hundred and ninety Allied personnel were awarded a badge, four Belgians, two Czechs, 244 French men (SAS, BCRA and SOE FR Section agents), four Dutch paratroops, 168 men from the *Kompagnie Linge*, and three Americans. These last were Second Lieutenant Richard Tice, badge No. 1669, Private First Class James Burnham, No.1670 and, very late in the war, Captain Cecil

Lee, No. 6534; none was awarded a Combat Wreath. Sixty-nine Britons, including Colin Gubbins and Peter Wilkinson, were presented with badges. As former members of No. 4 Mission to Poland, and great admirers of the Poles, they appear to have been invited to the opening of the training centre, as their badges are numbered 0019 and 0023 respectively. It is unclear whether or not they were already parachute qualified; the awards may have been 'honorary' as later the Polish Government in Exile went to the trouble of issuing a formal order to the effect that there were to be *no* such awards. (Official Gazette of the C.-in-C. and Minister Of Defence, Polish Government in Exile, No. 3 Year XXIV [of the State of Poland], London 20 June 1941 Section III General Staff C.-in-C. No. 773/III Position 30 [Abridged]. Parachute Badge No. 6. *The parachute badge cannot be awarded on an honorary basis.*

The French SAS men and agents had engraved on the reverse of their Polish badges *'Pour toi ma Patrie'*. Personnel who made at least one operational descent were awarded a numbered Combat Wreath, to be affixed to the outstretched claws of the stooping eagle on the badge. A few non-Poles were awarded the Combat Wreath; for example, the sole Frenchman to be awarded one was Sergeant Rene De Gaston (Parachutist Qualification Badge Number 5840) awarded Combat Wreath Number 2076 for an operational descent into the USSR; the date was thought to have been in late 1944 or early 1945. Based on the badge/wreath numbers, he must have gone through the PTC course near the end of the war and been immediately dropped into the Soviet Union – purpose unknown; the Wreath number is higher than those awarded to Poles for Arnhem. Twelve British personnel were awarded the Combat Wreath; Sergeant Maurycy Ballany, Lieutenant Eric Brown, Lieutenant Colonel Charles De Villiers (SOE), Lieutenant Philip Fell, Company Sergeant Major Donald Galbraith, Colonel Duane Hudson, Major Peter Kemp (MO1 SP/SSRF), Lieutenant A. McKee, Major Peter Solly-Flood (SOE), Colonel R. Stevens, Captain John Amore Trode and Major Gordon Wilson. As a matter of interest, Colonel Stevens, Major Wilson, Lieutenants Brown and McKee, and Sergeant Ballany were awarded Polish Parachute Badges, and Combat Wreaths with consecutive numbers presumably having been trained and then dropped for an SOE mission into Poland, or as liaison officers with Polish paratroops at Arnhem.

In addition to Polish Army personnel, 329 agents of Section 6 (or O.VI) of the Polish General Staff, called *Cichociemni*, 'The Silent and Unseen' were awarded parachute badges; allegedly trained only by Polish PJIs (Lieutenants Gorecki, Kruszewski and Gebolya), possibly at Largo. One hundred and forty-nine agents were also awarded the Combat Wreath (some Polish exile sources claim 316; they should know) for operational jumps, probably all into Poland. Another sixty-four Wreaths were awarded to O.VI personnel who jumped into other countries, thought to include Austria, the Czech lands, Germany, France, Hungary, Russia, Slovakia and Norway, as diplomatic, financial or command (operational orders) couriers, some to slave labour groups. The descents into Norway included a strange operation late in the war. This was carried out on 4 March 1945, and involved an RAF Dakota dropping seven French and eight Polish personnel into Norway. The flight took five hours and five minutes, so the operation was in central Norway although the departure airfield has not been identified. The pilot was Flying Officer Card, squadron not known, and the dispatcher was Sergeant A.H. Ross, a PJI from 1PTS, as were all RAF dispatchers.

Landing Safely

After the Great War the records of RAF clandestine air-landings and parachute drops into occupied France, Italy, Russia and elsewhere were lodged in the Public Record Office, and were consulted in the late 1930s by RAF and SIS officers. The SIS was going through a difficult time and had limited resources available for anything, but in 1938 was able to fund the establishment of a small company, the Aeronautical Research and Sales Corporation. It was registered in London, based in France, and conducted 'research flights over Germany and Italy using a US aircraft flown by an Australian, Sidney Cotton'. From those humble and illicit beginnings grew the efficient RAF and Naval air photography systems, and the Allied Central Interpretation

Unit, which together formed a vital part of intelligence support for Overlord.

By 1942 it had become clear to the Allies that the German and Italian armies in France and elsewhere in occupied Europe were not going to be ejected by a popular uprising. The only way the occupied countries were going to be liberated would be by force of arms. (There was a lingering hope that the main role of an invasion force would be to shepherd enemy forces back across their frontiers, and COSSAC had to plan for that contingency.) Whatever the shape of the campaign to liberate Europe, the first requirement was for accurate intelligence, and that meant agents on the Continent, and reliable systems for communicating with them.

On 10 October 1940 the first air insertion of a British agent during the Second World War took place. Air insertion and extraction of agents, escapers and evaders, mail and other items continued in all theatres until the closing stages of the war. As the SIS was tasked with collecting intelligence and as that was a paramount requirement for the War Cabinet and the Chiefs of Staff, the service had priority over any other organization for the use of air assets. Those included not just flights, but seats on transport aircraft for agents or couriers travelling by service aircraft to overseas commands, and tactical reconnaissance sorties to verify or amplify agent reports. The SIS also had priority for processing assessments and verification of sites for LGs, Landing Grounds, the generic name adopted by the Allied armed and secret services to cover both DZs, drop zones for parachutists, and LZs, landing zones for aircraft, gliders and, at the end of the war, helicopters.

Within the Air Ministry an Air Staff Director (ASD) controlled responsibility for each type of operation or activity. In the case of Special Air Operations flown by the RAF or FAA, and for a while, the US Army Air Corps and US Navy, the designated ASD was the Director of Intelligence (Requirements), and his main operational section was AI2c. The holder of that appointment was directly responsible to the ACAS (Ops), the Assistant Chief of the Air Staff (Operations), head of all operational matters in the Royal Air Force during wartime. Apart from coordination of all action relating to these operations within the Air Ministry, D of I(R) was also the principal contact with the Air Liaison Officers of SIS and

SOE. AI2c also liaised with the Admiralty, in the shape of the Deputy Director of Naval Operations (Irregular) for air-sea matters, and with the War Office as occasion required.

Within the RAF, to give one example, a staff officer from AI2c was in almost daily contact with the Air Defence of Great Britain control centre at RAF Bentley Priory, north London, to coordinate outbound and homeward flights by SD aircraft with the radar, night fighter and anti-aircraft authorities to avoid blue-on-blue incidents. This liaison over routes, times and IFF (Identification Friend or Foe) transponder settings also included the Admiralty Operations Centre for flights, such as Ascension sorties to recover information from Royal Navy manned inshore reconnaissance craft, i.e. fishing boats, by means of shortrange radio telephony. AI2c staff also dealt with setting 'pinpoints' for landing grounds and for issuing and updating definitive lists of these to user agencies and the SD stations for use by the SD squadrons. Pinpoints were issued in lists or amendments to lists, all classed as TOP SECRET. They were only handled by personnel with a high security clearance, in secure rooms to which there was limited access, and at other times kept locked in safes. The SIS and SOE did not generally use the same pinpoints for security reasons. One AI2c task was to ensure that pinpoints for each agency were well apart, and that their sorties were, if at all possible, tasked on different nights, although as D-Day approached that was not always possible due to demand for missions and shortage of aircraft. Careful examination of squadron and Air Ministry records indicate that a number of sorties carried agents for two organizations. (There was no problem about dropping supplies to two or even three landing grounds for different organizations.) The pinpoints for the SIS were issued on RED lists, and those for SOE/OSS on BLUE lists; the pinpoints were not at first allocated names and were referred to by a serial number or the code name for sorties. These were introduced in 1941 and were culled from separate lists created and issued by ISSB.

The names might be used as a reference for the landing ground which were rarely identified by name until the introduction of Eureka beacons, which sent out a signal pulsing recognition letters in Morse code. One example of an SOE pinpoint list updating the

125

filing reference numbers is: 'New B/20 Old 9F/60L 47o33'52"N 00o 24'23"W Notes; Used by Operations GAMEKEEPER, MATE, DYER, and CONJURER (all code names for resistance circuits; the pinpoint later received the unfortunate code name Migraine.)' The accompanying memorandum requested users refer to the 'grounds' by the reference number or by the name of any operation completed on it. AI2c issued the note marked MOST SECRET, to Wing Commander de Laszlo, the Air Liaison Officer at SIS HQ, with copies to OC 161 Squadron and Station Intelligence Officer, RAF Tempsford. An almost identical memorandum was noted as having gone to the Air Liaison Officer, SOE HQ, copies to OC 138 Squadron and SIO Tempsford.

The bald statement 'Issuing and up-dating lists of pinpoints' covered a series of complex activities and operations, and several organizations. Identification and verification of a piece of ground for use as an landing ground was a complex and time-consuming business. As part of their advanced training agents, who were likely to be responsible for receiving or dispatching people and material in the field, were taught how to select and manage landing grounds. Theoretical instruction included the characteristics of an ideal landing ground; long clear approaches, even, well-drained surface without ditches or ridges; prominent landmarks such as river bends nearby, close to roads and woods, far from military installations, and close to a farm. For SOE the topic was covered in Lecture A27, *Selection of Dropping Points and Reception Arrangements*. The syllabus covered: physical requirements of landing grounds, such as location far from enemy posts but near a farm; open ground, long field or meadow with clear approaches; a road or track and bushes, woodland or undergrowth nearby. Then followed selection of a site from a map and on the ground, confirming the map reference with the ground, and, if possible, finding the latitude and longitude of the site (from a map or surveyors report). The map name and number, the survey method used and the date to allow for magnetic variations of any bearings taken when selecting the site were also required. There were classes and field exercises in organizing, training and supervising reception parties; marking a site for an insertion or drop, storing weapons, and disposing of parachutes and containers.

Once in the field the results of the agent's research were passed to London wireless, pigeon or message in a mail pick-up by Lysander or Hudson. The reports were typed and checked against maps by the Air Liaison Section at SOE or SIS HQ, and at AI2c. If there were no obvious problems a tactical reconnaissance sortie was tasked to photograph the area around the pinpoint. (Usually a batch of potential sites would be photographed in one sortie along with other locations to avoid revealing areas of interest.) The air photographs, oblique and vertical images, were delivered to AI2c, checked and then sent by motorcycle dispatch rider to RAF Medmenham, yet another requisitioned country mansion, deep in the Buckinghamshire countryside. This was the Allied Central Interpretation Unit, manned by personnel from the British, Commonwealth and US armed forces. The ACIU did not just carry out photographic interpretation for intelligence collection or collation purposes, although that was the prime function. One part of the Army section dealt with ground (topographical) reports for possible military operations, varying in size from the Bruneval Raid to the entire coastal zone designated for the Overlord landings. The subsequent reports covered air photographs, maps with overlays showing distinct features or layouts, schematic representations of roads, canals and railways, and scale models of the terrain, with every building and feature present; true works of art and invaluable aids to planning. The sub-section dealing with these reports was always working under pressure especially after the invasion of North Africa as operations mounted from Britain became larger and more complex.

In late 1942 the section started being asked to prepare ground reports for the Directorate of Intelligence (Air) at the Air Ministry. These requests were accompanied by air photographs marked with the reconnaissance sortie number, date and time of the exposure, and the latitude and longitude of a piece of ground. The report had to describe the area around that 'pinpoint'. These requests were unusual in that no end-user of the reports was specified, and no stated purpose. As a result they were not allocated any priority, and were handled as and when time allowed. This did not go unnoticed, and a representative of D of I (Air), in the shape of Wing Commander A.R. Sofiano, contacted the head of the Army section indicating that he represented the end users, and the requests were very important, and would be increasing in number. One headache for intelligence and associated mission support sections, anywhere, is allocating priorities for processing information; every 'client' thinks their request is vital, and must be dealt with immediately. Patience and tact are therefore necessities, not just virtues, for duty officers and NCOs, especially in multi-national HQs.

The Army section was fully committed to ground operations so eventually the situation was resolved logically; the matter was air-associated so it would be handled by the Air Section. A Topographical Department was formed to handle all requests for reports for 'grounds'. As forecast the demand increased from fifty-seven reports in 1942 to 297 in 1943; everything was classed MOST SECRET, and had always to be dealt with as the highest priority. After the air photographs were received at the Topographical Department they were correlated to maps and any other recent prints of the area. The subsequent report covered all aspects of terrain, cultivation, foliage cover by season for woods close to the pinpoint, and any obvious landmarks as seen from the air. Each report was assessed as requiring around ten hours work by one of the staff to process from start to finish, spread over several days if additional photographic sorties were required. The end product, a folio of maps, three sets of annotated air photographs and a written report, was returned to AI2c where it was double-checked, and copies sent to the sponsoring agency, one to RAF Tempsford for the SIO, and one held on file. In late 1943 one fascinating request was to report on a two-kilometre square area of ground in central Germany. This was part of the planning process for an operation to rescue Wing Commander Douglas Bader, captured in 1941 after a mid-air collision. He was to escape from the POW camp, where he was making a nuisance of himself, and make his way towards the pinpoint. He was to be met at some stage by a team of thugs from the Small Scale Raiding Force, whisked onto a waiting Hudson and flown home, doubt-less to fly and, if allowed by HM Government, to fight again; the operation, as far as can be checked, was not mounted.

Gliders

The evolution of glider-borne landing techniques and their sub-sequent use by Special Forces after D-Day generally falls outside the scope of this book, but it is worth mentioning two simulta-neous experiments; one in Britain, the other in America. They involved the use of seaplane-gliders for infiltrating agents or Special Forces into hostile territory. In Britain a single-seat seaplane glider was developed and tested on Windermere. The aim was to develop a silent, possibly stealthy, i.e invisible to radar due to non-metallic construction and small cross-section, flexible means of delivering an agent and a small payload into coastal areas such as fjords or lagoons, or onto inland lakes and rivers. The glider, in broken-down form, was to have been carried on an MTB to within a few miles of the enemy coast, assembled, loaded with pilot and baggage, launched onto the sea, then towed into the wind at high speed, as in a ground-launch, using a winch. No informa-tion has been located about the problems of finding thermals (for lift) above the sea, of selecting landing areas, nor of marking them to show the wind direction. The idea had some merit, but required an agent who was competent in handling a glider at night (an art not much practised, then or now), and of landing on water. The design was based on a standard two-seat training glider made by the world-famous Slingsby Sailplane Company, of Scarborough, Yorkshire, and used by the RAF to provide cadets of the Air Training Corps with inexpensive air experience. The new design incorporated a strengthened and stepped 'planing bottom' to the fuselage, and replacement of the twin, side-by-side seats with a single central one plus a small baggage compartment. A prototype was built by Short Brothers Ltd., the well-known manufacturers of powered seaplanes, at their wartime shadow factory on the shores of Windermere. It was given flight trials, but no order was forth-coming. (The glider is on display at the Steamboat Museum, Windermere.)

Before the war the Germans developed similar gliders for training Lufthansa pilots for mail and passenger carrying seaplanes, but did not find the idea practicable. The US Navy also investigated the use of seaplane gliders for delivering small teams of men into hostile territory. The launch was envisaged as being from conventional airfields using a bomber as a tug; or from the sea, inshore or deep-sea, using a multi-engined seaplane, or even from aircraft carriers. Landing was to be on water, a beach or tidal flats. The US Navy financed a design competition, which included the construction and testing of one or two prototypes, and ten pre-production development aircraft. Three manufacturers (at least) submitted designs and built prototypes; both featured low-set wings as aids to flotation, stepped planing hulls and rudimentary undercarriages consisting of a single wheel under the centre of the fuselage. Trials were carried out, but the concept was dropped.

The SIS not only had priority for use of air assets for movement of agents and staff but also for obtaining air-associated equipment such as Eureka beacons and S-Phones, and use of training sites for their agents. All of these activities were based at or near the Royal Air Force station at Tempsford.

RAF Tempsford was the main operating base for the principal Special Duties units, 138 and 161 squadrons. Tempsford is about fifty miles north of London, and three miles or so south of St Neots in Huntingdonshire. It opened in 1941 and at one time or another during the war housed not only the two SD squadrons but also other units with secret roles. These included an Operational Training Unit, (11 OTU), 109 Squadron and 1418 Flight. 109 Squadron was part of 100 Group that conducted radio counter-measures operations for the RAF and other Allied services. No 1418 (Experimental) Flight was also part of 100 Group and tested airborne radio/radar detection and countermeasures equipment; including the Rebecca/Eureka homing system used by the SD squadrons. This system was a variation of an RAF standard method of letting aircrew locate airfields by means of two radio sets, one in the aircraft, and one on the ground at every airfield. The airborne set, the Rebecca element, transmitted an interrogation signal that initiated a response from the Eureka ground station. This was displayed in the aircraft on a small screen as a blip pulsing in Morse code the identification letters of the airfield, e.g. TP for Tempsford. The screen was marked with a vertical scale, and if the blip was left of the line the beacon was to port, and vice-versa for starboard. The pilot turned into the signal until it was centred on the scale, and held that course until the airfield (or landing ground) marker lights came into view. The range to the ground beacon was indicated by the gradual descent of the blip down the scale that was marked with a scale of miles, starting at fifty for the early sets. A battery-powered Eureka transmitter was developed for landing grounds. It was small and light, about 14lbs/6kgs, and could be broken down into a single man portable bundle of bits and rods, and came complete with webbing pouches and carrying straps. The set could be transported in one or other of the camouflaged carrying methods devised by the R&D Section of SOE. These included a bundle of firewood, a workman's tool box or an oil drum.

The name 'Rebecca' was taken from Recognition of Beacons, according to Sir Robert Watson-Watt, who devised and bestowed the name, as he was allegedly authorized to name all the British service radars, presumably in concert with the ISSB to avoid duplication. Sir Robert did not claim invention of the code name Eureka; it was too well known and too obvious a choice for homing equipment. The Eureka set was devised by Charles Bovill, a former radio engineer with HMV, the world-famous record company. The RAF had approached him about signal beacons for the SD sorties and Eureka was born. He was then asked, by whom is unclear, possibly AI2c again on behalf of SIS or even someone in that service, about a secure means of communicating with agents in the field. The result was the S-Phone which surpassed both services' requirements, expectations and hopes by a very wide margin. S-Phones were simple, man-pack ultra-high frequency radio sets which allowed agents to talk directly to the crews of aircraft or ships. The signal was transmitted in a tight beam which was almost impossible to intercept. The system had a very short range for ground to ground or shore to ship contacts but a long one for ground to air as long as the aircraft was within the signals 'cone'. SD aircraft running in to a landing ground would be flying at something like 400 feet above the ground and could be contacted when about ten to fifteen miles out. The Germans inevitably captured S-Phones, and tried to intercept the signal beams by flying low, slow Lysander-lookalikes, Henschel Hs 126s, fitted with UHF detectors at night around areas of known resistance activity. The same aircraft were also used to fly spotting missions at night, looking for marker lights or bonfires, sometimes using infra-red detectors. The Resistance got wise to this and organized dummy landing grounds and lit random bonfires all over the place. S-Phones were used by SIS for briefing and debriefing agents in the field, as described below.

Somersham, the Unknown Airfield

Landing ground or reception committee training for agents from all of the British and Allied secret services was initially carried out at STS 51. Due to a number of problems with the operation of Eureka ground stations and S-Phones in the field, a new course was introduced, lasting for two weeks, held at STS 40, based in Howbury Hall, Waterend; part of the village of Renhold, near Bedford. No more than twenty-four students, in two syndicates of twelve, were accepted on this course. The syllabus was covered in ten continuous working days, which included four night exercises, two operating S-Phones to orbiting aircraft, and two landing ground reception committee ones, with live drops guided in by Eureka and S-Phone. In addition there were twenty-four hours of outdoor air-ground S-Phone practice with aircraft, in twelve two-hour sessions, and one two-hour session with Eureka. The reception committee exercises were carried out on a large stretch of requisitioned farmland next to the village of Somersham, north-east of Huntingdon, twenty-five miles or so from STS 40. It was one of the most important Allied airfields of the Second World War, but no reference will be found to 'RAF Somersham'. It was officially a Q, or decoy, site; a simulated air station designed to seduce *Luftwaffe* bomber, late night-intruder, aircraft away from operational stations. Somersham was one of three Q sites around RAF Wyton, an important Bomber Command airfield. (The others were near Colne, south of Somersham, and near Haddenham, east of Wyton.)

The development of decoy airfields, or simulated air stations, stemmed from the widely held pre-war theory mentioned earlier that 'the bomber will always get through to its target'. Part of the British government's response to this threat was a wide-ranging search for solutions other than the production of more, and better, fighter aircraft, pilots and ground crew. One solution, or one part of a comprehensive solution, was to move the targets, in the sense of presenting apparent (in current jargon, virtual) targets such as iron works, steel plants, power stations, railway marshalling yards and shipyards. A national decoy authority was established in July 1940, tasked with masking live installations i.e. camouflage, and simulating alternatives, the decoy sites. These included dummy airfields, army camps and even towns, as well as decoys; active installations simulating a real, and adjacent, military or civil activity. All were located in open land near the target to be protected, or, as in the case of a decoy airfield, near several. Two main types of decoy airfields were developed – QL sites (L for Lighting), which worked at night and attempted to lure the enemy with lights arranged to look like a real operational airfield and K sites; daytime airfields equipped with dummy aircraft. By the end of December 1941 around 100 Q-sites had been built and brought into operation, a figure that eventually rose to 171. Between them they had received more than 350 enemy air attacks, twice as many as their parent air stations, which they were protecting. In addition, important industrial centres and factories were protected from night bombing by QF sites; F for Fire, which simulated burning buildings, ignited by incendiary or high explosive bombs.

Somersham had two locations, a QL array referred to as A Site, and B Site, the K location. The lighting array, in the form of an elongated Y, was in fields near Pidley Parks and Woodhurst, east of RAF Wyton and south-west of Somersham village. The QL site probably lured night bombers away from Bomber Command stations, but the K site had two roles, the second much more important than decoying bombers. It was a secret within a secret, so little known that even the late Group Captain Hugh Verity, a meticulous recorder of SD activities, only mentions Somersham once, in passing. It was the principal training area for two elements of Allied special operations; firstly, to practise agents in organizing landing grounds in enemy occupied territory, and, secondly, to familiarize aircrew with delivering people, pigeons or packages by parachute, or air-landing. Every SD squadron, whether full-time – 138 and 161 Squadrons and their Polish-manned flights and the US Carpetbagger units – or RAF Bomber squadrons with SD tasks

133

as a secondary duty, practised at Somersham. On one occasion Hugh Verity recorded eight night landings and take-offs in forty minutes at Somersham. To be precise, Somersham had not two but seven roles. The one role of the QL site has been covered. The B site at location K had six. The exact location of B Site is the cause of some debate even within the village but is thought to have been at North Fen, north-east of the village. It was used as:

i)   a simulated air station
ii)   as a secondary satellite airfield for RAF Wyton where aircrew could practice 'touch-and-go' approaches
iii) to provide night 'fly-bys' and 'touch-and-goes' for SD and Carpetbagger squadrons
iv) to train agents in reception committee procedures, including Eureka and S-Phone operations
v)   to practise aircrew in day and night airdrops
vi) dropping trials for the STS 61, SOE container packing station at Gaynes Hall, south-west of Peterborough

Dropping trials included testing ways of delivering pigeons by parachute.

Warbirds

Homing pigeons were delivered to Resistance circuits with a broken wireless or no operator – 'pianist' – in the jargon of the times, but also for routine transmission of information. Messages of surprising length could be written on very fine paper with a map-pen and rolled round a sliver of wood and inserted into the pigeon's leg-cylinder. Pigeons were dropped onto landing grounds with other supplies. They were delivered in baskets or panniers with a static-line parachute. They could also be dropped on or near landing grounds in small parachute-retarded pods holding one or two birds. The pods held small containers of food and water covered with a thin clear covering which the hungry birds could peck open if not found soon after landing. Some of these pods were dropped at random during routine SD operations after the main delivery or deliveries, or spontaneously to a remote farm or village after a failed main drop. The aim of this activity was to generate military, economic or political intelligence from non-Resistance sources by providing an opportunity to communicate with Britain. The Germans responded by issuing shotguns to troops in coastal defence posts, and allowing the troops to eat any pigeons they shot, once the message containers had been forwarded to the nearest Intelligence section. The order to use the shotguns reportedly came straight from the Führer himself. This was in response to the growing use by the Resistance, SIS and MI9 of pigeons due to the increasing efficiency of the German radio-intercept system, and partly because some were dropped into Germany to make the authorities waste time hunting for the birds and their containers.

In Britain the National Pigeon Service 'called up' more than 200,000 birds during the war. The birds served in every theatre, and with many branches of the armed forces and with secret services in enemy territory. The importance of the birds to SOE is demonstrated by the (approximate) figures of 'drops' to DZs for the nights between 30–31 May and 6–7 June 1944. In sixty-eight sorties by 138 and 161 SD Squadrons, twenty-five included pigeons to a total of 484 birds, usually in batches of ten birds. One of the first things an agent did on landing by parachute or dismounting from an aircraft was to release a pigeon with a standard message announcing safe arrival, just in case the plane was shot down on the return journey. The bird might be carried within the agent's clothing usually in an old sock with a hole in the heel.

STS 61 was the main SOE packing station for containers, packages and panniers, although a carpet-manufacturing factory near Worcester was used during the run-up to D-Day. The system was very like mail order; a catalogue, recently re-printed, was perused by agents and an order dispatched by wireless or carrier pigeon. The RAF made the delivery as soon as possible. Containers for *coup de main* parties were packed in a segregated area by an SOE officer; they were for SSRF teams 'in country', and may have included special ammunition for assassination missions. There was another packing station nearby, at Holmewood, a few miles south of Peterborough. This was OSS Area T, sited next to Station 162

135

Glatton, actually closer to the village of Holmewood, and linked to it by roads and aircraft taxiways. It, too, was very busy around D-Day. Area T started out with 253 all ranks, and ended with over 600. (No reason has been discovered for not basing the Carpetbagger squadrons there; it was certainly requested by OSS, but rejected by the USAAF command; possibly because the B-24s were painted shiny black quite unlike the natural metal ones used for bombing or for maritime patrols – and AS 162 was next to a main railway line.) There was a mansion at Area T, Holmewood Hall, built in the nineteenth century and therefore more comfortable than some of the stately homes. The OSS used it as an officers' club (mess) and to house agents prior to deployment. In that sense it was the American equivalent of Hassell Hall, close to RAF Tempsford.

Departure

Hassell Hall was one of at least three locations scattered around Tempsford as a holding point for agents and Special Forces personnel about to be inserted into enemy territory. (The other two confirmed locations were Tempsford Hall and Gaynes Hall.) Hassell Hall does not feature on the lists of SOE sites compiled by the late Gervase Cowell, former SOE Adviser to the Foreign and Commonwealth Office, but he acknowledged that it was probably incomplete, and unlikely ever to be complete as many SOE files were apparently destroyed in a fire after the war. It is thought that Hassell Hall was used at one stage to train agents in reception committee procedures, possibly for SIS/MI9, but no objective evidence has been located to confirm or deny that suggestion. Other areas around Tempsford airfield used by agents and others include the now demolished Gibraltar Farm. The farm buildings were used to receive, then store, containers, packages and panniers for each night's mission. From there they were loaded onto the bomb racks or into the fuselages of the SD aircraft by a specially selected and trained team of ground handlers. They were technically 'Trade Group Zero', old RAF slang for GD men, General Duties men, long gone but sadly missed as they could turn their hand to any task, usually but not always, legal. At Tempsford they were assisted as necessary by armourers, who fitted bombs when carried for diversionary or deception purposes by the SD aircraft. Also stored were bundles of leaflets, also used for deception purposes but equally PWE's 'ammunition'.

The farmhouse was used as the final holding area for the Joes. They were received on arrival from Hassell Hall or the other locations and were escorted by an SOE or SIS officer. They would change into operational dress, civilian clothes appropriate for their destination, and have belongings thoroughly checked to ensure there was nothing incriminating on the person or hand luggage. Once the dispatching officer in the farm received final confirmation from the Station Operations Room that the sortie was 'on', the Joe would be taken into another room and helped into a coverall and a parachute harness and taken out to a barn, the nearest building to the airfield. (The barn has been preserved as a museum.) As the aircraft rumbled along the perimeter track running past the barn the Joe would have a final word with their escort and be guided outside, then helped onto the aircraft which scarcely halted.

A specimen training flight from Tempsford to Somersham took place on 30 October 1943. This was flown in a Halifax Mk V, LW 272. The pilot was from the USAAC, Captain Robert L. Boone, and his diary contains a brief note on the flight. 'Flew 1:00 in Halifax today – made 2-day drops.' From information gleaned from other documents this can be expanded to provide a more detailed story.

Captain Boone was one of a team of thirteen personnel from the 36th and 406th Bomb Squadrons on temporary duty, from their (temporary) base at Air Station 120, or RAF Bovingdon, Hertfordshire. The temporary duty was for familiarization with SD air operations, and the team included six officers and five enlisted men, in this case all NCOs. Not all were going to fly; Lieutenant Robert D. Sullivan was to be the Group Intelligence Officer, and Major Robert W. Fish, another pilot, was going to be the Adjutant of the new Air Group.

The short training mission was an air-experience flight for a pilot from one of the Carpetbagger squadrons, the rest of the crew being from the RAF; there may have been other US personnel on board as observers. The one-hour mission involved an approach

137

flight of about seventy miles, including detours around the circuits of several airfields. These included normal circuit training from training stations, and pre-operational radio and engine-check flights from Bomber Command bases making ready for raids on targets in Germany and France. The cross-country flight was also good practice for the crew, as the air gunners and second pilot were involved in spotting landmarks for the navigator. The navigator also had to plan the route to Somersham, and to operate the Rebecca set. Other members of the crew may have been cross-trained to help with the set as in other SD crews. After the Rebecca set picked up the Eureka signal the navigator would have conned the pilot on the approach to the landing ground in much the same way that a bomb aimer (if RAF, correctly Air Bomber; USAAC – Bombadier) did on a bombing run. In this instance instead of saying port or starboard he would have used left or right for the US pilot. During daylight, pilots new to SD operations wore blue goggles to simulate the hours of darkness. The Halifax would have overflown the landing ground as on an operational mission to check for lights for a night drop, and for a day drop any ground signals such as a smoke grenade or smoky bonfire. During the final run-in to the landing ground the pilot or second pilot would have been talking to the agent in charge of the reception party (for a day run an RAF instructor) by S-Phone. As this was a daylight-training mission there would have been several dry runs over the landing ground before any items were dropped.

The RAF instructors would have been SD squadron aircrew on ground tours between operational ones. The SD squadrons were technically part of Bomber Command, which had a rule that after thirty operational sorties over enemy territory aircrew were posted onto ground (staff officer) or air training duties. After about six months away from operational flying they were then returned to a squadron for a further thirty sorties, again followed by a ground or training tour. Some aircrew completed three tours, and some made over 100 sorties, but as the loss rates on bombing raids were high statistically most aircrew could not expect to survive for long. That rule was not always adhered to in SD squadrons due to pressure of events. 138 Squadron aircraft were used for air-sea rescue operations during dark periods of the moon; these sorties (and minelaying ones) counted towards the thirty.

Sometimes agents awaiting deployment would take part in day training missions, to help themselves and the aircrew. The RAF instructors would have been teaching landing ground procedure and the finer points of Eureka handling. The trainee agents would have checked the wind direction and set out the marker lights as for a night drop; all good practice, and sometimes carried out wearing blue welder's goggles after a couple (if they were lucky) of unblinkered sessions. One agent would have been operating the S-Phone, and the others would have been getting ready to receive the containers or panniers. That meant ensuring they were well away from the centre of the landing ground just in case any of the parachutes failed to deploy. The panniers and containers would have been stuffed with old clothes or sacks and bricks or stones. Once on the ground the agents would have removed the parachutes and hauled the containers and panniers to the side to find out the hard way just how heavy and clumsy they were. The parachutes would have been removed, rolled-up and checked in to the RAF ground party, or the senior member. Parachute silk was like gold dust in a war-starved Britain; it was ideal for making female attire, and one parachute could attract a lot of favours from Tempsford WAAFs, Land Girls working on Midlands farms, or Bedfordshire factory girls. Once the second drops had been completed there might have been more practice approach runs, but more than likely there would be other SD aircraft inbound for either drops, touch and go circuits or practice landings.

Air-delivered supplies such as weapons, radio sets, medicines, printing materials and bottles of printer's ink (for PWE clandestine newspapers and posters) were packed into long metal containers, referred to as bidons (tin-can, oil-drum) by the French Resistance, fitted with a parachute pack at one end. The first RAF containers were large, clumsy, heavy and difficult to maneouvre and unload. The Polish Army and Air Force, services with some experience of the subject, designed a simple lightweight container which could be broken down into eight or so manpack size units on the ground; it quickly became the Allied standard, and its derivatives serve to this day around the world. The containers were carried on

139

standard RAF and Fleet Air Arm bomb racks under the wings or in the bomb bays of the delivery aircraft. Other supplies were packed into standard British Army wicker hampers, like large picnic baskets, and rolled out of the aircraft to fall free onto the DZ. The containers were released by the bomb aimer, after he had opened the bomb-bay doors, which is why most accounts of special duties' drops mention the aircraft circling the dropping zone. The marker lights and any signal bonfire were not visible at a distance and the pilot wanted to reduce all unnecessary drag on the final run in the area of the DZ in case he had to take swift and violent evasive action if the site had been ambushed by German night fighters or mobile flak guns. Once the doors were open and the aircraft aligned with the lights and at the correct height, the bomb aimer or pilot activated a toggle or push-button bomb release when the lights drifted into the graticules of the bombsight; some aircrew preferred to judge the moment to drop by eye alone. Panniers were dropped by the dispatcher in response to the Red On/Green On light in the cargo/parachutist bay, the light again activated by the bomb aimer or pilot. Panniers were hitched together in a string; once one went they all went, one after the other, and the dispatcher had to keep well out of the way, on the far side of the 'Joe-hole'.

In some parts of France freestanding Eureka beacons were established away from landing grounds for use by SD sorties unable to find their designated landing grounds, or spooked by flak or a night fighter. The navigators of these aircraft could transmit a Rebecca signal on a standby frequency which would trigger a Eureka beacon and a drop would be made when the blip reached a certain point on the vertical scale, usually at the 'two miles out from the beacon' point. This was a sensible way of getting supplies to the Resistance circuits, and avoided a waste of time and resources. A simple extension of this was the installation of a complete grid of Eureka beacons in France, complete with a controller with a stock of batteries and charging engines, and spare parts. For both systems the frequencies and beacon call-signs changed on a random basis determined by AI2c and passed to the field operators by radio or air-landed courier.

The purpose of all these complicated but effective management systems was to support special agents, and later Special Forces, in the field. There may have been relatively few SD flights into France, for example, in comparison with the streams of bombers and reconnaissance aircraft crossing the Channel in the months before D-Day, but they often produced better results in terms of damage to the enemy through sabotage or intelligence gathering. As D-Day approached the SD Squadrons (and their naval equivalents) became even busier as the number and type of special agents, formations and units increased, as will be described next.

Chapter Eight

Special Operations

From early 1941 the issue of an Allied invasion of the Continent increasingly occupied the attention of the Joint Planning Staff. They had to plan an amphibious invasion and also consider the follow-on, possibly a prolonged advance in constant contact with the enemy, across France, the Low Countries and into Germany. Any advance would be conducted on a broad front by one or more armies, each comprising two or three corps, each with three armoured or infantry divisions. Each of these formations would advance along corridors allocated by the senior ground force commander. There was nothing new in that concept; there really was no other way in which to allocate ground in a conventional land campaign but to divide it into what, in the Great War, the German and Austro-Hungarian Army called *gefechtstreifen*, 'fighting strips'. What was new was the growing realization among the JPS and field commanders that these corridors might extend from the English Channel at least as far as the western frontiers of Germany, or even the River Rhine. Few, if any, Allied officers considered they might one day reach as far as Berlin and the Baltic. These corridors were not defined in 1942, when even the notion of an Allied invasion of the Continent was only being turned into plans. And in the course of a battle or series of battles the boundaries of corridors could change in response to the tactical situation. But within a corridor, irrespective of its width, depth or the flexibility of its boundaries, it was the responsibility of the commander to decide on how to fight the battle, albeit in accordance with directives from the next command echelon, which in turn were generated in response to directives from the overall commander, in this case that of the invasion force.

In the event of an invasion, the Allies would initially cross territory where the population would be friendly. Embedded in that population ahead of the liberating forces would be resistance movements, expected to assist the invaders. These irregulars might also get in the way of friendly fire, or be destroyed in open combat with enemy forces. The questions for the planners, the high command and politicians were,

1. Should resistance movements be encouraged to undertake partisan or guerrilla warfare?
2. Should they be restricted to sabotage and assisting the civil authorities in shepherding the population away from danger?
3. Should they be told to keep out of the battle altogether?

Among other organizations examining these questions was SOE. There was an obvious role for resistance forces in sabotaging transport systems and enemy fuel stocks, and in cutting telephone wires to force the enemy to use radio and so expose signals traffic to intercept and jamming. One idea in particular reached fruition; the provision of direct support to conventional land operations from behind the enemy front lines. This involved deploying small teams of Allied troops into enemy-held territory ahead of the advancing invasion forces, to organize and help resistance groups in carrying out small but vital operations in concert with the main force battle plans. These would include bridge demolition, or countering enemy demolition, and blocking roads to force enemy troops and armoured fighting vehicles onto open roads or into open country where they would be vulnerable to air attack. Other tasks included attacking HQs and supply dumps and ambushing dispatch riders, staff cars, supply and repair units. This idea eventually became the Jedburgh operation.

Jedburgh Teams

The Jedburgh concept was devised by Peter Wilkinson, by late 1941 a lieutenant colonel at SOE HQ. In 1940, after Dunkirk, he had been invited by Colin Gubbins to join him in a new venture being developed by MI(R), the Auxiliary Units, ostensibly part of the Home Guard. He later moved with Colin Gubbins to SOE where their time with the Auxiliary Units provided the very best introduction to the problems of clandestine warfare. In 1942 Wilkinson was responsible for planning resistance operations before, during and after an invasion of the Continent. In May 1942 a joint meeting was called between the three bodies most likely to be involved with clandestine operations in the event of an invasion of France. Those attending were the DCO, the Deputy Chief of the General Staff, Home Forces (responsible for providing British troops for the invasion force), SOE's Director of Operations, Colin Gubbins and various staff officers. Topics discussed included the role of the Resistance along the lines noted above. The question of manpower for these tasks was addressed, in part, by proposing that the Allies harness the energies and enthusiasm of the large numbers of young men (and women) of the Maquis. The Resistance leaders would be fully occupied with sabotage so would be unable to help, even if they wanted garrulous and excited young people anywhere near their circuits. If the maquisards were to be controlled, SOE organizers would be needed. These would sensibly include officers capable of advising Resistance leaders (a touchy task), and taking operational command of a group for a specific mission, and instructing civilians in weapon handling, minor tactics, demolition and counter-demolition. That implied recruiting nationals of the countries to be crossed by the invasion forces, or British or American officers fluent in French, Walloon or Dutch. The teams would require wireless operators, and be able to manage reception committees. It was also envisaged that the tactical adviser and radio operator might be accompanied by a guide. The original intention was to drop these small teams with enough weapons and ammunition, medical supplies and food to arm a platoon-sized group; forty people. The teams would be inserted around the inland limits of the 'invasion area', not specified but already known to a few people. Normandy was within range of Allied fighters but at the limit of *Luftwaffe* ones, and was also the best stretch of beach of three along the French coast in terms of exits. That reflected the knowledge that the Germans viewed their U-boat bases in that region as being vital to interdicting Atlantic convoys, (this discussion having taken place at the height of the Battle of the Atlantic). The ports housing the bases had been turned into bastions manned by forces that could sally against the flank of an invasion force, landing anywhere between Cherbourg and Dunkirk. Also, at that time there was still a fixation about landing expeditionary forces in harbours. In that context Hitler regarded Cherbourg as a key Allied target, based on its use by the Americans in the Great War, its proximity to the Atlantic sea lanes, and its rail links with northern France.

The concept was accepted in principle by all attending the meeting. It was further agreed that the teams would be formed from servicemen. They would not join SOE, so if captured would not be treated as spies. They would, however, be recruited, trained, briefed and deployed by SOE, and operated at the direction of the invasion force commander. The teams and their protégés would not conduct espionage, but if tactical intelligence came their way they were to try to report it as quickly as possible to their parent organization or the nearest army headquarters. The Home Forces representatives requested that during the beach landings, the groups should carry out offensive operations against enemy road, rail and canal traffic, telecommunications, and *Luftwaffe* air and ground crew. It was also requested that during the second phase, considered as being advance in contact with a retreating enemy, the groups should work within Allied lines. Their tasks would include guarding key locations, providing labour parties for moving supplies or repairing roads, and acting as guides for road convoys or for cross-country movement of vehicles or troops. In addition, it was requested that men from the groups be organized into raiding parties capable of crossing no man's land and penetrating the German forward zones. No doubt shades of the First World War, and not altogether unrealistic in some ways, but ignoring such matters as politics, discipline and payment.

What's in a Name?

On 6 July 1942 Colin Gubbins wrote to A/DP, the acronym for the Head of SOE's Intelligence, Security and Propaganda Section, Commander John Senter RNVR, stating that:

> A project is under consideration for the dropping behind enemy lines, in cooperation with an Allied invasion of the Continent, of small parties of officers and men to raise and arm the civil population to carry out guerrilla activities against the enemy lines of communication. These are to be recruited and trained by SOE. It is requested that 'Jumpers' or some other appropriate code name be allotted to this personnel.

'Jumpers' was not allocated; it may already have been earmarked for use elsewhere, or may have been too close to the reality of the teams' role to be usable. Commander Senter allocated the name Jedburgh to the project. As far as can be determined, the name was taken from a list of small British towns, allocated to SOE by the ISSB. Nine examples have so far been identified with operations involving teams: Bardsea, Dunstable, Daylesford, Dodford, Datchet, Dunchurch, Darowes, Jedburgh and Massingham. The first is a modest seaside village in the north-west of England, the last a hamlet in Norfolk. Jedburgh is small, tidy little town in the Scottish Borders, famous for its rugby teams and the insular attitude of its inhabitants ('if yer nae fae Jed'art yer naebody'). Over the years a number of theories about the code name have been hatched by veterans, historians, authors and enthusiasts. These include:

> Jedburgh was the seat of guerrilla warfare in the Middle Ages

> Jedburghs was the name applied to Scottish border raiders in the Middle Ages

> Jedburghs were Scottish 'special troops', favoured by King Robert the Bruce (c.1314)

> Jedburgh axe was a fearsome hand-held weapon used in border fights to unseat, then slaughter, horsemen

146

Jedburgh justice was a summary procedure whereby a person is sentenced first and tried later

Jedburgh township in South Africa was captured by British infiltrators during the Boer War

Jedburgh is where Colin Gubbins thought of the concept. He didn't

Jedburgh is where he thought of the name (not his responsibility) while travelling on a train through the town. It is at the end of a branch line and there does not appear to have been any SOE establishment nearby but the fishing in the little rivers around the town was good, and he was reportedly a keen fisherman!

Now that the project had been approved in principle within SOE, and given a cover name, Peter Wilkinson started to turn idea into reality. That included demonstrating to GHQ Home Forces that the concept worked, which meant trials during major exercises. Fortunately the C.-in-C. Home Forces, General Sir Bernard Paget, took to the proposal from the start. He was an imaginative and vigorous leader, reportedly one of the best trainers in the history of the British Army, and had made a name for himself in Norway. Despite being a product of pre-1914, horse-and-cart era training, he welcomed new weapons and systems. In 1942 he was considered by many to be the land force commander for the invasion in all but name, if not the Supreme Commander. No secret was made of this view, so he was willing to test any plan which might make the invasion easier. He was also highly skilled at bureaucratic in-fighting and power politics.

In August the Chiefs of Staff Committee advised SOE that the requirement for the tasks envisaged for Phase Two of the invasion, the use of civilians in military duties such as sentries, building defences or carrying out raids, was no longer to be within the remit of the proposed teams.

In December 1942 representatives from SOE and GHQ Home Forces finished shaping the Jedburgh concept, including a stipulation by GHQ that Jedburgh personnel would operate in the uniform of their parent regiment or corp. The reasoning was that if captured in normal field uniform they would probably be treated as prisoners of war as defined by the Geneva Convention despite being in the company of what the Germans called 'terrorists'. Also, as the team members would not be noted as Special Forces they would be spared implementation of the Führer's Commando Order. GHQ also requested, sensibly, that each Jedburgh team should include one English-speaking officer, warrant officer or senior NCO from the country in which the team was to operate, and one from the nation providing the Army it was supporting. At around this time the Belgian and Dutch governments-in-exile relaxed their prohibition on allowing their servicemen to fight on foreign territory, which helped recruiting for the Jedburgh teams.

At that stage SOE envisaged that the teams would consist of a tactical leader or coordinator of resistance forces, a demolitions expert/weapons instructor, and, possibly, a 'guide'. This last role appears to have meant a scout or pathfinder; a soldier who would work with resisters to select routes to and from objectives, conduct CTR, and prepare sketches and sand models for briefings. However, those attending the December meeting decided that the final composition of the teams, and the nature, role and structure of any support elements could only be agreed once SOE and the command elements of participating formations had assessed the results of the field trial.

Exercise Spartan

As it happened, while the Jedburgh paper was wending its way through the corridors of GHQ Home Forces, that body was planning a major exercise for the following spring. Exercise Spartan would practise the command and control of formations likely to be involved in an invasion, and involved ten divisions, four independent brigades and two tactical air components. It followed two similar exercises, Bumper, in autumn 1941, involving around 250,000 troops in twelve divisions, and Victor in spring 1942. That was smaller but tougher as it incorporated lessons learned from Bumper, and from operations in North Africa and Russia, or as

148

much as could be gleaned by the British Military Mission in Moscow. An exercise allows senior commanders to assess the standard of training achieved by participating formations, and to evaluate tactics and techniques. An exercise that goes well is one where lessons are learned, not one where everything goes without a hitch. Bumper and Victor had revealed serious deficiencies in just about every aspect of command, control, communications, intelligence, tactics and logistics at every level from Army down to sub-unit. Victor in particular had revealed to the Allied military and political authorities that the forces earmarked for the invasion were not yet ready for a real war. Therefore another exercise was planned for early spring 1943 to reassess the ability of the nascent invasion force to meet the demands of a prolonged, mobile offensive against a determined and experienced enemy who would be operating over familiar terrain. Spartan would be the last chance to sort things out before the invasion, and the last chance of command for some officers. It would provide an excellent opportunity to test the Jedburgh concept and GHQ Home Forces requested SOE to provide twelve teams and support staff to provide one corps with sufficient clandestine warfare capability to exert an obvious influence on the ability of the enemy forces to conduct defensive operations.

Spartan would be very demanding as it would involve, for both sides, an advance to contact, then a battle with one side defending and the other attacking. Around Northampton, was a 'German' Army occupying a foreign country and tasked with conducting a mobile defence against an Allied Army Group which was to break out of a bridgehead on the south coast. Each force was supported by a tactical air component, evenly matched as the exercise did not realize how weak the *Luftwaffe* was in France, even at that time. The ground and air commanders were co-equals in the exercise which caused some headaches and arguments, and led to changes for Overlord. The two forces were not allowed to conduct any air or ground reconnaissance beyond the 'forward line of troops' as defined in the exercise instructions. The opposing commanders therefore had, in theory, no clear idea of the terrain other than what could be gleaned from maps. The Exercise Directing Staff (Umpires) also attempted to ensure that no reconnaissance of the battle area took place before the start of the exercise, official or unofficial, which doesn't mean it didn't take place. The 'German Sixth Army' consisted of two corps, VIII and XI, each with two divisions, and an independent area defence force, the Buckinghamshire Brigade Group, with limited mobility but plenty of artillery. In the later stages of the exercise Sixth Army was reinforced by the recently-formed Guards Independent Armoured Brigade Group, representing a *Panzer-Grenadier* division released from the OKW Theatre reserve and rushed to the battle area. GHQ Sixth Army also had under its command a full range of service and support formations, including a large number of engineer units for bridging and demolitions.

The attacking Allied 'Second Army' under General Andrew McNaughton, consisted of I and II Canadian and XII British Corps, with six divisions and one armoured brigade, plus service and support troops, including the Jedburgh force. General McNaughton fully supported the Jedburgh concept and his enthusiasm and backing ensured that it had a fair test; something for which he deserves full credit. Second Army was assumed to be within, but not defending, a bridgehead extending from near Southampton north to Andover then east to the North Sea. The Army was to advance north across the Thames and seize Huntingdon as a precursor to a major offensive by a follow-on force using the same axis.

GHQ Home Forces had not only agreed to incorporate the Jedburgh group and an associated guerrilla force into Spartan, but also espionage and counter-intelligence activity. The former simulated a LRDG-style Road Watch, and the latter was to operate against it and the Jedburgh teams using wireless interception services. These would not only test the survivability of friendly forces in enemy territory but provide realistic field training for Army Counter Intelligence Y-service (Direction Finding and Signals Intelligence) units. GHQ/COSSAC also wanted to test Allied counter-intelligence personnel in conducting rear area surveillance and security. (They did not know that the Germans knew an invasion was planned, and had started to make their own arrangements for stay-behind parties.) The Second Army therefore had access to intelligence from six road-watchers, who were assumed to have been inserted ahead of the invasion and breakout. They were to report the volume and nature of road traffic at key locations. The fact that the exercise did not include rail movements would not have mattered; the intention was to test the feasibility of observers collecting and transmitting traffic movements in close, and occupied, country. Also to be tested was the survivability of agents and Resistance groups in the face of vigorous counter-intelligence activity involving army Field Security and CI teams, civilian police, staff from MI5, the MI8 Radio Security Service and Army Y units. The last were radio interception units of the Army and RAF. ('Y' from the three triangulation points needed for a successful 'cut'; an accurate fix on a radio emitter.) The Army 'Y' units would try to 'capture' and locate the source of Jedburgh wireless traffic, and were in addition to the Special Wireless Sections, part of the HQs of British and Canadian Corps. As the Jedburgh messages were enciphered they were to be passed to Bletchley Park, for de-ciphering. The coordinates of the emitters were passed to the Field Security Sections of the relevant 'German' Corps.

As no Jedburgh teams or an associated command and communications system existed, a scratch force was hastily organized for Spartan. It used SOE staff officers, instructors and wireless operators, to provide:

1. Command and Liaison team at HQ First Canadian Army.
2. Communications team and LO at HQ I Corps.
3. A wireless relay facility at STN 55, Marwick House, Lerwick, Shetland.
4. Eleven three-man operational teams, code named Boykins.
5. Support staff for the partisan base, STS 14 (Briggens, Roydon, Hertfordshire).
6. 400 maquisards, men from 8/Royal Welch Fusiliers, happy to escape the boredom and petty tyranny of barrack life, field firing and minor tactical exercises. Another organization, probably SIS, supplied six agents equipped with radios.

GHQ Home Forces provided a treble-hatted team, acting as GHQ Allied Expeditionary Forces, *Armee Oberkommando West* and Exercise Control, with the final authority on safety, winners and losers. Exercise Control controlled the 'play', deployed the DS, produced post-exercise reports and attempted to ensure that issues identified were turned into lessons learned by the forces under the control of GHQ Home Forces. That body also ensured that the results, and especially those of intelligence-related activities, were immediately passed to the invasion planning team for possible integration into the slowly maturing plans for Overlord. (The COSSAC invasion planning staff was not formed until April 1943, after the exercise, but many of the nominees for it attended all or part of Spartan as observers or DS.)

Peter Wilkinson made early contact with Exercise Control, and found to his pleasure that the Chief Umpire was General Gerald Templar; they had served together and got on well, having similar approaches to many issues. General Templar, later to be head of SOE German section, and his fellow umpires were enthusiastic about injecting 'resistance forces and agents' into the game plan. The DS worked with Peter Wilkinson and his colleagues to devise a range of incidents, real and notional, to be inserted into the programme at inconvenient times.

GHQ Home Forces had allocated the Jedburgh group to the Second Army but it was left to Peter Wilkinson and General McNaughton to deploy them. They decided to allocate them to I Corps, First Canadian Army. The Army and its Tactical HQ had just been formed, as had II Canadian Corps and its Tactical HQ, and one of its two divisions, the (British) Guards Armoured, which was not only newly raised but new to armoured tactics. None of these formations had worked together, or, in some cases, as part of a large formation in the field. The exercise was therefore going to place great demands on many people, at different levels, and it was an act of considerable faith to accept the Jedburgh group into a new headquarters. Also, the decision to incorporate a new tactical concept into such an important exercise shows the degree of faith General Paget had in SOE, its staff and the concept, and in the ability of Andy McNaughton and the Canadians to assimilate a new tactical concept when already burdened with exercising conventional military operations with new headquarters.

Tactical Headquarters I Corps was deployed into the field near Liphook, Hampshire, and close to Tactical HQ Second Allied Army/First Canadian Army in Algonquin Camp, Witley Common, near Godalming, Surrey. The Jedburgh HQ team were co-located with Army Tactical HQ, but Peter Wilkinson shuttled between there and I Corps. He reported directly to what was called, in those days, the 'Brigadier General Staff', nowadays the Chief of Staff, Brigadier Guy Simmonds, a very bright Canadian Permanent Force officer who did not suffer fools, or foolish ideas, lightly. He later became Chief of the Canadian General Staff. Peter Wilkinson also made sure that General McNaughton, whose job it was to fight the 'war', was kept fully informed of the nature of the field test, and ensured he was aware of how to deploy the teams of Jedburghs and their resisters. The GHQ/SOE project team wanted to test four main activities in the exercise. Firstly, the probable utility of teams plus resistance groups in intervening effectively in a major battle at the tactical level, and secondly, where and when could they be deployed to best effect. Thirdly, what liaison and communications staff would be required in the ground force headquarters and at what level; Expeditionary Force, Army Group, Army, Corps or Division. Finally, the feasibility of inserting small groups of armed men into the rear zone of a battleground during mobile operations, and their chances of surviving in a hostile, and vigorous, active radio interception and counter-intelligence environment. The tasks allocated to the teams included demolition of key bridges and installations, attacks on demolition guards (counter-demolition/counter-scorched earth missions), *coup de main* operations against headquarters and communications centres, dislocation of supply lines and communications, and killing military policemen controlling traffic.

The Jedburgh team was welcomed into the bosom of the Canadian formations. McNaughton and Simmonds immediately grasped the potential of the concept and went out of their way to help. The success of the project was in no way hindered by the appearance of a large hamper of 'medicinal supplies' provided by the Officers' Mess, Wellington Barracks, to fortify the Jedburgh team against the chill air of an English spring. Spartan was officially 'dry', so the Jedburgh staff became very busy with secret briefings for Canadian staff officers and British DS.

The Jedburgh teams were based at Briggens but spent some nights in the field, or to be precise, in make-shift hides in Territorial Army Drill Halls, now used by Home Guard and Army Cadets Force detachments, both of whom provided enthusiastic help with domestic and cleaning chores. The Fusiliers were happy to be doing something different and, being officially scruffy and grubby, living their role to the full. Their officers represented resistance leaders, and the NCOs represented bother – but kept the whole thing running. The maquisards were briefed at Briggens prior to departing by bus for the scene of action. To passers-by or the police they were extras for a film set, or contract building and agricultural workers. The eleven groups were assessed as having successfully attacked and disrupted or destroyed several HQs and supply dumps, demolished several bridges, and knocked out key vehicles and installations for varying periods. The concept had been proven, and the hard work put in by Peter Wilkinson and his colleagues vindicated. The Exercise Control staff ensured that General Paget and General Frederick Morgan, COSSAC were made aware of the success of the concept, and Colin Gubbins was congratulated by a number of people in high places. The Jedburgh teams and their maquisards returned to barracks, so to speak. The six singletons also retired from the field. They, too, had done well, and their efforts were appreciated. They had demonstrated that even in the close country of the English Midlands a useful road-watch could be conducted by day and night, although direction finding was a problem. The concept had been proven and was used for Overlord.

The post-exercise debrief led to several main conclusions about Jedburgh operations in support of an invasion force:

1. Jedburgh teams would have to be allotted specific tasks, or a task, relating to the ground battle, and be inserted close to the probable operational area.
2. The period between the Army commander designating tasks and their initiation, could not be less than seventy-two hours, if the team was to be inserted, contact the Maquis/Resistance groups, secrete weapons and stores,

conduct reconnaissance, make plans, brief and rehearse all concerned, and mount the operation.

3. The immediate rear of the battle-line, however fluid, would be too well patrolled by the enemy to allow Jedburgh teams and their maquisard groups to operate; therefore they should operate in depth.

4. *Coup de main* tasks were better suited to fit, well-trained and disciplined commando or airborne teams, used to working together under duress.

5. There should be an evacuation plan in case the main campaign was stymied or defeated (this became Operation Mitchell, never needed, but to hand, just in case).

Manpower

Recruitment and training could now get underway. Both tasks proved bothersome. The original requirement for seventy teams was increased to 100. Each team was supposed to have three members: leader, wireless operator and demolitions/weapons instructor. However, some accounts indicate that two teams deployed with only two, and two with four, persons. Teams were to be a mix of British, US, French, Belgian or Dutch personnel, depending on the nation into which the mission was to be mounted. Eventually only one had a Belgian member, six had a Dutchman and two a Canadian. The Dutchmen appear to have included two South African officers, noted in one South African source as 1083 Reserve Captain J. Groenewoud of Cape Town and Reserve Captain J. Staal of Johannesburg; both killed and buried at Arnhem. (But one website indicates that Groenewoud was Dutch.) Two team members, Captain William R. Crawshay and Lieutenant R. Isaacs came from the 8th Battalion Royal Welch Fusiliers, inspired by what they had experienced in Spartan. Captain Crawshay's family had been connected with the Royal Welch Fusiliers for many years – his uncle commanded the regiment's 1st Battalion in the Great War – so there must have been something compelling about the Jedburgh concept to make him leave his regiment before the invasion. William had been appointed to a

Supplementary Reserve Commission in the Royal Welch Fusiliers in March 1939, and served with 1RWF in the UK before being posted to 8RWF; a hostilities-only unit.

During July 1943 the SOE project team arrived at the conclusion that seventy teams would be required for the cross-Channel invasion. This was on the basis of two Army Groups; 21st (British, Canadian, Allies) and 12th (US and French), each with ten divisions, and three Jedburgh teams per division plus five reserves per Army Group. (Eventually over ninety-three Jedburgh teams were formed, in Britain, North Africa, Italy and the Far East; some deployed more than once.) The problems facing SOE when seeking volunteers was to be repeated the following year when the SAS Brigade was trying find men to fill the ranks of 1 and 2 SAS. The problems were manifold. First, the British Army did not have a tradition of encouraging initiative among young officers and NCOs, unlike the German Army. Second, the regimental tradition discouraged the same group from seeking experience or opportunity outside the regimental, or even the battalion, family. 'Eager beavers' were deemed disloyal, and made to feel so. Third, by 1943 the Army had grown too big too quickly, resulting in a dilution of leadership, inhibiting the careful development of leadership qualities among subalterns and potential NCOs. Fourth, snobbishness ruled; a 'good man in mess', even if in other ways inadequate, was preferred over go-getters with poor table manners. Fifth, the Army in Britain was too big, meaning there were many appointments to be filled, irrespective of ability. Sixth, too many senior appointments were filled on the basis of 'a job for old Bonzo', i.e. duds, who further prevented the flourishing of initiative and sought comfort and security in demanding rigid adherence to orders, irrespective of their logic or sense. Seventh, the vast majority of training conducted by Home Forces was planned, conducted and supervised by officers and NCOs without recent, or any, battle experience, and hence was formulaic and uninspiring. (The 8/RWF War Diary for March 1943 reveals that the battalion was engaged in some mindlessly repetitive field firing training, practising battle-drills and minor tactics, interspersed with cleaning barracks; no wonder the men enjoyed Spartan. And one report on that exercise commented bitterly on the lack of opportunity for units to experience living and administering themselves in the field.) Finally, the Army had to compete with the other services for men with leadership potential. That was especially difficult when it was still surrounded by the aura of the slaughter at the Somme, Gallipoli and Ypres, and competing with the romantic images of the RAF, Royal Navy and Royal Marines. SOE and the SAS Brigade were looking for the same type of men as SIS, MI9, Phantom, the Reconnaissance Corps and the Glider Pilot Regiment.

Special Forces Detachments

SOE also had to find men for liaison teams, later designated 'Special Forces detachments', to be co-located with Army Group and Army and, as required, with Corps headquarters. Their role would be to maintain contact with Resistance groups and other bodies (MI9/X-1 organizers) in their operational area through SOE/OSS in London. In spring 1944 these two bodies set up SF headquarters for that purpose. The SF detachments were to be kept informed of plans and requirements by the operations and intelligence staffs of their parent Army/Army Group, and in turn to inform those staff of the local Resistance structure and capabilities. The detachment staff would then attempt to coordinate conventional and clandestine needs and abilities, and to harness the energies and local knowledge of overrun resistors and to protect them from enemy stay-behind parties, at that time an unknown quantity. These parties did exist, and caused some trouble after D-Day, but received short shrift, Jedburgh law, by invaders and locals alike.

US, British and Canadian SF detachment personnel were trained at STS 3 Stodham Park, Liss, Hampshire. The US detachments were larger than the others as manpower, especially of bright, well educated young officers, was much less of a problem. Their 'SF Dets' consisted of thirteen officers and twenty enlisted men, mostly graduates of the Intelligence School at Camp Ritchie, Maryland. The teams were also lavishly (to jealous British eyes) equipped with radios, jeeps and trailers, tents, camouflage nets and campbeds. The US detachments were also larger because they integrated most aspects of intelligence, counter-intelligence (including POW detailed, as opposed to immediate, front-line) interrogation, and secure communications staff. Four SOE detachments were raised, numbers 1–4, with the numbers 5–9 held in reserve. Initially five OSS detachments were raised, numbers 10–14, to support FUSAG, First US Army Group, and First, Third and Ninth Armies, with one in reserve. Three were later proposed, and two raised, in anticipation of further US Armies deploying to Europe in late 1944 and possibly requiring the formation of another US Army Group. That was a precaution, allegedly in case the Overlord forces advanced beyond Berlin and into Poland, to prevent it from becoming Russian territory again and also to tackle the rumoured Wagnerian Alpine Redoubt. (That did exist, to a certain extent, in the shape of a complex defence line running along the southern edges of the Dolomites in northern Italy, which is why so many SOE, OSS and SIS agents, plus an SAS team, and an Italian SAS unit, operated there in late 1944.)

Inter-Allied Missions

The SOE Special Forces detachments were smaller, and were co-located but in different tents, with SIS, MI9 and MI5 (counter-intelligence staff hastily commissioned for the occasion) liaison teams, each with access to, or their own, secure communications link to London.

At around the same time COSSAC realized that the addition of Jedburgh teams, SAS troops and operational groups would require careful coordination in the field, and not just in Allied military headquarters. The matter was raised with SOE and OSS, and they decided to raise yet another set of liaison teams to assist the leaders of Resistance circuits and their regional grouping in coordinating operations before, during and after D-Day. These were the Inter-Allied Missions, which were to consist of staff officers and communications staff, with medical and air liaison officers on call. These specialists were introduced into the system in case there were large numbers of battle casualties among the Resistance or clandestine warfare forces, or large numbers of weak or sick escapers, evaders and released POWs to be taken care of, or evacuated by air.

Bardsea and Sussex

The Jedburghs had at least one parallel body, the Bardsea Mission. On 14 July 1943 there was signed an agreement between Colin Gubbins and General Kukiel, Head of the Polish Army in the UK. It covered the raising and deployment of teams of military personnel to support the Polish Monika Resistance circuits in northern France in the event of a major German threat to them or the Polish communities around Lille and Valenciennes. The original idea was based on the Jedburgh concept, but the Poles refined and developed it into something more lethal. The mission was code-named Bardsea, and the teams as Bardseas or Bardsea Parties. The force is sometimes referred to as the Bardsea 'Operational Unit' and, incorrectly, as the Polish Operational Group, or the Polish Independent Parachute Company of Grenadiers. The operational unit initially had an Order of Battle for a command group and two operational companies. These would consist of a company HQ of seventeen men, and three operational groups, each of three five-man patrols. The Polish forces in Britain and Italy were chronically short of manpower so the ORBAT was refined to a single operational unit with a seven man command group, twelve Polish-manned teams each with five men, and four six-man liaison teams, three OSS and one SOE. The operational parties were allocated alphabetic code-names drawn from a list of Polish forenames – Adam, Bolek, Cyril, Dawid, Edek, Felek, Genek, Henio, Jasiu, Karol, Leon and Marek. The command group was code named Daylesford, and the liaison teams were OSS, Dodford, Datchet, Dunchurch and Darowes (SOE). The Bardsea commander and leader of Daylesford was Lieutenant Colonel Zakrzewski; Lieutenant Madeskyi was the operations officer. Team Darowes was led by a Major R.D. Guthrie, with Lieutenant G.A.H. Butler as his deputy. The OSS teams were headed by:

Dodford – Captain J.J. Kielbowicz (who was also the senior US/OSS officer on the mission), deputy First Lieutenant H. Wolfs.

Datchet – First Lieutenant S. Konieczko, deputy Sergeant Edmund Porada.

Dunchurch – First Lieutenant James G. Brown, deputy Second Lieutenant Stanley Gromnicki.

The Poles wanted to be armed to the teeth. Each man, including signallers and the doctor, were to be armed with a Sten gun and a Browning 9mm pistol, and to carry several types of grenades. Each team was to be armed with a Boyes .55-inch Anti-Tank Rifle. It would have been an effective stand-off weapon against *Panzer* laagers, lorry-parks, airfields and dumps, and made life difficult for enemy personnel in field or static headquarters. A Boyes would also have made short work of one of the German security forces favourite anti-ambush vehicles; a 'Q' truck, a tarpaulin covered, drop-side lorry fitted with a 20mm Flak gun. The SOE training coordinator allocated to the Bardsea project rather rudely dismissed these proposals, and the Bardseas had to be content with less. As they would have carried and used the weapons it should have been left to them to decide what was required. Another issue was shortage of training facilities; SOE undertook to train the Bardsea teams, but the only accommodation available was at either Inchmerry, or Warnham Court, near Horsham. Inchmerry was used initially, followed by Warnham Court. There the teams were given, and undertook eagerly, some very rigorous training at the hands of the SOE Bardsea training team.

The idea was developed with SOE and, later, OSS, who started raising two Polish operational groups, to be manned by bi-lingual paratroops from the 101st Airborne division in Britain. In view of objections raised by various governments about endangering the lives of 'slave labour' in Poland and other occupied territories, the role of these two OGs was to be modified, as will be described later. They were to operate in France as links between the Bardsea teams (described below) and the US First Army, as the Polonia enclaves would be within its intended corridors. OSS recruited sufficient personnel to man four six-man teams, including three US Navy wireless operators. The teams were trained at STS 63 Warnham Court, and joined the Polish and SOE teams for a final exercise, after which they were inspected by Colin Gubbins, who described them as the best fighting men he had ever seen. The Bardsea teams would have made a very useful addition to the Jedburghs, operating in conjunction with the 1st Polish Armoured Division in Normandy, but they were destined for something else, and were not involved in Overlord. There was a notion at one stage to use the Polish operational groups and possibly Bardsea teams, on Operation Dunstable. This was an abortive operation, intended to utilize the intelligence gathering, and sabotage potential, of Polish nationals working as forced labour by German industrial and transportation concerns.

Polish Ingenuity

The Poles were resourceful and at times outrageous. They established within Vichy France a sort of miniature Bletchley Park and MI8 (Radio Security Service) in one; a wireless interception and message deciphering station. This was located near Avignon, in southern France and was known to the Resistance and the Poles as Command Post Cadix. It was manned by cryptologists and radio-intelligence experts from Poland, Republican (anti-Franco) Spain, and the recently disbanded French Military Radio Interception Section. Cadix operated safely for many months until forced out of the country in 1943 when the Germans occupied Vichy France. The station monitored French, Swiss, Spanish and German police networks, and those of the *Abwehr*, the *Gestapo,* their Italian opposite numbers, the O*VRA (Organizzazione di Vigilanza e Repressione Antifascista)*, and *Wehrmacht* units, including *Feldgendarmerie* units throughout Europe. The command post also monitored the German Armistice Commission in French North Africa and Metropolitan France, and Vichy France government transmissions to and from the French colonial empire which stretched from Tahiti in the Pacific to Syria in the Middle East and as far south and west as the Caribbean and Guiana in South America. When the command post was eventually captured by the Vichy authorities and explored by the Germans, their wireless experts were fascinated, but the *Sicherheitsdienst, Gestapo* and *Feldgendarmerie* were enraged to the point of apoplexy, as many of their private looting and black market operations had been discovered, and some of the files leaked widely, so no one knew who knew what.

(The G2 (Intelligence) Section of the Irish Army also provided SIS with deciphered contents of German wireless traffic during the war.)

Operation Sussex

Throughout 1942 and 1943 one issue above others played on the minds of SIS; the security of the source of Ultra. If the Germans suspected that the Enigma system was being deciphered and many of their most secret signals read by the Allies, they would change the number of rotors in the encryptor or in some other way render it invulnerable to the experts at Bletchley Park. As the volume of Enigma decrypts increased and the Bletchley staff became better equipped and even more skilled, so did the demand for the product. The wider the distribution, the more chance of an inadvertent leak. The threat of such a leakage increased as the planning for the invasion of France started, and then accelerated. After the formation of COSSAC, the volume of wireless traffic within Britain increased, and continued to do so right up to the start of Overlord.

Stewart Menzies and SIS had to be prepared for the loss of Ultra and devised Operation Sussex. It was originally a purely British project, albeit with considerable help from the French, but in May 1943 the OSS was included. This was part of a general agreement struck between Menzies and Colonel David Bruce, Head of the OSS London Station, to share intelligence collection and distribution in Europe and elsewhere. The OSS team also obtained several squadrons of B-24 Liberators to supplement the woefully inadequate resources of the RAF and Polish special duties squadrons. OSS also bid for a flight of helicopters, either the R4 Hoverfly or the R5 Dragonfly. They were quoted as having a 450-mile range, and being capable of carrying three persons and bundles of cargo (or bombs) and seemed ideal for SD operations. (Alas, they were unstable, unreliable and slow, and the whirling rotor provided a large radar echo.)

The Sussex plan was based on the success of the LRDG road watch operations in North Africa, and COSSAC Intelligence Requirements Group studies of the post-exercise reports from Spartan relating to the six agents. The SIS planners discussed the question of intelligence targeting with the COSSAC planners, and it was decided that key traffic routes leading between Germany and France were obviously the best targets. COSSAC also indicated that the scheme should extend beyond a simple road-watch to include railways, canals (a major route for bulk goods between the Ruhr and France then and now) and static sites such as *Wehrmacht* and *Luftwaffe* repair depots, MT and AFV parks. The agent reports were to include numbers of vehicles, type, load and direction of travel, their tactical signs, radio call-signs on turrets (a feature unique to the *Wehrmacht*) and divisional and regimental emblems or symbols. Agents were also requested to try to find out from café, bakery or butchers' gossip and other means, unit ration (*Verpflugengesstarke*) and battle strengths (*Kampfestarke*).

The Sussex command team consisted of Commander Kenneth Cohen representing the SIS, Francis Miller for the OSS, and probably the most important member, a very senior French intelligence officer, Colonel Remy, the alias of Gilbert Renault-Roulier, former Parisian film producer and in 1943 head of the BCRA. Recruitment started in July 1943, followed by selection and training of personnel. The Sussex planners decided that the teams would be composed of native Frenchmen, and that they would be inserted 'blind', that is, dropped on unmanned (but ACIU assessed) landing ground, and that no one should know they were coming. The teams would consist of two persons, the observer/leader and a wireless operator, who would double as a recorder, using a two-way radio (US 'walkie-talkie') and noting the numbers of vehicles etc. observed by the leader. Miller and Remy disagreed with the 'blind' drop concept, without faulting the logic on which it was based. Remy, who referred to that idea as the Suicidex Mission, quoted the strong presence of *Milice* and German *Sicherheitsdienst* forces in the selected operational areas. These forces included *Nahfunkpeilungtrupps*, mobile direction finding teams, backed by German *Sicherheitungstrupps* and *Milice*. Remy was aware of their inroads into French-controlled circuits, and advised against the teams being dropped blind. It was therefore agreed that some pathfinder teams would be selected on the basis of being capable of travelling freely around much of northern and central France; salesmen, insurance representatives or claims adjusters, or something similar, and trained first. Among other things they would also be trained in selecting landing grounds, and in training reception committees to operate them without supervision so that the main group of Sussex teams could be inserted as soon as they were ready. The pathfinders were also to be capable of arranging food coupons, travel passes and other documents for the incoming team members, find standard accommodation for their own operations, such as OPs, safe-houses, wireless and Ascension broadcasting sites, funk-holes and runways or 'bug-out' paths.

The Sussex planners eventually came up with a target figure of sixty teams, each of two persons. The teams were to be distributed in two arcs across France, one from south of Bordeaux to the junc-tion of the Belgian, Luxembourg and German frontiers; the other about (and this is a very rough figure) thirty-sixty miles inland from the English Channel. The teams were to initially provide intelligence for COSSAC/SHAEF (Supreme Headquarters Allied Expeditionary Force), then for the Allied Army Groups advancing out of the bridgehead. The SIS-OSS deal allowed for a 50–50 contribution of resources, and the mission became two, Brissex and Ossex, all within the general framework of the Sussex Mission. Training commenced in early November 1943 for the Brissex pathfinder teams, but later for Ossex as, despite the best efforts of OSS to find French speakers in the US or Britain by December 1943, all recruits failed to meet the criteria of being able to pass as native Frenchmen. In the end Francis Miller had to turn to the French and in January 1944 the BCRA started recruiting in NATO (North African Theatre of Operations), the US term for French and Italian Africa, and quickly located sufficient persons for the Ossex teams and had them flown to Britain for training. This was carried out in several locations in England; the main centre was apparently Milton Hall, outside Peterborough, later to be ME 65, the Jedburgh training school. (The delay in opening Milton Hall for the Jedburghs was allegedly caused by the late recruitment of the Ossex teams.)

The standard Sussex training course lasted for twelve weeks, two weeks basic or conditioning training; a one week parachute course at STS 51; four to six weeks specialist training, wireless handling and Morse, map reading, close quarter combat and shooting, AFV and tactical sign recognition, and a week-long test exercise at Warnham Court. Then one week of leave and a further review period and some cross training, probably at Orwell Grange, south-west of Cambridge.

Ascension Flights

The importance of the Sussex mission is demonstrated by the fact that a special RAF unit was formed to provide it with communications support; the Ascension missions. These involved the use of an S-Phone link between an agent on the ground and an airborne interrogator/briefing officer in orbiting aircraft. The aircraft could be 200 miles or so from the agent, as the S-Phone was really a short-range line-of-sight radio-telephone strapped to the sender's chest (or mounted in a ship or aircraft). If the ground sender tilted back slightly the signal was transmitted like the beam of a torch, gradually widening as the distance increased, and travelling for a very long distance. It was short-range at line-of-sight due to the narrowness of the beam and subsequent difficulty in maintaining 'lock'. The RAF unit was the Special Signals Flight of 226 Squadron, based in Hampshire at RAF Hartfordbridge Flats, later renamed Blackbushe in December 1944. The flight was equipped with eight North American Aviation B-25 Mk II Mitchell twin-engined medium bombers, and one elderly but reliable twin-engined Avro Anson for training and practice (exercise support) flights. The Anson was based at RAF Booker, a small airfield outside High Wycombe as it was also used for S-Phone training by other parts of SIS, SOE and MI9, and, initially at least, OSS, at STS 40. Ascension missions started in April 1942, and shortly afterwards Flight Lieutenant Maurice Whinney was placed in charge of these operations and training until at least 1945. A number of Dutch MI9 interrogator/briefers, including at least one woman, Hilda Bergsma, later flew Ascension missions in S-phone fitted Mosquito fighter-bombers during the winter of 1944–1945, in the aftermath of Arnhem. Phantom personnel were also trained as interrogators/briefers and were, for example, very busy during the run-up to, and after, the crossing of the Rhine.

Each of the Mitchell bombers was equipped with a full S-Phone that included a special station for the airborne interrogator/briefing officer, close to the navigator's cubby hole behind the pilot. The country section at SOE, SIS or MI9 HQ initiated a sortie, either for a schedule issued to the agent prior to deployment or by wireless once in the field. Alternatively, either the agent or the section could request contact by wireless or, less likely, by courier. An Ascension plan might last for days or weeks, with contact missions flown at fixed times and days. A plan, or a single mission, was initiated a few days before the contact time the section completed on a RAF Form F177/17 Ascension OPERATION REQUEST. One example dated 30/6/44 is for Plan NYLON, Amendment 2, contact with a source in North West Belgium, starting on 1st June 1944, and to be flown in daylight on Tuesdays and Thursdays until further notice. The Tuesday missions were to be on station ready to call the agents at 0830 hrs GMT for thirty minutes, and on Thursday time on-station was to be 0930 hrs GMT. The Ground Aerial direction would be NE-SW, and the racecourse orbit area was to be between Orfordness, Suffolk and Point 52° 00' North/03° 00' East. The orbit was to be flown at 20,000 feet, and the distance between the orbit and the ground apparatus was given as 130 miles. There were no patrol areas to be avoided (these were either Allied night fighter loiter areas, where they waited for inbound *Luftwaffe* intruders following returning bombers to intercept them when they were landing, or other SIGINT orbits). The ground apparatus calibration chart, for tuning the airborne receiver (fitting the correct crystal) would be handed to the airborne interrogator, in this case named as Flight Sergeant Arthur. The ground aerial direction, NE-SW, is correct, at right angles to a line between the agent and the centre of the orbit. The aerial on the ground station of the S-phone system was like an old fashioned, i.e. 1950s', UK television aerial; an H with the central arm at right angles to the agent's body. The completed form was submitted to AI2c at the Air Ministry, where it was logged and processed, and a copy passed to the 'duty' squadron. Flight Sergeant Arthur, no forename located, was a French speaking airborne recorder, or in-flight contact. He and other RAF personnel doing the same job, if not already aircrew-qualified, were deemed to be radio observers, and were authorized to wear the appropriate brevet, an 'RO' in a wreath with a half-wing. He first flew what were to be called Ascension operations in April 1942, and as far as is known, continued to do so right up until the end of the war in Europe, and possibly afterwards.

The final test required a Sussex team to establish a road and/or rail watch for one week, based at Warnham Court. It was set in a large deer park, home to a large herd of red deer. Before the war the manor and policies had been purchased or leased by a Broadway impresario, Gilbert Miller, but it had been requisitioned for use by the Army early in the war. In 1941, the pride of the herd, a stag with forty-one points on his antlers, was found dead one day, possibly shot for moving target practice by soldiers. The head was later mounted, but disappeared after the war. (Gilbert Miller was supposedly a relative of Colonel Francis Miller of the OSS but no corroboration has been found.) The exercise routine included transmission of information to an orbiting Anson as SIS rules forbade all trainee agents transmitting Morse until operational. (No new signature to be noted and recorded by the Germans.)

Warnham Court offered seclusion, and Horsham a fair replica of the type of crossroads community to be sought out by the Sussex teams. Two main roads crossed on the western edge of the town, both busy each way, with military traffic. A third main road entered the town near its centre, creating another busy junction. On the north-west and west of the town were bridges over the River Arun, little more than a broad stream winding through water meadows at that point, but adequate for practising traffic counts; both bridges could be observed from several points, adding complexity to recording and reporting. A main railway line ran through the town, dividing the south of the town so offered interesting permutations for tracking military trains, as Horsham junction was always busy with military and civilian goods and passenger traffic. Finally, Warnham Court and Horsham had been used by other agencies for test exercises; the police were fully briefed, and experienced, in looking for 'spies'. The West Sussex constabulary was adept at interrogating strangers, and woe betide any Sussex agent who fell into their hands. One slip, one error that blew their cover story, and the fledgling agent was taken off the operation, and parked in the 'cooler' run by SOE's security section. The cooler was yet another grand house, a requisitioned shooting lodge, Inverlair, long since demolished but near Tulloch Station, on the West Highland line. It appears on lists of SOE installations as the Inter-Services Research Bureau Workshops, and was probably just that, a place providing repair or building for SOE schools in the Highlands, and for keeping rather disconsolate young people usefully occupied. They were kept there until any special knowledge they might have acquired during selection and training became 'time-expired'.

Inverlair also housed, for a short spell, Rudolf Hess, deputy to Adolf Hitler, after his mysterious and still not fully understood flight from Munich in southern Germany to a spot south of Glasgow in May 1941.

A brief calculation of the amount of time required for teams to pass through each phase of training indicates that the first tranche, agents for the Brissex teams plus a few spares in case any failed to make the grade, would have started to arrive at Warnham Court in January 1944. It is thought that several teams moved into Horsham each week, with a gap until the Ossex group was ready to be tested. No indication has been located of the test starting with a parachute drop; apart from lack of facilities there was possibly too high a risk of losing one member of a two man team during training to justify the extra experience. The exercises ended in late spring 1944, and were followed by more for Operation Proust, a follow-on to Sussex, but using only one person for the same mission.

The first insertion of a pathfinder team took place on the night of 7 January 1944, when an RAF special duties mission dropped a Major Soubestre, of the French Air Force, and his assistant at a landing ground in the département of l'Indre et Loire. This team went on to locate many potential pinpoints, and twenty-two were used as landing grounds. The team also set up over 100 safe houses and procured dozens of documents for incoming teams. A second, larger, pathfinder force of three teams was to be inserted on 5–6 February 1944 by 161 Squadron. They were to be dropped as party one of three flown in a Halifax II, piloted by Wing Commander Hodges. The other operations were four agents and two packages dropped blind from 600 feet near Loiret, followed by one agent, six containers and three packages to be dropped at Nevers but no reception party or recognition signal was seen. Operation Calangue, four agents, nine containers and two packages, were to be dropped near Châteauroux to a dropping zone where the reception team would flash 'H'. There was no sign of the DZ lights, or of the code-letter at the site, so the mission was aborted. The following night, 8–9 February, another 161 Squadron Halifax mission completed Operation Calangue. The containers and packages were dropped, or drifted, wide of the DZ and were lost. The teams had to contact the Resistance in breach of orders from their SIS controllers, but there was no other way of obtaining new equipment and supplies. By D-Day there were twenty-two teams in position, twelve Brissex, and ten Ossex, more or less all operational.

Vitrail

The first non-pathfinder operational teams were dispatched from the night of 9 April onwards. Among these was Team Vitrail, dropped on 10 April near Châteauroux. This team moved north into the general area bounded by lines connecting Le Mans, Chartres and Orleans. It was here in early June that Vitrail hit the jackpot and vindicated the entire Sussex mission. The two agents located a number of *Panzer* hides in the area and by careful observation and patient research gradually identified the units and formations. These indicated to SHAEF G-2 Intelligence staff that the area was being used as a harbour area for the *Panzer Lehr* division, the best by far of the twelve *Panzer* divisions in northern France. It was manned by the staff of several *Panzer* schools, officers and NCOs who knew every trick in the tank-on-tank battle trade, learned the hard way on the Eastern Front against Zhukov's and Cherniakovsky's armoured regiments. Not only was the *Panzer Lehr* manned by experts, it was also the best equipped *Panzer* formation in Normandy, with 237 AFVs – 99 *Panzerkampfwagen IVs*, 89 *PzKw V Panthers*, 8 *PzKw VI Tigers*, 31 *Jagd Panthers*, 10 Stug IIIs Assault Guns – and 693 half-tracks of various types, some mounting anti-tank guns.

On 3 June air reconnaissance of the harbour area near Le Mans revealed AFVs moving into a railway goods yard where rows of flat cars were lined up in sidings with vehicle loading ramps. The location of the station and the heading of the train seemed to indicate that the *Panzer Lehr* was going north to Alençon in Normandy a couple of days before the landings. Another report indicated that this was 1st Battalion, 6 *Panzer* Regiment, with *PzKw V Panther* tanks; one of the most dangerous threats to Allied armoured units equipped with ill-protected Sherman and Churchill tanks. More sources indicated other *Lehr* units moving out of their hides and depots, fuelled-up, camouflaged and with bedding rolls and packs slung on the turret Bergen-Bar. The entire *Panzer Lehr* seemed to be heading into the invasion area; the Germans seemed to have located the place and date of the landings.

On 5 June the Ascension flight servicing Vitrail received one message which, when deciphered, revealed that the *Panzer Lehr* division was only on a training exercise and the *Panthers* were bound for Russia. The secret had not leaked; and the *Panzers* were either on their way to the east, or back in their hides and depots, requiring cleaning, servicing and re-fuelling after an exercise, not poised near the Normandy beaches, waiting for the Allied landings.

Chapter Nine

Special Interventions

In mid-1943 the COSSAC concept of operations for the SAS during the invasion assumed it would be a self-sufficient formation capable of deploying mobile detachments by land, sea or air to conduct prolonged offensive operations behind enemy lines some 50 to 300 miles from the beaches, probably in conjunction with patriot forces. Apart from that there was no proposal for the command, control, organizational and logistical needs of the SAS Brigade, nor for a sponsoring higher formation; being a Middle East hostilities-only creation it was something of an orphan.

SOE considered bidding for the brigade but was, itself, fully occupied with other aspects of Overlord, such as the Jedburgh, Bardsea and Dunstable operations, and on-going activities in Norway and France. It was fully stretched and its efficient but fragile logistical infrastructure was incapable of servicing a motorized, multi-national brigade involving amphibious and airborne warfare. As the brigade was to operate mainly in direct support of 21 Army Group, the Director of Military Operations decided (in December 1943) it should be firmly embedded in an army structure, not part of any secret service. The Chiefs of Staff committee therefore refused to consider SOE's tentative bid, to the pleasure of various Army factions who were themselves jostling for control of the SAS, or indeed for their own survival.

A number of military bodies tendered bids for the brigade. They included the Directorate of Combined Operations which was facing an uncertain future after the recent departure of Admiral Lord

Mountbatten to south-east Asia. Another bid was entered by the British, Canadian and Polish manned 21 Army Group, commanded by General Sir Bernard Paget. As it was to be one of two Army Groups, the other composed of American and French formations, and as the SAS Brigade was to support both, that bid was not considered. COSSAC, despite being a planning group and not yet transformed into SHAEF, was also interested in controlling it and saw it as a strategic asset (and its own creation, in some eyes) to be deployed at the behest of the theatre commander, not subject to any intervening authority. However, COSSAC did not possess the necessary administrative machinery, nor a mandate, for raising a new, multi-national formation. In any case, the entire COSSAC body was in for a terrible shock. Many of its officers, or at least General Morgan and some of the British staff, attached themselves, spiritually and physically, if not organically, to General Paget and 21 Army Group, a purely Anglo-Canadian formation. Possibly there were hopes of preferment, but it was a tactical and political error as COSSAC was supposed to work impartially with both the British/Commonwealth/Allied forces and the US forces. Both Generals received a severe shock in late December 1943 when General Montgomery was appointed C.-in-C. 21 Army Group and Land Force Commander for the invasion phase of Overlord, and brought his Chief of Staff from the Eighth Army, General Freddy de Guingand, to fill the same role for the invasion. General Paget went to Cairo as C.-in-C., Middle East Forces, an operational command of a sort, (Greece, the Aegean, minor operations in Iraq and Persia), but subordinate to General Henry Wilson, Supreme Allied Commander, Mediterranean Theatre. General Morgan, who had laboured so long and so well as COSSAC, was appointed Deputy Chief of Staff, SHAEF, and worked faithfully and loyally for General Bedell Smith, the American Chief of Staff, as he had done when commanded only by the Combined Chiefs in Washington.

Airborne Forces

That left HQ Airborne Forces. In the summer of 1943 it was subordinate to the War Office, originally via DCO, and not part of 21 Army Group, and was only a supplier of forces as and when required. (In December it became technically subordinate to 21 Army Group.) Airborne Forces had a sound administrative structure, and recent, if extremely limited, experience of command of Special Forces when elements of SRS and 2 SAS in southern Italy were temporarily placed under command of 1st Airborne Division. That was mainly at the instigation of General Frederick Arthur Montague 'Boy' Browning, late Grenadier Guards, a protégé of Churchill and Mountbatten, and at that time adviser, Airborne Forces, to the C.-in-C. Allied Forces Mediterranean, General Eisenhower. General Browning had seen active service in the Great War as a junior regimental officer, and before moving to Airborne Forces had commanded 24 (Guards) Brigade, following more or less in the footsteps of Colin Gubbins. He possessed considerable personal charm and ability, and was eager for active command, but he was also a thruster. An RAF colleague said of him, '. . . he was like the hero of an uplifting Victorian novel: All the boys in the boat rowed hard, but Browning rowed hardest of all'. General Browning envisaged the SAS forming part of an Allied Airborne Army that would descend into Europe to open a road to Berlin ahead of an invasion force. In Italy the ostensible reason for his absorption of SRS and 2 SAS was to rationalize aircraft sorties, and make best use of equipment especially the perennially scarce parachutes. There was however, a suspicion in some minds that Airborne Forces wanted to assimilate any formation with a parachute or glider-borne capability; even Popski's Private Army was considered at one stage. (He tried for a long time to absorb the Polish Independent Parachute Brigade Group, but the Poles raised it for operations in support of the Home Army, *Armia Krajow*, in Poland, and resisted relinquishing control to SHAEF for a long time.) There appears to have been reasonable harmony on a personal level between the Special Forces and airborne units, which helped during preparations for Overlord. What was even more fortunate was that one of the general staff officers at HQ Airborne Forces was ideally suited for handling all matters relating to the SAS, and the secret services. This was Lieutenant Colonel Ian Collins, and his role in helping the SAS find its feet in north-west Europe is almost unrecognized. He was by profession a publisher, and also a world-class tennis player, having reached the semi-finals of the Davis Cup Men's Doubles in the early 1930s (beaten by a German team). He became GSO2 (SAS) at HQ Airborne Forces, and worked with the SAS until late in the war. There was, unfortunately, no similar Q appointment at Corps Headquarters.

Lieutenant Colonel Collins' appointment preceded the publication of a document that was to cause a serious controversy within the SAS. This was COSSAC Study Paper No. 6, issued 28 December 1943, entitled *OPERATION OF AIRBORNE FORCES (SAS) IN OVERLORD – DELAYING ACTION.* It was issued by Commander, Airborne Troops, 21 Army Group, and limited to seven copies. The first went to C.-in-C. 21 Army Group marked for Lieutenant Colonel Cox, G-Operations, and of the others No. 7 went to GSO 2 (Special Air Service), HQ Airborne Troops, 21 Army Group. It is not clear who drafted the specifically SAS elements of this paper, but it would not have been issued without General Browning's concurrence. The paper dealt with SAS operations in the enemy rear areas before, during and immediately after D-Day. These had been roughed-out by COSSAC in relation to the role of the Resistance in the ground forces concept of operations during the landings (Operation Neptune) and their immediate aftermath. The SAS operations were to be mounted in conjunction with an overall invasion schedule with three distinct phases:

1. Clearing the area around the beachhead (three days).
2. Clearing the 'invasion sector', roughly Dieppe to the Loire estuary (five weeks).
3. Clearing the rest of France (five months).

There was to be no call to arms to the peoples of France in case the enemy slaughtered everyone in sight. COSSAC attempted to make plans for SAS operations to fill the time and distance gaps between the Resistance/Jedburgh sabotage actions and the invasion beaches. This meant direct attacks on enemy formations either in transit, in holding areas, or manning defences.

Read in retrospect, Paper No. 6 seems simplistic, if not naïve, in some respects, but in fairness to the writers they were dealing with a new concept of operations, which was to be a small element in the largest military operation ever mounted. Many of the land, sea and air concepts, tactics and equipment were new, and few staff officers, whether from the Regular Forces, Special Reserve, Territorial Army, Canadian Militia, US National Guard or 'hostilities-only', had little recent experience on which to draw. And there was a clear understanding at many levels that this invasion could only be attempted once; if repelled or stymied in a tiny beachhead, as at Gallipoli, and, most recently at Salerno and Anzio, it would be a massive catastrophe. And above all, there was no David Stirling to guide the planners, and no other senior SAS officer in Britain; the Brigade had yet to be formed anywhere.

Lost Leader

The paper starts by appearing to state the obvious:

> SAS regiments are drawn up [to War Establishments] and units trained in such a way as to give the utmost flexibility from the operational standpoints. Each squadron is designed to be independently contained and administered.

The paper went on to note that experience had shown that Special Air Service troops could operate most successfully in small detachments of five to ten all ranks, working at night and lying up by day, and operating in thinly garrisoned areas 50–300 or more miles behind the front line. It also foresaw them linking up where possible with resistance forces and Jedburgh parties. The paper also outlined operational roles for the SAS troops. Priority One were operations in support of conventional ground forces during the amphibious assault stage of the invasion, while Priority Two covered 'strategic' operations during the subsequent breakout from the bridgehead and advance into Germany. Priority One tasks were to impose the maximum delay on the movement of enemy reserve formations against the beachhead until D+5. This was to include on D-Day, as a priority, to harass two *Panzer* divisions, either in their bases in Lisieux and St Lô, or during any move towards the beachhead. Both towns were cited as being within fifty miles of the coast, but are within fifteen miles of the coastline, and about

175

twenty-five miles from the landing sites. The planners also anticipated that on D-Day a number of enemy reserve divisions would start moving forward from harbour areas located along an arc from Rennes in eastern Brittany to Lille in French Flanders. Oddly, no assumed direction of these movements was assessed, but it could only be towards a simulated assault area in the Pas de Calais (if Fortitude South was successful) or the real beachheads along the Normandy coast. Apart from distances, which may have made tactical sense to the planners but were in direct contradiction to the earlier point about 50–300 miles behind the front line, it placed the landing grounds and operations in one of the most heavily garrisoned areas of the famed 'Atlantik Wall'. There was a secondary role; harassing the reserve divisions in an area within 50–100 miles of the coast; through some of the most densely populated areas of France. A third role was assistance in diversionary landings of an unspecified nature, at the time the paper was written apparently still being reviewed as Staff Study No. 22, but intended to be a large airborne operation inland from the beachhead.

The strategic role was to include harassing enemy lines of communication on roads, railways and, presumably, canals; attacking headquarters, communications centres and lines, supply and maintenance bases in conjunction with resistance groups, to destroy enemy aircraft on enemy airfields and fuel dumps, and to report on enemy movements and concentrations. These tasks were to be carried out by a force comprising five or six SAS regiments, each of approximately 400–500 all ranks, a total of 2,000–3,000 men. It was considered that 300 aircraft would be available for the SAS Brigade. It also indicated that the War Office had requested fifty American CG4 Hadrian gliders for insertion of some SAS detachments. The paper then contained four paragraphs devoted to timings; some hardly realistic. For example, it was stressed in order to conduct harassing actions against the *Panzer* divisions at Lisieux and St Lô, SAS troops would have to be landed five to six hours before the time the first wave of landing craft reached the beaches (Nautical Twilight plus one hour). That, it was stated, would give the SAS troops time to reach objectives, carry out tasks and withdraw to sheltered positions by CT, (Morning Civil Twilight D-Day). It was also stated that security difficulties could be overcome if diversionary forces were to land at the same time. The paper concluded with some well-intentioned but rather obvious hints about blocking roads '. . . as these detachments cannot carry sufficient explosives to blow up completely, undamaged bridges'. The final hint, *Capture and use of enemy AFVs and MT*, makes interesting reading.

The paper appears to have been prepared by staff officers with little or no experience of land battles in close country, and nothing of Special Forces operations anywhere, and there was no one present in the UK to study it with an experienced eye and mind. It was apparently not reviewed until a Commander SAS Troops, and some battle-hardened SAS officers arrived on the scene. That did not occur for another six weeks in the case of the brigade commander, and longer for the regimental appointments, some of which were filled by officers with limited battle experience, and none of true Special Forces operations. In other words the (flawed) concept of operations for the SAS was not reviewed by the officers to be responsible for the operations until less than sixteen weeks before they were to be mounted by a formation yet to be formed from scattered, under strength units from several nations.

The size of the new formation was set, initially, as headquarters and four to six regiments; four to support the invasion force, the other(s) held for contingencies such as Norway. As Overlord was to start in France the SAS formation was to receive a Demi-Brigade (a formation unknown to the British and French Armies), comprising the *3eme & 4eme Bataillons d'Infanterie de l'Air* (3BIA, 4BIA). Having solved sponsorship and format of the new formation and addressed, partly, operational roles, the questions of finding a UK base, recruitment and training had to be tackled. It was initially assumed that many SAS operational deployments would be made by air, either by parachute, glider or landing by special duties Hudson or US Army Air Corps Dakotas, or a combination of these methods. The question of seaborne landings was also actively considered; and various methods of extraction; sea, air and land. As a result the SAS would need a training base with ready access to an airfield (or airfields) capable of handling troop-carrying aircraft and gliders, parachute practice facilities, including storage and maintenance of parachutes, and landing grounds. Also required were cross-country driving areas, including woodland, and amphibious warfare facilities such as landing craft and beaches, and MTBs and rocky shores. And, of course, accommodation to house a brigade of an HQ and five or six battalion-sized units, preferably close to each other.

England was almost filled to capacity and more troops arrived daily from the USA, and anyway it had few locations that met the SAS requirements in full. Rocky Wales had few airfields and no amphibious warfare centres. That left Scotland, site of so many special training schools and centres but with space for more; and there was also the possible use, or suggestions of use, of the brigade in Norway to be considered.

The first proposal was to base the brigade near Perth, on the southern edge of the Highlands. It was a garrison city, housing the Highland area administrative headquarters, ordnance depots and workshops. It had a small but busy harbour, with easy access down the River Tay to the North Sea coast for amphibious training, and numerous army camps, small-arms, field-firing and demolitions ranges. For demolition and counter-scorch instruction there were many railway branch-lines, power stations and dockyards. The area was mainly farmland and forest, similar to northern France, and was well-endowed with mansions for housing headquarters or officers' messes, many with access to such necessities as salmon beats, deer forests and grouse moors. There was also a decided bonus, the Polish Parachute Centre at Largo, and over ten airfields nearby. There was RAF Woodhaven, a seaplane-base on the Tay opposite Dundee, home of 333 (Norwegian) Squadron, flying agents and material into Norway by Catalina flying boats. Pending the arrival in Britain of 2 SAS, the only SAS unit in existence, the British and French authorities agreed to incorporate the French Demi-Brigade into the new formation. On 6 December 1943 it commenced moving to the Perth area, the Etats-Major (HQ) and 3 BIA to Comrie, west of the city, followed by 4 BIA to Largo, soon to become 3 and 4 SAS.

In late summer 1943 the Directorates of Military Operations and of Training at the War Office started considering the training requirements of the SAS formation, and requested from AFHQ,

Algiers, the services of Lieutenant Colonel Bill Stirling and some senior NCOs as instructors. There was a pointless exchange of signals and no lieutenant colonel, but a Captain R.M.K. Bell, KOSB, and one or two NCOs had arrived in Britain by late October. (Interestingly the Regimental Headquarters, King's Own Scottish Borderers, have no record of a Captain R.M.K. Bell.)

After some well-deserved leave this small group assembled in an Army camp twenty miles or so east of Perth to establish an SAS Training Centre. This was Baltilly Camp, in Ceres, a village set among the low hills of central Fife, and just uphill from Largo. The 'Training Centre' was hardly more than a couple of Nissen huts but the training team prepared a two-week programme of theoretical and practical instruction on SAS techniques and tactics. The first course started on 27 November 1943, and consisted of forty officers and non-commissioned officers from 4 BIA who were based in Largo, followed on 12 December by a group from 3 BIA. Thereafter combined French and British groups arrived every two weeks until 21 February when the centre started moving to Ayrshire. (The British troops were recruited from across Home Forces.) Each course included several short exercises, and one or two special interest visits, one being to replica Atlantik Wall fortifications, perched high up on moors in the vicinity of Dunblane, in sight of the Stirling family estate at Keir.

Ore Again

At one stage during the winter of 1943–44 a detachment of 4 BIA and one of a Norwegian Independent Parachute Company spent some time in Peterhead, a fishing port on the north-east coast of Scotland. There were several airfields in the immediate vicinity and further inland, used by the RAF Banff and RAF Dallachy Strike Wings, each consisting of several squadrons of Mosquito and Beaufighter aircraft. Their main role was attacking German ore-convoys sailing from Narvik to north Germany. Further east, the Russians spent much time and effort, including extensive use of submarines, to attack convoys sailing from Lulea to Danzig and other Baltic ports. The Russians also mounted a major campaign to cross northern Finland to reach Lulea, or at least to get within

Stuka range, and to push the Germans away from Murmansk, entry port for Allied Arctic convoys. The Germans responded to the Russian campaign by deploying their elite mountain troops to the swamps and forests of Lapland.

The French and Norwegian troops at Peterhead were probably involved in a complex deception plan within Operation Fortitude North, as they reportedly were on 'signals exercises' using their native tongue, and accompanied by 'some Polish para radio operators'. RAF Banff was used for such ploys, such as in August 1943 displaying two Horsa gliders as part of Operation Tyndal. The Germans depended on Swedish ore right up to the end of the war, which is why they were so sensitive to any threat to Norway, to the extent of having many divisions tied up there right to the end. They also kept their last battleship, the *Tirpitz* there, as a counter to an invasion fleet, as well as a threat to Arctic convoys. The overall plot for Operation Fortitude North was designed to be played over a long period, with the intention of convincing Hitler – no one else mattered – that a massive American, British and Russian force was to invade Norway from the north. It would then advance south in concert with naval forces, cross over to Denmark, clear northern Germany and the heavily defended Friesian islands, and link up with a smaller invasion force which would cross the Channel by the Pas de Calais.

The area around Perth seemed ideal for the SAS Brigade but several complications arose in early 1943. Apart from re-locating other units and considerations relating to Operation Fortitude North, there was the danger of breaches of SIGINT from any wireless or radio along the east coast. These problems brought about a change of plan, and an area around Ayr, on the west coast of Scotland south of Glasgow was allocated instead. There were excellent rail and road communications with the south of England for access to supply centres. There were airfields at Prestwick, Dundonald and Turnberry, several large amphibious warfare training centres on the Firth of Clyde, and a vast tract of the southern uplands for training and field firing. The area was well endowed with power stations, mines, gas works, railways, road and rail bridges, harbours and docks for demolition instruction and practice. Ayrshire was already busy with over thirty military or naval sites of all types and sizes, housing some 16,000 service personnel and hundreds of coal miners, so a few more troops was thought to make little difference. There was also accommodation readily available for 2,000 plus troops in the area due to the departure of an infantry brigade. Finally, the area was relatively close to Headquarters Scottish Command in Edinburgh for routine administrative matters, and a long way from HQ Airborne Forces near London. The brigade headquarters would be in the tiny village of Sorn, one British or Belgian regiment each in Darvel, Newmilns and Galston, small lace-making towns in the Irvine valley, and one French battalion at Auchinleck, near Sorn; the other at Doonfoot outside Ayr (with some shuffling of units later). Ayrshire it was, but the accommodation would not be vacant until February 1944, which was just as well, because a bureaucratic wrangle between HQ Allied Forces, in Algiers and the War Office nearly deprived SHAEF of the bulk of the existing SAS units.

An Unseemly Squabble

The possible size and structure of the brigade had been agreed as had the source of some of the troops; Allied airborne forces. In Britain there was 1 Airborne Corps manned by British and Canadian troops, small units of French, Belgian, Dutch, Polish and Norwegian commandos and paratroops, and a burgeoning US airborne force and soon, this was in late 1943, several operational groups. Most important of all in north Africa there were thought to be two experienced British SAS units in the Mediterranean around which the Brigade could be built. The reality was that one of these units had been disbanded and the other was under-strength and with a large detachment operating (very successfully) behind enemy lines in Italy. The residue of 1 and 2 SAS were not stuck in north Africa by any default of administration or lack of transport, but by a reluctance of various headquarters to release them for Overlord. The ensuing paper battle is fully documented in File WO 104/4158 housed in the National Archives in London. It makes interesting, if depressing, reading. Interesting in a detached way, as it reveals the way such bureaucratic squabbles are conducted; depressing as resultant delays meant the SAS Brigade had only a few weeks to prepare for Overlord. An outline of the exchange follows, as it reveals many of the hurdles the Regiment had to overcome before deploying into north-west Europe. It is a wonder that any detachments were ready in time to support the opening moves of Overlord.

It should be noted that during the following exchange the War Establishment of 2 SAS (WE NA XII/410/1 dated 13 May 1943), allowed for a headquarters and headquarters squadron plus two operational squadrons, each of 153 all ranks, a total of 410 all ranks. However, Lieutenant Colonel Bill Stirling was firmly of the view that the unit should be increased to four operational squadrons. That would require a new establishment of around 700 all ranks if it was to be an effective force, with two squadrons on operations, one resting/re-training, and one preparing to deploy. In late 1943 the unit had 350 all ranks on strength, but leave, absence on training courses and sickness reduced the actual strength to 220, including about 100 non-operational personnel. That meant two under-strength operational squadrons with 60 instead of 153 troops.

On 28 September 1943 the DMO in London requested Allied Forces Headquarters Mediterranean in Algiers (AFHQ) to release some or all SAS units in the Mediterranean theatre for immediate return to the UK for Overlord. AFHQ replied on 30 September stating that due to future operational commitments in the Aegean it wished to retain 1 SAS, which was already committed in that area. However, the Special Raiding Squadron, quoted as being from 2 SAS, should rejoin 1 SAS, the balance of 2 SAS being dispatched to the UK. The same day the C.-in-C. Middle East, General Paget, whose command was subordinate to AFHQ, signalled the War Office. He indicated that Middle East Command now had a requirement for parties of troops totalling 1,000 men to provide support for guerrilla operations in the Balkans, and would appreciate the early return of SRS, quoted as being 'of 1 SAS' to help achieve that target. On 13 October AFHQ, copy to C.-in-C. ME, sent an urgent request for one squadron from 2 SAS to remain in the Mediterranean theatre for current operations, also stating that 2 SAS less one squadron could be released forthwith for return to the UK. Note that 2 SAS had the equivalent of only one full operational squadron on strength at that time. The War Office sought clarification of whether AFHQ meant to retain one squadron in total or two, one each from 2 SAS and the SRS. On 19 October AFHQ replied that the original intention was to retain SRS. 1 SAS, then operational in Italy, should be returned to the Middle East; one squadron of 2 SAS to be retained in Italy, and 2 SAS less one squadron to return to the UK. (As 2 SAS consisted of headquarters, a headquarters squadron and two under strength operational squadrons, and as 1 SAS had been disbanded, there would be very few trained SAS troops for the new brigade in the UK.) The waters were further muddied by a second paragraph in the signal indicating that Allied Forces Central Mediterranean (15 Army Group in Italy), strongly recommended that SRS should be returned to the UK to make up 2 SAS as 'this squadron had been abroad for a long period'.

The exchange rumbled on, and so did time. On 16 November GHQ Middle East Command signalled the War Office requesting that the whole of 2 SAS (and one commando unit) be retained for operations in the Aegean. That would have meant only the SRS would have been available for the SAS Brigade, and then only from January 1944. Precious months had been wasted in futile exchanges and on 2 December an added twist was the urgent requirement for Bill Stirling and six non-commissioned officers to return to Britain by air as instructors for 3 and 4 BIA. (The training team did not return until much later in December, and only after further prevarication.) D-Day was less than seven months away, but the paper war was not over. An immediate response from the Director of Military Operations to Allied Forces Headquarters, copied to GHQ ME stated, bluntly, that 3 and 41 (RM) Commandos, 2 SAS (less two squadrons), 1 SRS, and '1 SAS' (which had ceased to exist), were to move to the UK as soon as possible, preferably on the next convoy, as they were urgently required by 21 Army Group. AFHQ queried the need, and the War Office stated that the decision was firm, but 'required fullest details of your demands' to retain 2 SAS and the commando units. On 17 December AFHQ signalled that 'Special Raiding Sqdn 1 SAS Regt' and 3 Commando would be dispatched by the next convoy, and a further signal 'on 2 SAS Regt and 41 Commando' was to follow.

By 20 December no such signal had been received at the War Office, where someone was losing patience. A peremptory signal to AFHQ, copy C.-in-C. Middle East, stated, '. . . urgently require proposal for 2 SAS and 41 Commando. If decided they will return UK, essential they sail (convoy) MKF 27 as considerable reorg and trg necessary in UK. Request immediate reply'. Immediately AFHQ signalled, '. . . in view of 21 Army Groups urgent requirements have decided not to press for retention of 2 SAS (less Two Sqns) strength 150 all ranks . . . and will dispatch in MKF 27. And Lt Col Stirling and 6 NCOs will be dispatched by air soonest'. That seemed to resolve the matter, apart from the ambiguous strength of 2 SAS; '150 all ranks' represented only an under-strength HQ and HQ Squadron, and a weak operational squadron. However on 26 January 1944, just over four months before D-Day, a message from Winston Churchill to General Wilson referred, among other matters, to the fact that 2 SAS had been retained in the Mediterranean and that '. . . you should now have all the materials at your hand'; a fairly broad hint to stop asking for more men and to get on with the task. The Prime Minister went on to suggest that Major The Lord Jellicoe would make an admirable Commander (of Special Forces) and he, Winston Churchill, would be '. . . very glad to see him made a Brigadier at once, and thought from my talks at Cairo that this was going to be done. Pray let me know how these matters stand'.

The following day General Sir Leslie Hollis, Churchill's military secretary, prepared a short minute for the Prime Minister, noting that General Montgomery had asked that the whole of 2 SAS, amounting to 640 parachute-qualified troops, should be made available for Overlord. (No mention of the source of that figure has been located.) The regiment would assist in forming a belt of small independent parties around the beachhead area as a means of delaying the forward movement of German reinforcements during the early stages of the landing operations. Unless 2 SAS was available as a nucleus around which other volunteers could be trained and organized, General Browning did not consider that in the time available a force could be formed capable of carrying out the task. 2 SAS was in the Mediterranean theatre, earmarked for Operation Anvil, the invasion of the south of France, but had few other operational commitments in the theatre. The minute also noted that there were some 4,000 other special service troops in the Mediterranean theatre, including about 1,000 trained parachutists, three US Ranger battalions, each with a strength of about 500 men, and an independent parachute brigade group currently serving in the line; in all about 8,000 all ranks. It was considered by the British Chiefs of Staff that these forces were sufficient to carry out any future operations in the theatre. The minute concluded by stating that the chiefs of staff therefore recommended that 2 SAS should be returned to the UK to prepare for Overlord, and asked for the Prime Minister's agreement to that course. All that, six days after AFHQ assured DMO that all was sweetness and light.

Final Round

On 30 January the Chiefs of Staff secretariat, possibly following a gentle nudge from the Prime Minister's office, signalled AFHQ asking if there would be sufficient special service forces available for future operations. The signal indicated that it was thought there were some 4,000 special service troops plus a parachute brigade and three Ranger battalions in the theatre. On 31 January General Wilson responded by stating that it was essential that 2 SAS and all commandos should be retained in the Mediterranean theatre. He reasoned that they were not only particularly suitable for 'commando' operations on the Dalmatian coast (one of Winston Churchill's pet schemes) but were also for Operation Anvil, 'particularly if it was to be mounted as a threat and not as a major assault'. This message was repeated to the Prime Minister, but with an unctuous opening sentence, 'I am fully in accordance with your views that there is great scope for Commando operations in this theatre'. The signal closed with the comment to the effect that Jellicoe had not been forgotten as a commander for future operations 'when they take shape'. The signal was copied to the US Joint Chiefs of Staff in Washington 'for information'.

On 3 February the Chiefs of Staff, again possibly with a nudge from the Prime Minister, requested from AFHQ approximate strengths of all commandos located in the Mediterranean theatre apart from 2 SAS, and of the parachute brigade and the three

Ranger battalions. When no answer had been received by 7 February a sharply worded reminder crossed with the answer from AFHQ. This effectively ended the debate, as it revealed that there were some 16,840 Allied special service troops in the Mediterranean theatre, not including 938 others reported earlier, nor 2 SAS; a grand total of 18,418 all ranks!

Taking No for an Answer

General Wilson had overplayed his hand and been caught out; worse, he had tried to embroil the Americans in what was a British internal squabble. Advising the US Joint Chiefs of Staff was a serious tactical and political mistake, as they were far from enthusiastic about the Mediterranean theatre in general, and the Balkans in particular, especially any ploy in which Winston Churchill had a hand. Also, appealing past his own side, so to speak, did not make his already weak case any stronger in the eyes of the Chiefs of Staff and the Prime Minister. Despite all that, there was more wrangling before General Wilson received a personal telegram from the Prime Minister, dated 14 February 1944. It stated bluntly; 'Essential whole of 2 SAS returns UK (aboard) MKF 29'. The story was not quite over. On 17 February HQ Italy signalled AFHQ and the War Office requesting, sensibly, that as the detachment of 2 SAS then operating in Italy was performing most useful service, could it please stay? More signals followed, but on 22 February it was made abundantly clear to all concerned in the Mediterranean theatre that the squadron in Italy, less about fifty men operating behind enemy lines, had to return to the UK forthwith, and the rest were to follow as soon as they returned to base.

The object of all this wrangling, 2 SAS, languished at Phillippeville in Algeria until 23 February 1944, when it moved to Algiers to embark on convoy MKF-29 for the UK. The squadron in Italy was ordered to embark on MKF-30, despite continued requests by its commanding officer, Major Roy Farran, and a progressively ascending level of staff officers at HQ Italy for it to be retained.

The result of this squabble was that the new SAS formation had just over 100 days to prepare for D-Day, let alone for any precursor operations, and that HQ Italy was deprived of a very useful force, fully experienced in operating in Italy, at a most inconvenient time in the Italian campaign.

Postscript

In August 1944 3 Squadron, 2 SAS was dispatched to Italy, mainly at the instigation of veterans of the earlier and entirely successful venture there such as Major Roy Farran and Captain Ian McGregor, aided and abetted by Lieutenant Colonel Ian Collins. The squadron had few veterans of its earlier period in Italy but it served with distinction in that 'forgotten front', including an attempt to block vital Axis road and rail supply links with Austria and southern Germany by blocking the Adige valley with a rock fall.

Chapter Ten

Overture and Beginners

The initial intention was for the SAS formation to consist of brigade headquarters and four to six regiments. Brigade HQ was initially one entity but later divided into five elements; Tactical HQ, Rear HQ, Administrative Base, the SAS Training and Reinforcement Camp, and 20 Liaison Headquarters. Each of the regiments was, in theory, to consist of a headquarters and a headquarters squadron plus four operational squadrons, although the French had an additional company, later squadron; a training unit, or *Compagnie/Escadrille Leger*. Two of the regiments would be British and Commonwealth, two French and the others manned by Allied troops.

The EMIA, the *Etats Major d'Infanterie de l'Air,* was the headquarters of all Free French airborne forces and was non-operational. In early 1944 it moved from Camberley to share accommodation with the SAS Brigade HQ in Sorn Castle, although it had increasing responsibility for non-SAS and non-UK based Free French airborne formations. Twelve personnel of the EMIA attended parachute courses at 1 PTS in the winter of 1943–44, a sensible act as it created a sense of comradeship with the operational troops and a small pool of reserves. Later, when the first regiments moved south for Overlord operations, the EMIA divided; the majority of the staff went south to be in close contact with Brigade Tactical HQ, HQ Airborne Forces, SFHQ and General de Gaulle's HQ in London. A rear-echelon remained in Ayrshire for some months before moving south with the remainder of the SAS Brigade. At one stage an element of the EMIA was to deploy onto the continent with Tactical HQ of either SHAEF, 21 Army Group, or 9 Army Group, but as it was not equipped to take part in operations it remained in London.

The French Connection

A word about 20 Liaison Headquarters. This was a small, only twelve men, team of French or French-speaking British officers and other ranks, commanded by Lieutenant Colonel Oswald Cary-Elwes, a pre-war officer in the Lincolnshire Regiment. The role of 20 Liaison HQ was to handle all aspects of inter-Allied liaison, especially over supply and administrative matters between the British military and civil authorities and the EMIA, the HQ of the Demi-Brigade and individual French SAS Regiments. These matters included ensuring delivery of such essential supplies as rough wine, *pinard*, to accompany the daily institution of the Armies of France, *le Soupe*.

Lieutenant Colonel Oswald Aloysius Joseph Cary-Elwes was the correct man for the job. He had been at school in France and spoke colloquial French. He joined the British Army in the 1930s, and after Dunkirk was appointed Brigade Major of a Nigerian brigade. Not such an odd posting as it first appears; it was next door to Chad, where the Free French forces of General Leclerc were assembling. Later he served in the Middle East, and then in Algiers, accompanied throughout by his batman of many years, Corporal Eric Mills. His fluent French was derived from his family having been champagne shippers for three generations, something which put him in good standing with the French. His main role as OC 20 LHQ was to act as go-between for the French (and Belgian regiments), and the British military, civil and (at times) ecclesiastical authorities. Local contacts ranged from Brigade HQ through RAF Station Commanders and Station Warrant Officers, PJIs/Dispatchers and the aircrew of transport squadrons, air traffic control staff, RAF and Royal Navy, of the various Ayrshire airfields used for training flights and parachute drops (men, containers and vehicles), and later USAAF aircrew from the Carpetbagger squadrons. Civil authorities included landlords of requisitioned property, Ministry of Public Works staff repairing said property, the police, Procurators-Fiscal (Scottish prosecutors), courtroom staff, wine suppliers, angry mothers and fathers with daughters of obvious fertility, doctors and hospital staff, irate landowners bereft of game, finned, feathered or furry, and men enraged by strayed female servants/daughters/wives and, in one case, grandmother; the French and Belgians were long remembered with affection in parts of Ayrshire. Lieutenant Colonel Cary-Elwes sometimes also acted on behalf of the British military authorities with their French or Belgian counterparts.

Poisoned Chalice

The SAS Brigade formally came into being on 8 February 1944, when the War Diary was opened with entries about staff appointments. Brigade headquarters was housed in Sorn Castle, home of an ancient Scottish family, the Setons, lying in a hamlet a couple of miles east of Mauchline, in southern Ayrshire. Sorn Castle was described in an old guidebook as '. . . a most spacious, commodious, and comfortable mansion' and in 1944 all its facilities were needed to house the offices of Brigade Headquarters and its associated officers' and senior NCOs' messes.

The brigade was commanded by Brigadier Roderick William McLeod, Royal Horse Artillery. As a subaltern he had seen active service with a mountain battery in the North-West Frontier Province of India, no place for the faint-hearted, and later attended the Staff College at Camberley. He served on the staff of the 4th Infantry Division during the *Sitzkreig*, then in the War Office, followed by command of 1 Air Landing Light Regiment, Royal Artillery, 1st Airborne Division, and saw active service in Algeria and Sicily. In 1943 he returned to the United Kingdom with the division and was appointed Deputy Commander, 1 Parachute Brigade – and was suddenly offered command of the, as yet unformed, SAS Brigade. He had had some contact with SAS troops in Algeria and (fleetingly) Sicily, but had not operated with them and was unfamiliar with Special Forces tactics and requirements, and of the command and administrative methods evolved at either end of north Africa.

Brigadier McLeod may have been flattered at being selected to command a new formation but soon must have thought it was a poisoned chalice. He has left some interesting papers relating to his spell in command of the brigade; they are in the care of the Liddel Hart Centre for Military Archives, King's College, London. By all accounts he was not an officer to shirk responsibility, nor to be afraid to tackle some of the thorny issues, and personalities, he inherited with the appointment of Commander, Special Air Service Troops. He has sometimes been blamed for ordering the veterans of 1 SAS to wear red, not sand-coloured, berets. (2 SAS wore red ones from the start.) This is unfair; the order came from above and was based on the difficulty of manufacturing limited numbers of an unusual colour of headdress at a time when just about every British factory of any type or size was working flat out. The rest of Airborne Forces wore red berets, and were commanded by a Guards officer, with a great respect for uniformity. Whatever the reason, this major contribution to winning the war against National Socialism was sensibly ignored by veterans of 1 SAS whenever possible. (It took fourteen years before the sand-coloured beret was officially approved for wear by SAS troops in August 1959, but many serving personnel had laid hands on one before-hand, Moss Bros. having got wind of the change.) The French, sensibly, kept out of the debate, ignored everything they didn't like, and stayed in their black berets, but each regiment wore a different badge. (General Browning designed and wore a unique service dress jacket, with a button-over front like a Napoleonic hussar's plastron, or Great War RFC pilot's jacket; it had a zip at the neck, for reasons unknown. But he did wear a red beret.)

Brigade HQ formed a varied collection of veterans assembled in Ayrshire. Ayrshire is a pleasant place but in a wet Scottish spring it was a far cry from Kabrit or Phillippeville, and not to everyone's taste. The first to arrive were the remnants of 1 SAS, men from the defunct SRS, lead by Lieutenant Colonel Robert Blair Mayne. And here the military bureaucracy had another, unintended, swipe at the veterans of 1 SAS. The brigade, as noted, was established for one existing and one new British SAS regiment. On arrival at Alloway Paddy Mayne discovered he was CO, 3 SAS, as 1 SAS, a ME GHQ 'hostilities only' unit, had been disbanded. Therefore subsequent units would be numbered from 3 onwards, as for the French units, which would become 4 SAS and 5 SAS, and were not amused at losing their numbers 3 and 4, nor all overjoyed about being SAS, not *Infanterie de l'Aire*. It would also mean that the new unit would be junior to 2 SAS, seen as *arriviste* by the veterans of Kabrit. Brigadier McLeod wisely supported Paddy Mayne so thereafter a new 1 SAS regiment entered the Order of Battle of 1 (British) Airborne Corps, albeit wearing red berets.

The French Demi-Brigade left Comrie at the end of January 1944 and by mid February was ensconced in Ayrshire. Some of the units occupied billets in a hutted camp between Cumnock and the village of Auchinleck. The rest of the French units settled into a hutted camp near Auchinleck, a large village a few miles east of Ayr; others were a few miles away in Alloway. The accommodation in Cumnock was described in the War Diary, the *Journal de Marche de le Demi-Brigade d'Infanterie de l'Air*, as '*très satisfaisante*'. That was due in part to the presence of a large number of young and not so young ladies. Prior to the outbreak of war the British government made plans to build, once war had been declared, a number of Emergency Medical Service Hospitals around major cities. One of the EMS units for Glasgow was built in the grounds of Ballochmyle House, close to Mauchline. It specialized in plastic, reconstructive and maxillofacial surgery, for badly burnt patients, civil and military. In 1943 it had 1,200 patient beds, and over 2,000 female staff, many living within the hospital site and not totally uninterested in polite conversation with French paratroops.

The two French regiments, by then 3 and 4 SAS, were separated by a few miles, which is just as well as when they met socially, whether or not with the *pinard* taken, they fought. The cause was supposedly the date of allegiance to *le Grande Charles*. Political ideology does not appear to have had much bearing on the matter; the truth is that like all paratroops, anywhere, at any time, the French liked a punch-up.

The French were followed into Ayrshire and the brigade by a strong body of Belgian paratroops; fit, disciplined and eager to fight the German Army. They, too, had a long road to travel to Galston, Ayrshire.

No. 5 (Belgian) SAS Regiment

After the surrender of the Belgian Army on 28 May 1940 some Belgian troops found their way to Dunkirk, then Britain, where they congregated in west Wales. In August 1940 a new army was established, the *Force Belgique en Grande Bretagne* (FBGB), including the 1st Fusilier Company, soon enlarged into the 1st Fusilier Battalion. In July 1941 a second battalion was formed from an influx of recruits from Canada, the men from the first batch forming one complete company. This consisted of men who had been living or working in the US but who rallied to their nation's cause in 1940. As the US was neutral at that time they were dispatched to Canada, to Joliette, Quebec, where they were enrolled into the Belgian Army and underwent basic military training. Those who opted for the infantry were formed into a fledgling battalion, part of the Belgian Division in Canada. In the early days the battalion was little more than a large company, but it slowly expanded as more men rallied to the mother country. In 1942 a company from the Joliette training unit sailed for Britain under the command of Captain Eddy Blondeel, a man later to become one of the stalwarts of the wartime SAS, and in post-war years the founding-father of the Belgian Para-Commando battalion.

The majority of men in the Canadian detachment were formed into B Company, 2nd Fusilier Battalion, and the balance formed the nucleus of C Company. However, life as an infantryman did not appeal to everyone, and from 1940 there was a steady exodus from the two Fusilier battalions and other units in the FBGB, into SOE and the Commandos where they formed 4 (Belgian) Troop of 10 (Inter-Allied) Commando. In late spring 1942 the FBGB was invited to provide volunteers for a company of paratroops and B Company 2nd Fusilier Battalion volunteered en masse. They moved to Hardwick Hall for the standard course of pre-parachute fitness training, then to 1PTS for parachute training, then to RAF Brize Norton for training in air-landing (glider) techniques. In mid-May 1942 the unit became D (Parachute) Company, 2nd Fusilier Battalion, then in June detached from the battalion and became the Independent Belgian Parachute Company. In July 1943 the company became, briefly, D Company, 3rd Battalion [British]

Parachute Regiment, then D Company, 8th Battalion Parachute Regiment, and finally the Independent Belgian Parachute Company again.

In December 1943 the Company moved to Inverlochy Castle, outside Fort William and near Lochailort, for a special training course run by the Commando Basic Training Centre. In January 1944 the Company Commander, Eddie Blondeel, went to London for several meetings, and just before he was due back some of the officers were alarmed to hear from a British liaison officer that the company was moving to somewhere near Moscow. That proved correct, but the young Belgians, alarmed by visions of winter in Russia, were relieved to learn there is a village of that name in Ayrshire; Scottish humour is rarely subtle! The company duly moved south, mostly by train, but a vehicle party moving weapons and ammunition did indeed pass through Moscow, Scotland, in February 1944, to reach a hutted camp in the grounds of Loudoun Castle, outside Galston. There the much put-upon Belgian Independent Parachute Company found a spiritual home in the SAS. This led to yet more changes of title; first the Belgian Independent Special Air Service Company, then, in June 1944, Belgian Independent Special Air Service Squadron, and finally, in 1945, 5th (Belgian) Special Air Service Regiment.

Throughout its travels the Belgian unit showed great fortitude in the face of so many changes of location, title and role. It was noted for smartness and discipline, in and out of barracks, and avoided the Belgian Commando policy of separate Walloon and Flemish-speaking sub-units; the SAS unit deliberately mixed the two groups to foster team spirit and a sense of identity – and some of the troops recruited in the US had American-English as their first language. In March 1944, purely for purposes of developing inter-operability, the Belgian Squadron was teamed with 1 SAS and 4 SAS into a Group A for all aspects of training, with as much use of French as possible for one week, then English the following week, and so on. Group B consisted of 2 and 3 SAS; the language idea was good but there was not enough time available to both groups to make it work properly.

No. 6 (United States) Special Air Service Regiment

This was long held by students of Special Forces and enthusiasts of all things SAS to be a flight of imagination. There was a comparatively well-known Italian SAS unit which conducted an airborne raid in the closing days of the war, and also the short-lived (1947–1949) Canadian SAS Company, OC Major Guy d'Artois, ex-SOE. There have been, long ago in the 1950s, vague rumours of a Polish SAS unit, and of an American one. However, as sometimes happens, there was some truth behind part of the hearsay.

In late 1943 there was, as noted above, a proposal for the SAS Brigade Order of Battle to include five or six operational squadrons, the four above plus one multi-national European along the lines of No. 10 (Inter-Allied) Commando and possibly derived from it, and an American one. The fifth, European, squadron was in the end restricted to the Belgians, but the Dutch and Norwegians were also thought to have been approached about incorporation of parachute-qualified commandos or volunteers from their infantry.

The concept of a Polish squadron made sense; the Bardsea teams mentioned earlier would have benefited from being Jeep-borne, but at the time of writing no documentary evidence has come to light to support that ancient rumour. The rumour of an American SAS Regiment was dismissed as improbable, not the least because of the long-held US antipathy to having any of their personnel, units or formations commanded by foreigners. Other people had also heard a rumour about an American SAS unit, and in 2001 written evidence of the proposal was located. It can be found in the National Archives, Kew, in File WO171/369 War Office: Allied Expeditionary Force, North West Europe (British Element): War Diaries, Second World War, Airborne Corps HQ Troops: June 1944 Directive 3 Paragraph 2b Special Air Service Troops Order of Battle to be:

HQ Special Air Service Brigade
F Squadron Phantom

1st (Br) SAS Regt	2nd (Br) SAS Regt	3rd (Fr) SAS Regt
4th (Fr) SAS Regt	5th (Bel) SAS Sqn	6th (US) SAS Regt

The 6 SAS is thought to have been an SOE/OSS idea, and to comprise the NORSOG, the French and US Marine Corps operations groups, augmented by volunteers from 1st Ranger Battalion then arriving in Britain, and from parachute and glider units.

It appears this proposal was made by HQ Airborne Forces, HQ SAS Brigade and Special Forces HQ regarding the coordination of offensive operations behind enemy front lines before, during and after the invasion. There were to be a plethora of organizations inserting individuals, small teams or units into the rear areas. These included SOE, PWE and OSS agents and couriers, Jedburgh teams, Inter-Allied Missions, Operations Groups, OSS Weather Jumpers, Brissex, Ossex and Proust operatives, MI9/OSS-Y agents and POW Recovery Teams, Bardsea parties and SAS detachments. Any attempt to streamline the organization, communications and administrative apparatus would have been considered, and as the OGs and Bardsea parties may have appeared to some eyes to be in certain ways akin to SAS units, there was a degree of logic in the idea. Whatever else might have come about from a US SAS Regiment, mounting OGs etc. on armed jeeps would have made them even more formidable than they turned out to be in action in France. At some stage Lieutenant Colonel Serge Obolensky may also have been involved in discussions, but whether the members of NORSOG, a salty bunch at the best of times, would have taken to wearing red berets is an interesting point. But the proposal seems to have disappeared, in much the same way and apparently at the same time, as the Americans refused to accept the primacy of SOE (and SIS) in directing clandestine warfare on the Continent.

To return to the SAS Brigade which, by March 1944, included not only the five fighting units, but also a Brigade headquarters, with a combined total of forty-two all ranks including the brigadier, his batman and a signaller. That leads to communications.

Attached to Brigade headquarters, was F Squadron, Phantom. This new squadron was commanded by Major Jake Astor and had a strength of about 100 all ranks, each one expert in long-range wireless communications. Many Phantom personnel had also been trained in battlefield reconnaissance and observation, and in SIGINT to intercept Allied and German tactical radio networks. The men of F Squadron rightly considered themselves an elite, and had the task of keeping their own skills up to the mark (reading and sending Morse had to be practised constantly if fluency was to be maintained). They also ran the brigade wireless net, manned a rear-link to HQ Airborne Forces, and trained wireless operators for 1 and 2 SAS. The original SAS Signal Troop, Royal Signals, was a distant memory, and its Middle East War Establishment (MEVI/1095/1) was not relevant to the Overlord concept of operations. It included a base station, an RHQ section with five Jeeps FFW (fitted for wireless), a 3-ton truck, twelve operators, a cipher sergeant and two cipher operators and a cook among twenty-three all ranks, four Jeep-mounted squadron detachments (including one Greek one) and an Army HQ detachment. The European battleground would require something different, and it came from Phantom (with some help from the BBC). The Belgians and French had their own operators. HQ Squadron, 1 Airborne Corps Signal Regiment, also provided considerable help to the brigade. The regiments were equipped mainly with the famous J, or Jedburgh, wireless set, complete with aerial pack, hand/foot generator and spare parts packages. Brigade HQ was provided with a selection of teleprinters and high-powered wireless sets for contact with HQ Airborne Forces, Special Forces HQ and 21 Army Group and other, lower, headquarters. Transmissions to and from the field went through other locations and were sent mainly by means of very powerful transmitters owned and operated by the BBC. That body also trained some SAS personnel (and that may have included some from F Squadron) in the use of these transmitters, and in broadcasting for daily news bulletins, to be much appreciated by the detachments in the field.

Also available for SAS and Phantom patrols was a steam-powered generator; the boiler made by Stuart Turner Pumps Ltd., and the generator by Arthur Lyons & Co. Ltd. The boiler could be heated by wood chips, coal or even dried dung. It solved the problem of electricity supplies, and of the irksome hand-generator issued with Jed sets, but it was heavy (90lbs/50kgs) and noisy unless well-insulated or buried in a mini-bunker.

Departure of Bill Stirling

As soon as the matters of unit designations and berets had been resolved, more or less, a major row erupted over the tactical deployment of the brigade in France. At issue was the nature and locations of the missions allocated to the five regiments for the period D-1 to (approximately) D+15. The planners wanted the brigade to deploy, pre D-Day, detachments into the immediate rear of the coastal defence zone with the task of interdicting German reinforcements. They also wanted other detachments to attack *Luftwaffe* communications centres and airfields on D-1, and selected headquarters beyond the scope of Jedburgh-lead Resistance groups.

These targets had been selected by planners with no experience of Special Forces operations, and may have made tactical sense but flew in the face of experience and logic. The problems included making heavy drops in a flak-rich area; a large formation of *III.Flak-Korps*, later found to have over 100 88mm, and 120 multi-barreled 20mm guns, was deployed around the Somme estuary and Bayeux areas into which some of the SAS detachments were supposed to drop. Other issues included lack of ground cover and lack of time to reconnoitre routes and to conduct CTR, the impossibility of finding jeep routes in the dark and negotiating them in vehicles during curfew. Not the least were the dangers inherent in harassing alert, well-trained and angry *Panzer* divisions equipped with dozens, if not hundreds, of tanks, self-propelled guns, armoured personnel carriers and armoured cars.

The argument was vigorous and sustained. On the one hand were Lieutenant Colonels Stirling and Mayne, on the other staff officers from I Airborne Corps and SHAEF, with more or less helpful interjections from SFHQ and with Brigadier McLeod in the middle. On one side were the traditionalists – the ' do-as-you-are-ordered-or-resign because Sir knows best' school; on the other were the voices of experience of Special Forces operations. The issue of targeting seems to have been resolved fairly quickly. Airfield attacks were out of the question. The 320 or so *Luftwaffe* fighter, bomber and reconnaissance aircraft available to support the German defence forces were based well away from the invasion area, in well-defended airfields sited in thickly populated and intensively farmed countryside, regularly patrolled by mobile security units of the *Wehrmacht* and *Milice*. Interdiction of German reinforcements and supply columns was accepted without question, with the sensible proviso that each jeep should be equipped with either a British PIAT (Projector Infantry Anti-Tank), or a US 2.75-inch Rocket Launcher (Bazooka), both capable of disabling light armoured vehicles used by the Germans in France. The PIAT had, officially, a maximum effective range of 115 yards against moving armoured vehicles, and 350 yards against static vehicles, airfield dispersal sites or houses. The 2.75-inch Rocket Launcher had a quoted maximum effective range of 150 yards against armoured vehicles, but was neither reliable nor effective against anything better armoured than a half-track. Most SOE personnel, and Jedburgh teams, were trained to use the PIAT bombs fired from spigots – lengths of steel tube, spiked into tree-trunks, aimed with a modified rifle sight, and fired from a discreet distance by a long wire; a handy ambush weapon, and deadly if fired in barrages against tank laagers or supply dumps. Some SAS may have been taught that technique, but it did not fall comfortably into the 'shoot-and-scoot' European countryside tactics gradually evolving in Ayrshire as 6-pounder anti-tank guns, to be towed by jeeps, arrived along with trailers and machine guns which were married-up and tested. They could be landed by glider, and dropped (with difficulty) by parachute, and had first been issued to 2 SAS in Algeria. The original War Establishment had allowed for six 3-inch mortars and six 6-pounders (plus six 2-inch mortars for target illumination at night), although there are few records to indicate they were ever fired, let alone used on operations.

The main debate centred on operations in the coastal strip, the land between the Normandy coast and a line between, roughly, St Lô and Lisieux. The Resistance had supplied detailed information about the defences along the coast, and about field-works in the immediate hinterland. They had also provided information to supplement air reconnaissance of the whole of Normandy (and much of the rest of northern France) to assist the patient experts in Allied map-making units, and the British Ordnance Survey, in compiling 1:50,000 and other maps of the future battle area. Anyone with the smallest grasp of land warfare looking at maps, or of a few of the millions of pre-war holiday photographs provided by the British public, of the countryside around Bayeux and Caen would realize the idea of jeep-mounted operations there was seriously flawed. (The Inter-Services Topographical Department on behalf of the COSSAC planners had obtained the photographs by public appeal for snaps of the French coast and countryside; the result was overwhelming.) In the end the planners were made to see sense, and the SAS operational areas were moved further inland, and the targets changed. The task of inter-dicting enemy counter-attack forces in the rear of the fortified zone was to be dealt with in three ways. First by ground-attack aircraft armed with cannon and rockets or bombs; the dreaded *Jabos, Jagdbomber*, greatest goblin in German soldiers' battlefield demonology. The *Jabos* were to be controlled by RAF or USAAF air liaison teams operating with the leading units, and by the pilots searching for targets of opportunity during sweeps. Second, naval gunfire, controlled by RAF, Fleet Air Arm and USAAF fighter pilots until Air Observation Post light aircraft could use Normandy landing strips. Third, army heavy (155mm) and super-heavy (8-inch) artillery, scheduled to be available from D+2.

The decision to use ground attack aircraft was based on the know-ledge that Rommel would fight as close to the landings as possible, meaning on the beaches or in the coastal defence zone. As no German knew where the landings would take place, the key anti-invasion forces, the *Panzer, Panzer-Grenadier* and artillery (especially *nebel-werfer*, 'fog-throwers', multi-barrel rocket launcher) units, were based inland, ready to move as directed once the landing point was identified. That intention had been in part deduced by the planners' reading of Rommel's known battle tactics, but also by a flow of information from France and other sources, some unlikely. These other sources included SIGINT processed by Bletchley Park and the US equivalent, Arlington Hall, a former boarding school for girls outside Washington and manned by the Signals Intelligence Service. Both stations had deciphered signals traffic from key sources which revealed accurate information on the German forces and defences in France and Belgium. The main source was encoded traffic passed along a radio-teleprinter link between the main *Wehrmacht* HQ in France, that of the C.-in-C., Field Marshal von Rundstedt, and the

OKH in Berlin. The first operational Colossus 'computer' installed at Bletchley Park broke the code. The signal traffic revealed, among other things, regular detailed returns of the numbers and status of units, personnel, equipment and supplies, including ammunition states. The returns covered all units and formations in Army Group B, comprising the First and Fifteenth Armies, roughly north of a line running from the Loire estuary through Orleans to Lake Geneva, as well as returns from units in Army Group G, everything south to the Pyrenees and along the Mediterranean. Although the main area of interest for the SHAEF planners was the north, anything about *Panzer* or *Panzer-Grenadier* divisions in the south was needed, if only to plan how to interdict any move towards the invasion area. And that meant most of all, keeping aware of the location and status of the *2 SS Das Reich Panzer*, and the *17 SS Panzer-Grenadier*, divisions. If they arrived at the beachhead before a strong anti-tank screen had been formed they could cause havoc. All the more reason to ensure that the SAS were out of what would be a free-fire zone for Allied fighter-bombers, and to have a very powerful interdiction force such as rocket-firing ground attack aircraft on station above it during daylight hours.

One outcome of the argument was that Lieutenant Colonel Bill Stirling expressed, in writing, his lack of confidence in the abilities of his commanders. This action, it was in all probability coolly deliberate action, not a gesture, helped focus minds in airborne forces and 21 Army Group. In a major war a lieutenant colonel and commanding officer is an important person, but not all that important, so there may well have been some machinations by the Tartan Mafia on behalf of the brigade, not the man. Whatever the exact story, and it is unlikely that it will ever be known, Bill Stirling resigned his appointment as Commanding Officer of 2 SAS, voluntarily or otherwise. He does not appear to have made any statement about the reasons for his resignation; probably working on the basis of one of the precepts of leadership once taught to young officers; never explain, never complain. Later, David Stirling said of his older brother in the context of this sensible disagreement with a fatally flawed concept, '. . . he lost the battle but won the war'. Thereafter he was employed on minor administrative tasks, and left the Army soon after the war ended.

Major Brian Franks was appointed CO 2 SAS. He was an avuncular hotelier, well used to dealing with crises, real or imagined, and handling disaffected or disgruntled souls of all walks of life. He turned out to be an inspired commander, and helped 2 SAS settle down after its disjointed birth and disturbed formative years.

More Problems

The role of the SAS was further complicated by two decisions made at the highest levels of the Allied command, and that meant the Supreme Allied Commander Europe (SACEUR), General Eisenhower. (The SAS Brigade and SOE/OSS were theatre-level assets; their battlefield roles were set by SHAEF, although its operations were allocated in accordance with the missions of the Army Groups, or subordinate Armies, to which the regiments were in deep support.)

The first decision was that no uniformed Special Forces were to deploy onto the Continent before H-Hour (the hour at which the invasion was planned to start) on D-Day. The reason was to preserve secrecy of the date and possibly the location or at least general area, of the landings. That decision covered the SAS, OGs, the Jedburgh teams and Inter-Allied Missions, and stopped a number of operations stone dead in their tracks. It also covered, or appeared to cover, the Pathfinders for the British and US airborne divisions. These were to drop one hour ahead of the main force, and mark the DZs, and later glider LZs. They would use Halophane lights (low light source but wide visibility lenses of rippled glass), Eureka beacons, conventional marker lights, and smoke grenades to indicate the wind direction on the dawn and dusk LZs and S-Phones for ground-air contact. The risk of their being captured, or their bodies found, in time to initiate a full alert by the Germans was considered unlikely. In any case their presence was considered so important to the overall success of the Utah and Sword Beach landings as to justify dropping them as planned.

The second decision was less dramatic and related to the problems of MI9. By late 1943 a considerable pool of evaders, and some escapers, was forming in northern France and southern Belgium as the *Gestapo* and *Milice* closed in on ratlines in southern France when it was occupied after the Allied landings in Algeria. These pools, usually congregated in rough camps in woodland, were mainly composed of aircrew evaders, but with a sprinkling of escapers from many Allied nations and services, many needing medical treatment but all undernourished. The Belgian and French organizers were desperate to have these 'packages' moved to safety, so SFHQ and MI9, in the shape of Colonel Crockatt, once of MI(R), requested help from the SAS Brigade, by way of HQ Airborne Forces. A number of operations for removing the packages were planned, and that involved the harried senior SAS officers in more briefings and discussions. Some of the suggestions involved insertion of SAS jeep-mounted patrols, landed by glider or Dakota on rough strips prepared by American airborne engineers, complete with small bulldozers, all landed by US CG4 Hadrian gliders. The jeep patrols were to escort columns of packages, on foot or in lorries or buses, to the airstrips for evacuation by Dakotas or snatched gliders, with fighter cover. Commonsense prevailed, and in any case the 'snatch' equipment was not readily available in Britain until well after D-Day. The SAS were to be involved in successful recovery operations, Operations Marathon and Bonaparte. Later veterans were to say that of all their operations these were the ones which gave them most satisfaction.

SOE's Air Supply Section, medical staff from Red Cross and the Royal Army Medical Corps, and nutritionists from the Ministry of Food in London, devised an Invalid Ration Load capable of sustaining 200 'weakened' men for one day, fitted into a standard Mark III, parachute container, for dropping to these camps. It consisted of two kegs, each weighing 90lbs/ 43kgs, containing identical loads of meat extract, arrowroot powder (for alleviating diarrhoea), condensed milk, sugar, tea, boiled sweets, salt, cigarettes, matches, and chocolate. Two boxes within each container contained brandy (two bottles) and 20lbs/9kgs of Army biscuits, the infamous, but nutritious, 'Biscuits; Hard, 32-Hole'. These loads were dropped to MI9 reception committees and were a boon in the weeks before D-Day, as travel and movement of food supplies inside France was reduced to almost nil due to Allied bombing and then Resistance sabotage.

In April 1944 another formation was co-located with the brigade and may have received some help with training, pay and rations. This was S Force, one of a series of 'lettered' small task forces set up to conduct special operations in support of the landings, or of subsequent operations in Europe. For example, T-Forces (there were ostensibly two, one British and Commonwealth, the other US, but by some accounts each nation had several) were to seize, search and restore or maintain in working order technical installations in the occupied countries and Germany. Another part of their work was to acquire, by fair means or foul, any technical material that might be of value, militarily or commercially, to the Allies, or at least to the nation deploying the team which either got there first or spotted and acquired the prize. S-Force was a land-based deception force, equipped with US White Scout cars, sort of shortened M3 half-tracks with four wheels and no tracks. Why it was attached to the SAS Brigade in Ayrshire remains unclear, unless it was just for 'pay and rations'. One source has suggested that there was a proposal to insert a mobile deception unit into the enemy rear areas on D-2, part of Operation Fortitude South and S Force was certainly tasked with a move to southern England with the brigade, but the exact relationship remains obscure. (S Force teams did land in Normandy, but no one knew what to do with them until that ever-resourceful Canadian General Guy Simmonds found work for them in their proper war role.)

S Force probably made few calls on the SAS Brigade, which was just as well as it had enough administrative problems of its own. These were growing rapidly, and increasingly diverging from the not inconsiderable requirements of the airborne forces and their parachute, air-landing and base formations, which included virtually every arm and service of the army, and some of the Royal Air Force. The requirements of the SAS Brigade were in many ways unique, and were a hybrid of army, air force, navy, commando, airborne and SOE supplies and equipment, further complicated by coming from units provided by three nations, two with limited visible means of support; someone has to pay for military supplies, after all. The obvious solution was for the brigade to have its own base organization and, after some debate, that proposal was agreed to by the War Office, with several provisos. The main one was that all supplies or equipment common to all or most units in the

Airborne Corps would continue to be supplied by that formation's base organization; sensible, but a nightmare for the brigade quartermaster staff, as the SAS base was at some distance from that of the corps.

The new administrative system was implemented in early May, less than five weeks before D-Day. The brigade was still stationed in Ayrshire, but about to move to Gloucestershire, to a holding area prior to deploying into action. The new base area was to be at Williamstrip Camp, near the village of Down Ampney, about eight miles from the brigade holding area at Fairford, although another site at Coln St Aldwyn, north of Fairford was also used.

Operational planning for the brigade had been started before it was formed, and evolved with help from veterans as noted above, up to and beyond D-Day. More operations were planned than took place, as the tactical situation changed. As the saying goes, 'no plan survives contact with the enemy (or reality) unscathed'. It was during that phase of development that the distance between SFHQ and Ayrshire was most felt to disadvantage. (Apart from Ian Collins and the QM branch, HQ Airborne force did nothing except slow communications down.) Possibly the greatest problem facing the British regiments was lack of officers, not just squadron commanders, with any operational experience, let alone airborne or special operations.

The plans drawn up in late winter/early spring 1944 for SAS operations in support of the first two phases of the invasion – establishing a beachhead and clearing the invasion area – envisaged insertion of around fifty missions. (Ultimately only twenty-eight were mounted, plus three others, one part of Fortitude South, the other an unsuccessful assassination attempt, and a successful POW recovery mission.) One of the major outcomes of the 'Bill Stirling incident' was the deletion of the tasks to delay the *Panzer* forces assumed to be in the St Lô and Lisieux areas. Instead of the bizarre plan and timetable for SAS operations, a more sensible alternative was adopted. This involved three airborne and air-landing operations, Coup de Main, Mallard and Tonga, intended to isolate German *Panzer* forces from the invasion beaches.

Jeeps and Gliders

The result of the protests by experienced SAS officers, supported by Brigadier McLeod, was that the planners moved the operational zones away from the beaches towards the outer edge of the invasion area. The prime requirement was to insert the SAS detachments where they were needed to support the overall battle-plan, and where there was an active resistance group and, if at all possible, one designated to receive a Jedburgh team. There was no question, and never had been, of any possibility of independent operations. The only means of insertion was by air, but in order to deliver as many jeep-mounted detachments as quickly as possible using the minimum of aircraft, gliders were to be used. At one stage it was envisaged that there would be a significant number of glider and aircraft insertions and extractions, using existing or new landing grounds, to move not just SAS detachments but also troops from either the British and US airborne divisions into France; the idea of the Airborne Army again. As a result several RAF pilots, seconded to Airborne Forces to act as Ground Liaison Officers during the early days of the invasion, were dropped into France along with SAS teams.

The British manned gliders were owned by the RAF but crewed by Army personnel serving in the Glider Pilot Regiment. Early in the war some Air Force officers had reacted with near-hysteria to the possibility of Army personnel being competent to fly aircraft, forgetting that the RAF was born of the Army (and to this day RAF officers wear brown gloves with black shoes; a remnant of that heritage). When the issue was first raised in 1941 the then Deputy Chief of the Air Staff, Air Marshal Sir Arthur Harris, later to be AOC Bomber Command, expressed the view that:

> . . . the idea that semi-skilled, un-picked personnel (infantry corporals have, I believe, even been suggested) could with a maximum of training be entrusted with the piloting of these troop carriers is fantastic. The operation of gliders is equivalent to forced landing the largest sized aircraft without engine aid – than which there is no higher test of piloting skill.

He, once an infantry bugler, not even an NCO (serving with the Rhodesian Regiment in German South West Africa, at the start of the Great War) and later in that war an excellent pilot, was incorrect, hence the Glider Pilot Regiment. In 1944 'heavy drop' technology was in its infancy as the Allies lacked transport aircraft capable of carrying large loads internally and disgorging in flight. In Europe Stirling and Halifax bombers were adapted to carry large parachute loads, such as jeeps, or a jeep and 6-pounder anti-tank gun, slung under the fuselage, which did little for handling the aircraft in flight. During dropping trials there was a significant level of damage to such loads, despite strenuous efforts by the Central Landing Establishment and the Parachute Test and Trials Unit, RAF Henlow, to reduce the rate of fall, oscillation, and impact. HQ Airborne Forces had decided to insert as many jeep-equipped detachments as possible by glider. Accordingly a special detachment of the Glider Pilot Regiment was formed to support the SAS Brigade, and SOE/OSS missions such as the Bardsea parties. The original plan involved a detachment of twelve American CG4 Hadrian gliders, and twelve two-man crews. To make best use of limited manpower twelve SAS men were to be cross-trained as co-pilots; they would revert to their operational roles after landing. The Hadrian was used as it was reusable after delivering vehicles; the entire front of the cockpit could be swung upwards for loading and unloading, whereas the British Horsa nose had to be removed, the nose wheel discarded and ramps used to unload vehicles. (In theory the nose could be re-mounted, and the control cables re-connected, but that rarely appears to have happened.) The Hadrians, it was hoped, would be recovered by either C-47s landing and towing them off, or using the new 'snatch and go' technique, originally developed to remove raiding parties from the scene of their missions, mainly used (in Burma) to remove unloaded gliders for a second trip.

The SAS Brigade headquarters canvassed its regiments for volunteers to undertake the special, less intensive training course than even the attenuated Assistant Glider Pilot one. Six men are reported to have completed their course and qualified, entitling them to wear the small co-pilots brevet on their chests. (Glider pilots proper wore a large brevet, or wing, to a design worn now by Army Air Corps pilots.) General Browning qualified, as he was photographed wearing one, but not a parachute badge. The group included a Captain (later Lieutenant Colonel) Paul Murphy who also served in SOE. In the end only eleven crews (possibly including six SAS men) were posted to X Flight, created for landing SAS units behind German lines. (A GPR flight usually had eight crews.) The Flight was to be equipped with Hadrian gliders, capable of carrying one jeep and a trailer, or one jeep and a 6-pounder anti-tank gun, and the pilots were selected on the basis of having flown Hadrians into landing grounds on Sicily on Operation Ladbroke, the airborne element of Operation Husky. For many of the British pilots that was their first long flight in a Hadrian, and nineteen were accompanied by a USAAF pilot flying as a volunteer co-pilot cum instructor; a gesture much appreciated by the British pilots.

Ready at Last

Whatever the means of insertion, the SAS were as ready for war as time and circumstances allowed. Their first operation in northern Europe, however, was not offensive operations in support of the Resistance. It was a strange and much misunderstood deception manoeuvre designed to help the Allied divisions spearheading the invasion assemble on their DZs and landing grounds free from German interference.

Finale

Titanic IV

Operation Titanic IV was the first operation carried out by SAS troops in north-west Europe. Six men and one aircraft were involved, and although Titanic IV is mentioned in several books about the regiment it is usually dismissed as only a small part of a deception ploy, implying that it was almost an irrelevancy. Closer scrutiny confirms that it was indeed a tiny part of a huge plan encompassing, but not restricted to, Operations Fortitude North and South, without which the invasion of Normandy would not have been successful.

Hitler's Hunch

Hitler guessed that if the invasion was stymied, on the beaches or inland, the Allies would not be able, or willing, to try again for a long time; something which would allow at least forty divisions to be released for service in the *Ostland*. He, and the OKW, the *Oberkommando der Wehrmacht*, the German Army High Command, assessed that any landing in France would be followed by another, either in Norway (the Allied Operation Jupiter plans) or in the Balkans. To counter those threats he ordered eleven divisions to be kept in Norway, and twenty in the Balkans, but only forty-one in France. His intuition (or remarkably sound tactical judgement) about the proposed landing site mentioned earlier was correct, as was the assessment of Admiral Theodor Krancke. The

Admiral based that on three separate elements. First, *Luftwaffe* photo-reconnaissance flights over south-east England and the Thames estuary (some made by fast, high-flying jet-propelled Arado Ar234 aircraft, out of reach of Allied air defences), failed to reveal any build-up of landing craft opposite the Pas de Calais, the Germans' favoured landing site. Second, Allied bombers had pounded *Kriegsmarine* shore batteries and control centres between Boulogne and the north coast of the Cotentin peninsula, all covering approaches to the Seine, Somme and Douvre estuaries. Third, the railways leading to the Pas de Calais had also been heavily bombed, but not those leading to Cherbourg and Brittany. Both Hitler and the Admiral guessed that the Allies would use airborne forces against the Cotentin and Brittany, and both took what precautions they could. Hitler in particular recalled the terrible casualties suffered by *Luftwaffe* airborne troops in Crete, and those of the Allies in Sicily, and ordered preparations to be made accordingly. During May three new units were deployed to the Cotentin; the *91 Luftlande-Division* was switched from Nantes, its intended destination, to La-Haye-du-Puits, west of Carentan, *Fallschirmjäger-Regiment 6* was moved into the area around that town, and the *Stellungs-Werfer-Regiment 101* positioned south of Cherbourg. The *91 Luftlande-Division* had two regiments (six battalions) of infantry and various artillery units, and a former reconnaissance turned mobile infantry battalion, *Fusilier-Bataillon 91*, mounted on bicycles for anti-paratroop operations. The *Fallschirmjäger-Regiment 6* was very strong for that theatre and time, with fifteen companies; twelve rifle and three heavy weapons. They were manned by fully trained paratroops, most having completed nine descents, including three at night. They did not have parachutes in France, but had the confidence brought about by successfully completing paratroop training. Each rifle company had twice as many machine guns as *Wehrmacht* infantry ones, and there was a good range of support weapons. No. 13 (Heavy Mortar) Company had eight heavy machine guns and nine 120mm mortars; deadly in the hands of well-trained crews, such as men who had survived the *Ostland Kreig* to become instructors to paratroop units. No. 14 (Tank Hunting) Company was equipped with four 7.5cm anti-tank guns, thirty-four *Panzerschreck* Rocket Launchers and six heavy machine guns, and No. 15 (Assault Pioneer) Company had two 8cm mortars and six machine guns. The *Stellungswerfer Regiment 101* had three battalions of heavy multi-barrelled or multiple-racked rocket launchers, the dreaded 15cm *Nebelwerfer*, (fog-throwers), 'Moaning Minnies' to the Allies, and 24cm *Heulen Kuh*, 'Howling Cow' or *Stuka zu Fuss*, Foot Stukas, to the German foot soldiers. Each battalion had three batteries, each with six launchers, giving fifty-four units, most with eight barrels, providing impressive firepower to the defending forces. The regiment was trained in anti-airborne tactics, and was divided between the east and west coasts of the Cotentin, and could move between each as required. In other words, the Germans had strong forces ready to meet the Allied airborne forces, and any deception manoeuvres to conceal the exact location of the landing sites were going to be important.

Operation Titanic was the overall code-name allocated to simulated paratroop landings behind the German coastal defence zone, intended to disperse German anti-paratroop forces (usually battalions of light infantry mounted on bicycles) and to draw attention away from real landings. Titanic was part of Operation Taxable, itself a small but vital part of Operation Fortitude South, the deception plan for Overlord.

The original Taxable plan included several simulated paratroop landings, of which Operations Titanic I–IV are the best known. Only IV was mounted due to lack of transport aircraft, and scarcity of SAS troops due to the delays in getting 1 and 2 SAS back to Britain.

Titanic I was to simulate an airborne division landing on a DZ north of the River Seine, in an upland area called the Pays du Caux, south of St Valery. The aim was to lure enemy reserves, especially the formidable *12 SS Panzer-Division Hitler Jugend*, north of the river and away from the invasion beaches and the few (deliberately) undamaged bridges over the river, leading to the Juno and Gold assault areas. A subsidiary aim was to reinforce the Germans' fixation that the invasion would be in the Pas de Calais, further reinforced by deception operations off the coast between Le Havre and Dieppe, simulating an invasion fleet heading for the Pas de Calais. One involved motor launches towing barrage-balloons painted with metallic varnish to provide strong returns on German sea surveillance radar screens. Other devices on the launches produced smoke, and 'loud nautical sounds'. The launches would advance beneath orbiting RAF Lancaster bombers from 281 Squadron dropping aluminium chaff called 'Window', to augment the balloon's radar-signature. A similar operation involving 617 (Dambuster) Squadron, dispensed Window off the Pas de Calais, and around the Somme battlefield of the Great War, just behind the coastal defence zone. (The use of 617 Squadron further demonstrates the importance of this deception plan.)

Titanic II was to simulate an airborne landing in eastern Normandy, intended to hold enemy mobile groups west of the Seine and away from the beachhead area.

Titanic III, a simulated parachute drop south of Caen, was to coincide with Operation Tonga, landings by the British and Canadian 6th Airborne Division north of the city; the aim here was to lure enemy reaction forces south, away from the real DZs around the Orne bridges.

Titanic IV was to coincide with US landings west of Utah beach, on the eastern side of the Cotentin peninsula. It (IV) would be to the west of St Lô and was intended to draw enemy forces away from the coastal area. Titanic IV would operate in conjunction with Operation Bigdrum, involving more launches fitted with deception gear, and supported by radio countermeasures Short Stirling and B-17 aircraft, all jamming German sea surveillance and coastal artillery fire-control radars on the Pointe de Barfleur, the north-east tip of the Cotentin peninsula. Another part of Bigdrum, closely associated with Titanic IV, was simulation of a massive stream of aircraft approaching the Cotentin peninsula from the west, as if to make a parachute drop between Coutances and Avranches. This was to be simulated by Window dropped from more RAF Stirlings. This force would leave the English coast at Portland Bill and fly south and around the Channel Islands. Window would be scattered from a point just outside the pre-plotted radar envelope of German defences on Guernsey and Jersey. This false stream of aircraft would parallel the course taken slightly later by US aircraft carrying the 82nd and 101st Airborne Divisions on Operations Chicago, Elmira, Galveston and Hackensack, for the seizure of the landward ends of roads running on embankments crossing low-lying ground behind the Utah assault areas; ground that had been inundated by the Germans as a defence measure. The JPS regarded the role of these airborne divisions as critical to the successful exploitation of the Utah landings. The second airborne wave would include gliders carrying bulldozers to enlarge the exits from the roads and to make gun positions, and anti-tank guns to repel the expected counter-attacks by *Panzers* and *Panzer-Grenadiers* in half-tracks. Therefore anything which might ensure the success of Chicago, Elmira, Galveston and Hackensack was to be welcomed.

Their secondary mission was to protect the southern flank of US VII Corps landing on Utah, and also to be prepared to exploit southward through Carentan. The latter task was to be carried out by destroying two bridges on the main Carentan highway and the railroad bridge west of it, by seizing and holding the la Barquette lock, and finally by establishing a bridgehead over the River Douve north-east of Carentan.

The 101st was to be reinforced by its glider-borne infantry and artillery units landing at dusk on D-Day. The 82nd Airborne was to protect the approaches to Utah from the German *91 Luftlande Division*. On 25 May it was reported by SIS or the Resistance as harboured north of Saint Saveur le Vicomte. (The German forces in Normandy were certainly weak, but one of their generals said later that although badly equipped, '. . . *his best weapons were his young NCOs, battle-hardened in Russia*'.)

Intervention

The decision to drop two airborne divisions followed by glider landings was disputed by Air Commander-in-Chief, SHAEF, Air Marshal Sir Trafford Leigh-Mallory. He felt that dropping two airborne formations close together was disastrous, on the basis of airborne operations in Sicily. He had earlier objected strongly to US troop carriers overflying the peninsula which was known to be studded with flak sites, carefully plotted and reported by Resistance. The troop-carriers would have to overfly these at low-level and in a full moon to reach the DZs. Leigh-Mallory does not appear to have offered an alternative plan for securing the exits to the area and the

Carentan bridges. He predicted, although no objective evidence used to support his view has been located, that possibly only 50 per cent of the paratroops and 30 per cent of the glider-borne forces would land safely. He added that severe aircraft losses would jeopardize the numerous airborne operations planned to support the Allied advance into Germany. This intervention delayed a final decision on Titanic IV, among many other operations, including the entire airborne and air-landing assault on the Cotentin peninsula. In that time Leigh-Mallory appealed to the senior British officer in SHAEF, Air Chief Marshal Sir Arthur Tedder, General Eisenhower's Deputy Commander. Sir Arthur ruled that the airborne operations must proceed, but that failed to placate Leigh-Mallory. On 30 May he again wrote to General Eisenhower, re-stating his contention. General Eisenhower and his inner staff considered the matter but insisted the airborne operations had to proceed, writing (to Leigh-Mallory) that, '. . . a strong airborne attack in the region is essential to Overlord and must go on . . . every single thing which may diminish these hazards must be worked out to the last detail'. Eisenhower afterwards said that deciding against the advice of his senior air commander was harder than deciding to proceed with the invasion after listening to the weather forecast for the invasion period.

But the point had been made – Titanic IV was far from trivial – it was very important. It would reduce the risk to the paratroops and their glider-borne colleagues when they were landing and once they were on the ground. The operation assumed even greater importance if the force that landed had been decimated by flak or enemy night fighters.

SAS Tasking

The Titanic IV mission was allocated to the SAS Brigade because, although it was to be in direct support of the 82nd and 101st Airborne divisions and into the American sector of the invasion area, there were no US troops available; no 6 SAS, for example. (The seven-man USMC OG would have been ideal.) The task was allocated to 1 SAS; some accounts state the task was 'offered' to Paddy Mayne by a junior staff officer, and that it was rejected on the grounds that it was an 'intelligence' operation, then 'offered' to, and accepted by, Lieutenant Colonel Franks, 2 SAS. No evidence has been found to support these contentions. The live element of Operation Titanic IV was conducted by troops from 1 SAS; three men from A Squadron, Lieutenant Frederick James Poole, Troopers Dawson and Saunders, and three from B Squadron, Lieutenant Norman Harry Fowles and Troopers Hurst and Merryweather. They faced considerable opposition. Enemy forces in the south Cotentin reportedly included four major formations. *243 Infanterie-Division* was tasked with the static defence of the west coast of the peninsula and had its headquarters in Périers, north of Coutances. Further south was the elusive *91 Luftlande-Division*, and to the east was *354 Infanterie-Division,* which had a counter-attack role against sea or airborne landings along the coastal area of Normandy. It was based east of St Lô, with its headquarters in the small country town of Canisy. The fourth formation, *Schnelle Brigade 30*, was based to the south-west of St Lô, with headquarters in Cerences, south-west of Coutances. The brigade had at least one mobile unit trained in quick-reaction anti-airborne operations, mounted on bicycles; a primitive mode of transport but sufficient for patrolling roads and country lanes quickly and silently. The SAS Brigade Operational Instruction section on enemy dispositions then went on to state that:

> . . . all that is certain is that on D-Day the towns in the area will be full of troops at a high state of readiness; some of these troops may be on their way to the beaches. A vigorous response to Titanic IV is probable; formed units could easily be on the DZ within one and a half hours and motor-cycle or cavalry patrols should be reconnoitring within half an hour of landing.

On 27 May the bulk of the SAS Brigade moved from Ayrshire to holding camps near airfields in the Cotswolds. The troops arrived late on 27 May and those detailed for operations between D-Day and D+14 moved from Cirencester station to a holding area, a transit camp near RAF Fairford. The camp held a large number of men as the teams for Operations Titanic IV, Bulbasket,

Houndsworth, Dingson, Samwest and Gain were incarcerated there, along with the brigade command and administrative staff; nearly 500 men.

The two teams for Titanic IV were selected by the commanders of A and B Squadrons. The six men were apparently not told of their mission until after they arrived at Fairford. An account of this appears in *Operation Bulbasket* by Paul McCue. This extract is based on the personal testimony of Captain Peter Tonkin, OC A Troop, B Squadron, 1 SAS, a veteran of commando operations in the Middle East, and of SAS and SRS operations in North Africa, Sicily and Italy. He took part in Operation Bulbasket, and dropped into France on D-Day; the book gives full account of the mission. He was briefed about Bulbasket on 29 May, in the makeshift operations room (a marquee) at Fairford, by Paddy Mayne and the brigade Intelligence Officer, Captain Michael Foot, later Professor M.R.D. Foot.

While Tonkin was reasonably happy with his own briefing, he was horrified when he learned of the orders given to two other officers. To quote:

> Lieutenants Fowles and Poole, both relatively new to the Regiment, were to undertake an operation called 'Titanic' which involved two officers and four troopers parachuting into the Carentan peninsula and accompanying large-scale droppings of dummy paratroops. Once on the ground their job was to create the maximum amount of noise and confusion, thus attracting German units towards themselves and away from the invasion beaches. The thing which does stick firmly in my mind is that the two 'Titanic' officers were briefed separately but on the same day I was. They were new to the SAS and to active service. We – the old hands amongst us – were appalled at the suicide nature of the job they were given but successfully resolved the doubts they had by telling them what a wonderful job it was and how we were jealous. I am positive the next day (30 May) Titanic was cancelled. [The day of Leigh-Mallory's final intervention.] They were so disappointed that we (stupidly) cheered them up by showing our genuine concern and relief that it was off and we had quite

216

a few drinks in the Mess. I am also positive that the day after that Titanic was put on again and I can remember the two of them coming out of Paddy's command tent as white as sheets. We were so disturbed that Harry Poat (Major and 2 I/C of 1 SAS) told Paddy of the circumstances. I believe he told them it was volunteers only and they had the right to withdraw with honour.

The two subalterns elected to continue. The mission required the six men to attract notice by attacking traffic on the St Lô-Périers road, the present day D900, during the hours of darkness. It carried the traffic between the headquarters of VIII German Corps in St Lô and *243 Infanterie-Division* in Périers, and the SAS action would, it was hoped, establish the presence of live paratroops on the ground. They were then to lie low until overtaken by the Allied offensive, assumed at the time of the briefing to be 18 June.

After talking to Paddy Mayne, Lieutenants Fowles and Poole carried on with their preparations. These included studying the 1:250,000 scale maps (Sheets T3a and 8) of the area around the DZ. This was at Grid T3569, near the village of Marigny. On 30 May the teams left Fairford and travelled to another holding station, this time slightly less austere than the tents at Fairford. They were housed in Hassell Hall, and joined the Bulbasket and Houndsworth teams who had spent a couple of days in London being briefed at SFHQ on the finer points of their operations with the Shipwright Resistance circuit, and the respective roles of SOE agents in the field, and of Jedburgh teams. There is no record of the Titanic team being briefed on the presence of the Resistance in their prospective operational area, but it appears that the local circuit had been informed by SFHQ of the likely presence of a small party of paratroops in the area.

Departure

On 5 June Paddy Mayne travelled to Hassell Hall for a final word with his men. It is not clear whether the four troopers were allowed to eat and socialize with the officers; even if the regiment was considered egalitarian by the standards of the time they were probably more comfortable apart. The Hall was busy with SOE agents, their conducting officers and staff officers from SOE as well as the SAS officers. The SAS officers spent much of the day with jigsaws, watching a film and chatting with two young women who helped them with the puzzles. The SAS troops obviously did not know who the two women were; Paul McCue reveals that one was Violette Szabo, about to depart on her second mission to France. It was her last; she was captured by the Germans, interrogated and sent to Ravensbrück concentration camp where she was executed in 1945. Also close by were the three members of Jedburgh Team Hugh who were to fly with the Bulbasket reconnaissance team in Halifax MA-T, a Mark V version, on Mission Politician. The three Jedburghs were a French weapons/demolitions instructor, Capitaine L.L. Helgouach, wireless operator, Lieutenant R. Meyer, and the team leader Captain William Crawshay, 8 RWF. (For his subsequent actions in France William Crawshay was awarded a DSO, a *Croix de Guerre*, and appointed to the *Legion d'Honneur*.)

Just before 20:00 hours the Titanic and Bulbasket teams collected their Bergen rucksacks, radio and weapons and travelled by car to the airfield to collect their parachutes and pigeons. Tempsford appeared to be filled with aircraft. Among the first aircraft to take-off were the Halifax aircraft of 138 Squadron flying the two Titanic missions. Seven were allocated to Titanic I (plus four Stirlings from 149 Squadron flying from RAF Methwold, Suffolk to deliver Window) and one for Titanic IV; other Stirlings were to drop Window for Titanic IV.

Titanic I went ahead as planned, despite a low cloud base of 1,000 feet over the DZ areas, which lay about 250 feet above sea level. Seven Halifax BII aircraft from 138 Squadron took part. Four dropped the dummy paratroops and packages through the Joe-holes, and three, plus the Stirlings, dropped Window. The operation appears to have gone as planned.

Arrival

The eighth Halifax, NF-M, flown by Flight Lieutenant Johnson, carried the Titanic IV teams and containers. It took off 'on time', and was logged back into Tempsford at 03:00 hours on 6 June; the log entry simply states 'Dropped Party'; the RAF had played its part, and delivered the SAS teams to the DZ. The troops had jumped but it was not as simple as the log indicates.

The Halifax made an accurate landfall near Avranches and commenced the run-in to the DZ, and when the aircraft was estimated to be eight minutes away the navigator appears to have switched on the dispatcher's red standby light. But for some reason, stated as a malfunction in the lights, it changed to green, Go, almost immediately. When that happens there is no time to think; dispatcher and paratroops are staring at the light, mesmerized. When it changes the dispatcher screams 'Go', and they go – fast. The result of the malfunctioning light was that the two teams were dropped about seven minutes ahead of schedule, at 00:20 hours. They may have been momentarily flummoxed by the malfunctioning lights, and there appears to have been a slight pause before No. 2 in the stick followed Lieutenant Fowles through the Joe-hole; just a few seconds, enough to scatter the first man from the others. And to make matters worse, the last man, Lieutenant Poole, tripped over his leg-bag and 'rang the bell', knocking himself out in the process. (He must have been last as no one reported seeing him stumble.) The majority landed some two kilometres north-west of the intended DZ.

No report of dropping containers or the sight of Very lights or the sound of simulated rifle fire have been located. When the parties rallied it was discovered that Lieutenants Poole and Fowles were missing. The four troopers buried their parachutes and, as the visibility was good, carried out a prolonged and widespread search for the containers. None were located, nor was there any sign of the two subalterns. The four troopers were on their own. As it was now 03:00 hours, and there was a glimmer of light in the east, they decided to follow as best they could the instruction issued at Fairford. They spread out around the DZ and planted their Lewes bombs and withdrew. The bombs exploded, but failed to attract any immediate attention. The party moved to the north away from the landing area and hid in a thick hedge. They stayed there all day and saw no movement apart from a patrol of German bicycle troops on the St Lô-Carentan road. That evening, at about 20:00 hours, they were contacted by a member of the local Resistance, named as Monsieur Edouard le Duc. How he located them is not known, unless they were spotted by a farmer or farm worker in or near the hedge. Monsieur le Duc advised the team – in what language they communicated is not known – that he would lead them away from the area later that night. He departed, but returned after about three hours, and led them westwards for about two miles to the ruins of an old abbey, possibly the Maison de Marais, next to the present day D 900, between St Lô and Périers. Monsieur le Duc helped the troopers find a hiding place, and then departed. The party remained hidden throughout D-Day, undisturbed and content to be safe; sounds of battle would have been faintly heard from the east. Monsieur le Duc returned early the following morning, at around 01:00 hours, bringing some food and cider but leaving soon afterwards. Later that morning the troopers' spirits rose considerably when Monsieur le Duc returned with Lieutenant Poole. He looked somewhat battered, and after the Frenchman departed explained what had happened since leaving the aircraft. Apparently when the jump light changed from red to green and the dispatcher yelled, or screamed as most do, he, Poole, in his haste to leave the aircraft had stumbled and 'rang the bell' on the far side of the Joe-hole. The next thing he remembered was coming-to on the ground, still in his parachute harness. He checked his watch and realized he had been unconscious for about forty-five minutes. He managed to disentangle himself and buried the parachute. He also wrote a brief note explaining the circumstances of his arrival, and that there was no sign of the other troops. The message was dispatched by his pigeon, which had patiently endured the exit, uncontrolled descent and long wait before its temporary owner came to his senses. At some stage he appears to have lost the MCR-1, and there is no record of how, or where, he disposed of his Lewes bombs. At some time on D-Day he appears to have made contact with a farmer who hid him and advised Monsieur le Duc.

The party remained in the abbey for three days. They were not idle, and established a daily routine for camp tasks, such as they were, and patrolling the immediate area, moving out as much as four miles, but finding nothing of significance. They were supplied with food by members of the local Resistance, who took consider-able risks in moving about in the rear of a battle zone full of nervous enemy troops. The nervousness was caused not just by the invasion, which many German soldiers instinctively realized spelt the beginning of the end of the Thousand Year Reich, but also by Resistance operations throughout the Cotentin. According to a detailed report prepared in July 1944 by OSS SF Detachment 10, attached to First US Army, and in the immediate post-landing days working with VII Corps pushing westwards from the Utah beaches, there was prolonged and vigorous action by the local Resistance circuits throughout the Cotentin. This included action on 5–6 June in accordance with Plan Vert, sabotage of railway lines across northern France to cause a delay of six hours to rail movements. (Six hours because the logistical elements of the Overlord battle plan for D+5 onwards depended on these lines.) In the Cotentin the main line linking Cherbourg and Paris was cut at Lieuxaint between Valognes and Carentan; also the Cherbourg – Coutances line near La-Haye-du-Puits. 'Inter-urbans', rural tramways, and narrow-gauge railways were also severed, and the turntable at Valognes put out of action, isolating the station's complement of railway engines in the engine shed. Also in accordance to a plan devised by COSSASC and SOE/OSS, and initiated by a BBC coded broadcast ('It is hot at Suez'), there was a concerted effort by all circuits to cut telephone and telegraph communications between Cherbourg, the Channel Islands and the rest of France. Particular attention was paid to cutting underground cables around Périers, and to keeping them cut. This little town was a communications hub through which ran many lines linking headquarters and defence sites. (The cables had been located and sabotage sites selected during the previous year; at one time there was a large file of reports and maps plotting German and *Milice* power and telecommunications links in France, based on Resistance surveys. The author and some others studied part of it in the 1950s but at the time of writing it had not been traced in the National Archives or any other location.)

The railways were strongly guarded as a group of enthusiastic 'unregistered', or freelance resisters, had sabotaged the Cherbourg turntable shortly before the landings, and the Germans had doubled the guards at key points, and reinforced their roving patrols.

It is worth mentioning that the report also describes in some detail the use of Resistance men as volunteer guides, an idea discarded by COSSAC during the planning phase of the Jedburghs. 'Guiding' included leading groups of paratroops, dropped well away from their DZs to their assembly points, showing infantry and engineer patrols safe routes towards, into or through enemy defence lines, and going into enemy held territory themselves to obtain information on troop dispositions and strengths. The Americans were much more innovative than the British in this respect, and also trained some Resistance men as observers and inserted them by parachute or Piper Cub light aircraft into enemy territory. These men were sometimes equipped with wireless sets, if short-term or 'tactical' observers, returned through the front lines on foot or were overrun by advancing forces.

On 10 June Monsieur le Duc once again appeared at the abbey, and once more with a pleasant surprise – Lieutenant Fowles. The Frenchman departed soon afterwards, and the rest of the troops were able to recount their experiences since leaving the aircraft. Apparently Lieutenant Fowles had landed one field away from the DZ and had spent a considerable time searching for the others and the containers. He hid for a few days, occasionally sniping at some German soldiers but without apparent success. He also cut a few telephone wires strung along the side of a road leading to a German headquarters, again without being hunted. At some time in the afternoon, without volunteering an explanation to his colleagues, Lieutenant Fowles left the abbey but returned again at 23:00 hours. That night the group held a discussion and it was decided to stay in the abbey until overrun, in accordance with the order issued in England. Their rations would have been running low by that time, but the food from the Resistance would have helped.

Nothing much seems to have happened for the next two weeks. On 25 June, well past the date the Allies were supposed to arrive, Monsieur le Duc appeared with three US paratroops; escaped prisoners of war. They were all from the 508th Parachute Infantry Regiment, 82nd Airborne Division. They were Captain Berry, a medical officer, and two unidentified privates, one wounded. All three had been dropped near Edenville on the night of 5–6 June, but well away from their DZs, as with many of the US paratroops. This was due to three things:

i)   inexperience of the crews of the C-47s, many flying their first operational missions but captured next day.
ii) scattering of the C-47s when overflying the many flak sites around Cherbourg and the northern Cotentin.
iii) the C-47s were flying in threes, with only the lead aircraft in each V fitted with a Rebecca receiver, and when descended into the low cloud shrouding the Cotentin that night, in the run up to the DZs many of the Vs were scattered, and dropped their paratroops as opportunity presented.

After being searched and briefly interrogated the US paratroops had been in trucks in company with other prisoners and German wounded and driven south along main roads. The convoy was spotted by USAAF fighter-bombers and strafed. As the trucks were crowded, many of the occupants were wounded or killed and the trucks were brought to halt. In the subsequent confusion the three paratroops escaped into the woods at the side of the road. They were later located by some local people, and passed to the Resistance who took them to the SAS troops.

The Americans had little in the way of food so the supply situation became serious. It was resolved, in part, by foraging for vegetables but these could not be cooked as lighting a fire was out of the question and the supply of Hexamine tablets for the SAS men's cookers had long since been exhausted.

On 28 June there was a very unwelcome break in the monotony when paratroops of *Fallschirmjäger-Regiment 6* took possession of a nearby village, Remilly-sur-Lozon. Monsieur le Duc had maintained contact with SAS troops after delivering the US paratroops to the hiding place and, when confirming the presence of the Germans, added that they knew there were Allied paratroops in the vicinity, and that the party should therefore move away from the area as soon as possible. That night he took them about three kilometres south, back to the vicinity of the original DZ. They remained hidden until the following night, when he returned and

223

led them further south, for about two kilometres, to another hiding place, described as an old brushwood cabin where they hid for three days and nights. The wounded private seems to have been able to keep up with his companions, and his wound is not mentioned.

It was now 2 July and food was in very short supply, so the party decided to move north in the hope of being overrun by the Allied advance. The party moved out that night but made slow progress across the fairly open countryside, which was intersected with small tracks and roads, frequently patrolled. The party had to cross the River Taute, little more than a wide, slow stream at that point, but with muddy fringes. It was reached over open country, and it took some time for the group of ten men to negotiate the area. On the night of 8–9 July the party moved north again and arrived near the village of Raids, on the main road between Carentan and Périers. They went to earth about 400 metres from a German position being mortared by Allied troops. According to Trooper Hurst the party had many near misses from overshoots, but felt moving would be too dangerous. The following morning it was decided to recce the area ready for a break across no man's land that night, 9–10 July. The party were not well concealed, and unlucky. At about noon they spotted two German soldiers, reported as 'paratroops', advancing towards their position. The Germans spotted them, and threw several grenades before making off. The grenades exploded among the party. Captain Berry, Lieutenant Fowles and the uninjured private were slightly wounded, but Hurst was seriously injured in both legs, and Merryweather in the back. Neither could raise themselves far off the ground, let alone walk. The uninjured members of the party, Lieutenant Poole and Troopers Dawson and Saunders, carried Hurst and Merryweather to a nearby farm, helped by the three Americans. Lieutenant Fowles left the group, apparently intent on finding and silencing the Germans. The farm was about 150 metres from the scene of the incident, and only 700 metres from the nearest friendly forces, US troops advancing down the Cotentin peninsula towards Coutances. In the farm Captain Berry did what he could for his colleagues. They did not have much time to ponder their fate or decide what to do next, as their presence in the farm was, to quote Trooper Hurst, '. . . revealed by the French', possibly the farmer and his family leaving the premises in a hurry to avoid getting caught in a battle. The Germans must have interrogated the French, because they did not mount an attack on the farm, merely surrounded it as if aware the occupants were wounded. The cordon was formed by about forty German paratroops dressed in camouflage suits and heavily armed with automatic weapons. Hurst later described them as being very young, white-faced and nervous. The senior German, a sergeant, shouted to the party to come out. The party had no option but to comply. They left the farm building carrying or supporting the wounded members, and were lined up, or laid down, in a row. They were lightly searched for weapons which were carefully removed and placed out of reach. The escape equipment carried by the SAS troops sewn into various places in their uniforms was not found.

Prisoners of War

The Germans escorted the party to a nearby position, a line of trenches along the north edge of a sunken lane, some of the Germans helping to carry the wounded SAS troopers. The party was escorted past the defence line and into an orchard and over to a hut that the Germans were using as a headquarters. Each man was briefly interrogated by one of the German officers, thought to have been a captain. The only questions asked of the troops were their number, rank and name. No other information was sought; the Germans probably realized their prisoners had no information of any tactical use in the current engagement.

After two hours the party were moved to an advanced dressing station where a German Army medical officer attended to their wounds. They were also given some evil-tasting cigarettes, and some sweets and confectionery. The wounded were, by now, feeling the cumulative effects of the tension of the last few weeks in enemy territory, lack of hot food, or even any reasonable food, being mortared by their own side, their injuries, and the trauma of being captured so close to safety, and the fear of being summarily shot. They were moved again, to an old monastery being used as a makeshift surgical station. The operating theatre was a large room full of straw and 'pretty filthy' according to Hurst. Some of the Allied wounded were operated on by the German surgical team, who also had about fifty of their own to look after.

Here Lieutenant Fowles reappeared. He was badly wounded in the back, and was carried into the monastery by a German soldier, and attended to by the German medical staff. At some point the three unwounded SAS troops, Poole, Dawson and Saunders, were taken away. They had a chance of a few words with Hurst before leaving, as he was just about to be taken into the operating 'theatre'. A couple of days later, on 13 July, he was taken by road to a temporary military hospital in Rennes, a long, uncomfortable and dangerous journey in a *Wehrmacht* lorry; one of a convoy of twenty vehicles filled with wounded soldiers, enemy and Allied, intermingled and lying on straw. The tops of the lorries were marked with a large Red Cross, and luckily the prowling *Jabos* left them alone. The hospital was in a school, and held about 400 casualties, including some from the 6th Airborne Division. Merryweather arrived at the hospital the day after his colleagues, and was reunited with Hurst. The patients were looked after by one or two German surgeons, six French doctors and about eighty French nurses; the standard of medical care was described by Trooper Hurst as being 'good'. He added that the food was poor, consisting of nothing but lukewarm coffee for breakfast, black bread and beans for dinner, and pasta in the evening. He was unable to eat due to his condition, and was sustained by intravenous injections. On 2 August American forces were reported to be close by, and the Germans departed. It took four more days of skirmishing around the town, and some street fighting, in which the Resistance took part, before the city was clear of enemy forces.

The hospital was immediately visited by a US Army medical team, and some support troops. The patients were examined, and their wounds re-dressed with proper materials; the German and French staff had been very short of everything, including bandages, swabs and wound pads. More to the point, serious food in the form of US tinned rations, and good, hot strong coffee was supplied while beer, cigarettes and candy were handed out to all and sundry. The next day, 6 August, a US Army medical unit moved the patients into ambulances for a short but fairly comfortable drive to the US 35th Evacuation Hospital, located between Rennes and Fougères. There the two SAS troopers – they had lost contact with Lieutenant Fowles – were injected with penicillin and plied with good food; they were warm, comfortable, and free.

Postscript

All six SAS men survived the war. On 5 November 1945, when 1 SAS Regiment was about to be disbanded, Lieutenant Colonel Blair Mayne formally signed three Army Forms B638 *Commendations For Awards*, for Lieutenant Frederick James Fowles, Lieutenant Norman Harry Poole and Trooper Anthony Merryweather. The forms were countersigned by Brigadier J. M. Calvert DSO, MC, Officer Commanding Special Air Service Troops, and by Field Marshal Sir Bernard Law Montgomery. The awards of two Military Crosses and a Military Medal were for Operation Titanic IV.

The presence, and the efforts of the six men, supported by Monsieur Edouard le Duc and his compatriots in the Resistance, had seriously delayed the deployment of *Kampfgruppe Meyer,* the main reserve available to *Generalleutnant* Dietrich Kraiss, commanding *352 Infanterie-Division*. On 5–6 June the *Kampfgruppe* was close to St Lô, within a few miles and therefore easy striking distance of the US DZs north of Carentan, and of Omaha and Gold beaches. General Kraiss could not deploy his reserve against any of these targets in the critical hours of 6 June 1944; *Kampfgruppe Meyer* was moving west, towards an alleged mass parachute drop west of St Lô.

Monsieur Edouard le Duc, a former pilot and aged twenty-eight, was captured and shot by the Germans; it is not clear if that was for general Resistance activities, or specifically for helping the 'paras'; US and SAS.

A German Appraisal of Allied Air Landings by General Kraiss

During a war, the success of one side and the failure of the other are interrelated. In general, the success of the defender's measures can best be judged by the degree to which the attacker, as the active party, has been able to realize his goal.

The Allied air landings in Normandy in June 1944 were carried out in close tactical collaboration with the amphibious operations. The Germans expected the air landings to take place further inland, and to be aimed at more strategic objectives. Defensive measures were taken accordingly. The choice of landing areas for the overall operations came as a surprise and, consequently, the defensive front was such that in comparison with other areas it was inadequately fortified and was held by weak German forces. The majority of the German reserve was committed elsewhere and was only reluctantly released for action.

The German reserves were almost completely tied down by the air landings, real or threatened, making it impossible to launch effective counter-attacks against the amphibious assault. Consequently, the attackers were able to gain a foothold on the coast and, within a short time, to establish contact with the airborne elements.

The tactical objective of establishing a bridgehead was thus accomplished despite German countermeasures.

Bibliography

Beesley, P., *Very Special Intelligence,* Greenhill, London, 1977

Bird, A.D., *A Very Private War,* Greenhill, London, 2003

Bowman, M.W., *The Bedford Triangle,* Patrick Stephens Ltd., London, 1988

Cave Brown, A: *The Secret War Report of the OSS,* Berkeley, New York, 1976

Carell, P., *They're Coming!,* Schiffer, Pennsylvania, 1994

d'Estes, C., *Decision in Normandy,* Dutton, London, 1983

Darling, D., *Sunday at Large,* Kimber, London, 1977

Dodds-Parker, D., *Setting Europe Ablaze,* Springwood, London, 1983

Draper, A., *Operation Fish,* Cassell, London, 1979

Ellis, L.F., *Victory in the West, Vol.1, The Battle for Normandy*, HMSO, London, 1962

Ensminger, T., *Spies, Supplies & Moonlit Skies; Vol. I, Carpetbagger Squadrons,* Private, Ohio, 1998

— *Spies, Supplies & Moonlit Skies; Vol. II, The French Connection,* Private, Utah, 2003

Erskine, D., *The Scots Guards, 1919–1955,* Naval & Military Press, London, 1956

Foot M.R.D., *MI9 Escape & Evasion 1939–1945,* Bodley Head, London, 1984

— *Resistance,* Paladin, London, 1984

— *SOE in France,* Greenwood, London, 1984

— *SOE the Special Operations Executive 1940–46,* Mandarin, London, 1986

Ford, R., *Fire from the Forest; the SAS Brigade in France, 1944,* Weidenfeld & Nicholson, London, 2003

Friedhof, H., *Requiem for the Resistance,* Bloomsbury, London, 1988

Garlinski, J., *Intercept,* Methuen, London, 1995

— *Poland, Britain and SOE,* Allen & Unwin, London, 1969

Garnett, D., *Secret History of the PWE 1939–1945,* St Ermin's Press, London, 2002

Griffiths, F., *Winged Hours,* Kimber, London, 1981

Hampshire, A.C., *The Beachhead Commandos,* Kimber, London, 1983

Harrison, G.A., *Cross Channel Attack*, Center of Military History, Washington 1989

Hastings, S., *The Drums of Memory,* Pen & Sword, Barnsley, 2001

Heimark, B., *The OSS Norwegian OG in World War II*, Praeger, Connecticut, 1994

Hinsley, F.H., *British Intelligence in the Second World War, Vols. 1–4,* Cambridge University Press, London, 1979

Kozacuk, W., *Enigma,* Universities of America Press, London, 1984

Lewes, D., *Jock Lewes,* Pen & Sword, Barnsley, 2000

Marks, L., *Between Silk and Cyanide,* Free Press, London, 1998

Marshall, R., *All the King's Men,* Heinemann, London, 1988

McCue, P., *Operation Bulbasket,* Pen & Sword, Barnsley, 1996

McKenzie, C., *The Secret History of SOE,* St Ermin's Press, London, 2000

Merrick, K., *Flights of the Forgotten,* Weidenfeld & Nicholson, London, 1989

Miller, R., *Behind The Lines,* Pimlico, London, 2002

Otway, T.B.H., *Airborne Forces,* HMSO, London, 2000

Peskett, S.J., *Strange Intelligence,* Hale, London, 1981

Powys-Lybbe, U., *The Eye of Intelligence,* Kimber, London, 1983

Reymond, J., *D-Day Fortitude South,* Maidstone Libraries, 1986

Richards, Sir Brooks, *Secret Flotillas, Vol. 1,* Frank Cass, London, 2003

Rigden, R., *SOE Syllabus*, PRO, London, 2001

Seaman, Mark (Ed), *Secret Agent's Handbook of Special Devices,* PRO, London, 2000

Stenton, M., *Radio London and Resistance in Occupied Europe,* Oxford University Press, Oxford, 1994

Verity, H., *We Landed by Moonlight,* Crecy, Manchester, 2000

Vickers, P., *Das Reich,* Pen & Sword, Barnsley, London, 2000

West, Nigel, *MI5; British Security Service Operations 1909–1945,* Bodley Head, London, 1992

— *MI6 British SIS Operations 1909–1945,* Weidenfeld & Nicholson, London, 1983

— *Secret War; The Story of SOE,* Hodder & Stoughton, London, 1992

Winter, H.W., *Special Forces in the Desert War*, HMSO, London, 2001

Wilkinson, P., *Foreign Fields,* Taurus, London, 1997

Zetterling, N., *Normandy 1944,* Fedorowicz, Winnipeg, 1997

Index

233